THE RIDGEFIELD LETTERS

RICHARD N. WILLIAMSON

THE RIDGEFIELD LETTERS
IN THE *LETTERS FROM THE RECTOR* SERIES

THE COLLECTED WORKS ✦ VOLUME I

© 2019 BRN Associates, Inc.
All rights reserved.

ISBN (paper) 9781940306001
ISBN (Kindle) 9781940306025
ISBN (ePub) 9781940306032
ISBN (PDF) 9781940306049

For more information,
or for additional titles, contact:

Marcel Editions
An Imprint of the St. Marcel Initiative
www.stmarcelinitiative.com
c/o BRN Associates, Inc.
9051 Watson Rd., Suite 279
St. Louis, MO 63126
(855) 289-9226

Marcel EDITIONS
A S⸀ MARCEL INITIATIVE IMPRINT
Jesu Christo Regi æterno milito
—MARCELLUS CENTURIO, A.D. 298

St. Louis, Missouri ✺ 2019

CONTENTS

NO. 1 | MAY 24, 1983   1
Picking up the Pieces

NO. 2 | JUNE 9, 1983   3
Support from *The Angelus*

NO. 3 | JULY 8, 1983   5
SSPX Consolidates

NO. 4 | AUGUST 6, 1983   7
Growth and Litigation

NO. 5 | SEPTEMBER 3, 1983   9
SSPX Stays on Track

NO. 6 | OCTOBER 3, 1983   12
Misleading Arguments

NO. 7 | NOVEMBER 1, 1983   15
The Archbishop's Balance

NO. 8 | DECEMBER 12, 1983   18
The Archbishop Rebuilds

NO. 9 | JANUARY 10, 1984   21
Rome in Confusion

NO. 10 | FEBRUARY 2, 1984   24
Scandal of the New Code

NO. 11 | MARCH 1, 1984   27
The Archbishop Unswerving

NO. 12 | APRIL 1, 1984   30
A Century of the Devil

NO. 13 | JUNE 5, 1984   33
    Advance and Betrayal
NO. 14 | JUNE 30, 1984   40
    Gratitude
NO. 15 | AUGUST 1, 1984   43
    Assassination and Evangelization
NO. 16 | SEPTEMBER 1, 1984   48
    May Politics Be Immoral?
NO. 17 | OCTOBER 1, 1984   52
    Consecration to the Immaculate Heart
NO. 18 | NOVEMBER 1, 1984   55
    The 1984 Indult, Sign of Hope
NO. 19 | DECEMBER 1, 1984   60
    Consecration and Christmas
NO. 20 | JANUARY 1, 1985   64
    Weighing the 1984 Indult
NO. 21 | FEBRUARY 1, 1985   70
    Petition of the SSPX to Rome
NO. 22 | MARCH 1, 1985   75
    Rome – Not So Hopeful
NO. 23 | APRIL 1, 1985   80
    Corks and Nets
NO. 24 | MAY 1, 1985   83
    April 1983 – A Doctrinal Split
NO. 25 | JUNE 1, 1985   88
    The Archbishop Comforted by US Visit
NO. 26 | JULY 1, 1985   93
    The Archbishop Not Hopeful of Rome
NO. 27 | AUGUST 14, 1985   98
    The Ongoing Standoff
NO. 28 | SEPTEMBER 10, 1985   103
    Conciliar Church Mentally Stricken
NO. 29 | OCTOBER 1, 1985   108
    Cardinal Ratzinger Stricken by Council

NO. 30 | NOVEMBER 1, 1985   113
    The Archbishop's 80th Birthday

NO. 31 | DECEMBER 1, 1985   118
    Romans Fiddling While Rome Burns

NO. 32 | JANUARY 3, 1986   123
    First SSPX Ordinations in the Argentine

NO. 33 | FEBRUARY 1, 1986   128
    Infallibility and the New Mass

NO. 34 | MARCH 1, 1986   133
    Replace Bishops Who Betray?

NO. 35 | APRIL 1, 1986   138
    The Joys of Spring

NO. 36 | MAY 1, 1986   143
    The Archbishop's Mounting Fears

NO. 37 | JUNE 6, 1986   148
    Faith's Ebb and Flow

NO. 38 | JULY 1, 1986   151
    Happy Servants, Unhappy Trials

NO. 39 | AUGUST 6, 1986   155
    Insider Describes Horrendous "Rome"

NO. 40 | SEPTEMBER 3, 1986   161
    Assisi Meeting – False Ecumenism

NO. 41 | OCTOBER 2, 1986   166
    The Archbishop Resorts to Cartoons

NO. 42 | NOVEMBER 1, 1986   173
    Assisi: Save the Wolves?

NO. 43 | DECEMBER 1, 1986   178
    The Blessed Virgin Describes Christmas

NO. 44 | JANUARY 6, 1987   183
    Another Joint Statement of Two Bishops

NO. 45 | FEBRUARY 1, 1987   188
    Death of John B. Williamson

NO. 46 | MARCH 3, 1987   193
    "Rome" – Appearance Without Substance

NO. 47 | APRIL 1, 1987   199
   Communism, The Rotting of Christendom
NO. 48 | MAY 4, 1987   203
   Assisi Explained: Hell is Empty!
NO. 49 | JUNE 1, 1987   211
   The Fifth Age of the Church
NO. 50 | JULY 1, 1987   215
   Episcopal Consecrations Pondered
NO. 51 | JULY 30, 1987   220
   Answered Prayers
NO. 52 | AUGUST 10, 1987   222
   A Handsome Dominican Building
NO. 53 | SEPTEMBER 10, 1987   226
   Three Items of Good News
NO. 54 | OCTOBER 1, 1987   229
   Episcopal Consecrations Decided
NO. 55 | NOVEMBER 1, 1987   234
   Chronology of Contacts with Rome
NO. 56 | DECEMBER 9, 1987   239
   The Archbishop Will Consecrate Regardless
NO. 57 | JANUARY 10, 1988   243
   Liberalism Against the Family
NO. 58 | FEBRUARY 2, 1988   249
   The Consecrations are Justified
NO. 59 | MARCH 1, 1988   255
   Weak Arguments Against the Consecrations
NO. 60 | APRIL 2, 1988   262
   The Story of Dorothy
NO. 61 | MAY 1, 1988   267
   The Consecration of Russia
NO. 62 | JUNE 1, 1988   273
   Will Rome Approve of the Consecrations?
INDEX   279

NO. 1 | MAY 24, 1983

Picking up the Pieces

MANY OF YOU will have received Archbishop Lefebvre's letter of April 28, addressed and sent out to all friends and benefactors on this seminary's mailing list as then available, and certainly all of you by now will have learned of the painful and scandalous division amongst the priests of the Northeast District and the Seminary of the Society of Saint Pius X (SSPX) in the USA. However, perhaps not all of you, as coordinators of the Society's churches, chapels, and missions in the Northeast District, have yet received official notification of the results of that division.

As Provisional District Superior, I wish then to inform you that on April 27 the Society's Superior General, Archbishop Lefebvre, in accordance with the Society's Statutes, officially dismissed Fr. Clarence Kelly as District Superior, Fr. Anthony Cekada as District Bursar, and Father Donald Sanborn as Seminary Rector. Furthermore, on the same day, in accordance with Canons 681 & 653 of Church Law, the Superior General dismissed from the Society altogether, for the grave scandal of rebellion against his authority, four priests: Fr. Clarence Kelly, Fr. Anthony Cekada, Fr. Daniel Dolan, and Fr. Eugene Berry. By joining with these four in their rebellion, five more priests dismissed themselves: Fr. Donald Sanborn, Fr. William Jenkins, Fr. Joseph Collins, Fr. Martin Skierka, and Fr. Thomas Zapp.

Hence, not one of these nine priests is any longer a member of the SSPX. They are henceforth independent priests without a bishop, no longer under Archbishop Lefebvre's responsibility or authority. They can hold neither office nor title within the Society; they cannot represent it, nor solicit funds in its name. Nor have they any further connection with the Northeast District Incorporation, and anything that they were to attempt to do in its name, or in the name of the Society they have rebelled against, would be misrepresentation and deceit. Thus, even if they have inserted their personal names as Directors of Corporations owning certain chapels or churches of the Society, then inasmuch as these properties were acquired by their acting in the general estimation as agents of the Archbishop on behalf of the Society, they have only a fraudulent title to these properties.

Coordinators, please take note. For legal problems arising, consult and please inform Mr. Alfred Skidmore J.D., the Society's attorney on Long Island.

For pastoral problems, let all those wishing to stay with the Society under Archbishop Lefebvre contact at the Society's seminary in Ridgefield any of the three priests still in the Society in the Northeast District; either Fr. Roger Petit, the District's new Bursar, or Fr. Dominique Bourmaud, or myself. We will do what we can to come to your aid, because Archbishop Lefebvre wishes to abandon no person desirous of committing himself to his care.

May the Holy Ghost inspire us in this Octave of Pentecost with His gifts of Wisdom and Fortitude to find out and to pursue God's will for each one of us, and may Our Divine Lord keep all our hearts and minds in that peace which He alone can give.

NO. 2 | JUNE 9, 1983

Support from *The Angelus*

INSTEAD OF ANOTHER issue of *The Verbum*, the seminary is sending you this month the latest issue of *The Angelus*, from Dickinson, Texas.

Besides maybe enabling you to get to know this monthly magazine of the Southwest District of the SSPX in the USA, this issue in particular offers to its readers several articles which will be of special interest to you.

In addition to the picture story on "Our American Seminarians" and "Ridgefield Diary" which concerns your American seminary directly, "A Interview with Father Schmidberger" and "News from St. Mary's" give you the opportunity to make the acquaintance of the future Superior General of the Society, upon whom so much depends.

Above all, "Clarification of Misinformation" on page 2 makes the public dispute between the Society and the nine priests who are no longer members, take a great step forward, by making material available to refute many of the untruths and misjudgments currently circulating. Our thanks and congratulations go to our colleagues in the South for all that is so useful in this article, and in this issue of *The Angelus*.

Richard N. Williamson

Also enclosed is a Subscription Form for the Spiritual Exercises being given by the Society in the Northeast this summer. Let us not be surprised if, following Our Lord, we run into all kinds of troubles, for "All that will live godly in Christ Jesus shall suffer persecution." (II Tim 3: 12), but let us take up spiritual arms, for instance the Spiritual Exercises, against this sea of troubles: "Watch ye: stand fast in the faith: do manfully, and be strengthened." (I Cor. 16: 13)

Thank you for all loyalty and support, past and future – may our Divine Lord bless you and His Mother reward you.

NO. 3 | JULY 8, 1983

SSPX Consolidates

AFTER THE DRAMATIC events of the spring within the Northern District and seminary of the SSPX in the United States, the latest news is that both are consolidating, like the International Society as a whole.

The Society throughout the world is consolidating by the succession of Rev. Fr. Franz Schmidberger to Archbishop Marcel Lefebvre as Superior General of the Society. This does not mean that the Archbishop is quitting the Society, or ceasing to administer world-wide the sacraments of Confirmation and Holy Orders to followers and seminarians of the Society, it merely means that he is handing over to Fr. Schmidberger the arduous day-to-day task of administering and governing the ever-growing Society. Thus he is resigning as Superior General but not as Bishop, and he will still be readily available to give advice to Fr. Schmidberger whenever needed.

The Society's Northeastern District is consolidating by the restarting of Missions on Long Island, in Philadelphia, Detroit and Minneapolis, which in addition to the major centers in Armada and Chicago, and several other smaller centers, are enough to fully stretch the Society's three priests in the North! Fr. Schmidberger will

Richard N. Williamson

be visiting in person Philadelphia, Detroit, Chicago and Minneapolis on July 11, 12, 13, and 15 respectively, so that Catholics will have a chance to meet in person the new Superior of the Society to whom they may be entrusting their spiritual welfare.

The Society's seminary in Connecticut is consolidating by the tranquility restored amongst the twenty-one seminarians and the priests remaining after the departure of one third of the seminarians and three out of five professors, including the former rector, Fr. Sanborn, to whose five and a half years in office the seminary and seminarians owe so much. The Seminary's academic year closed out, on schedule, at the end of June, and the seminarians are taking a well-earned rest until the seminary reopens in September, with the prospect of around a dozen vocations, several fine young men, entering. Thus the long-term future of the Society and its American Seminary are not in doubt, but in the short term we must live, and we need your help. Our special thanks go to those who have faithfully continued contributing to the "St. Aloysius Gonzaga Fund" despite all the contradictions. Please continue – the seminary must not go bankrupt for the beginning of the new school year!

May God bless you, and Our Lady protect you, and St. Joseph reward you!

NO. 4 | AUGUST 6, 1983

Growth and Litigation

IN THE PRESENT state of difficulties between the SSPX in America and nine of its former priests, with litigation, alas, imminent, you must be wondering what is happening, or likely to happen, to the seminary...

Even before questions of property and buildings, come questions of people: where a seminary is concerned, of priests and vocations. As for priests, the seminary should have in the autumn a full teaching staff as soon as Fr. Pierre Delaplace from France and Fr. Wolfgang Goettler from Germany can join us. Fr. Delaplace was ordained only this June, Fr. Goettler has been working as a priest for two years already in Austria and Germany. Both will be great assets, and welcome in America's more and more international seminary.

As for vocations; besides a dozen and more serious applications to enter the seminary already received, the mail has brought me in the last week alone another half dozen applications to the seminary or the Brotherhood! Of course, not all these may prove to be serious, or well suited, but with only thirteen rooms left at our disposal, we have a serious problem of accommodation, and it is most likely that by September 24 when the new seminarians enter, we may have to be turning some applicants away for lack of space.

Hence the problem of buildings and property is indeed a problem. As for the property, the Society enters into litigation with a preliminary hearing on August 8 in New York State, on a suit involving not only the seminary property but also many other properties throughout the Northeast District. As for the construction work on the seminary, the imminence of dispute over title had brought this to a close, but the Society's new Superior General, Fr. Franz Schmidberger, could not stand the thought of several hundred thousand dollars' worth of materials being left exposed to rot by wind and rain, so he decided to enter upon a direct contract with the construction company to ensure that the building already there is fully protected by the time winter comes. Hence, construction work will start again, also on Monday. Please then resume your contributions to the Building Fund if you had interrupted them, and be assured that we have as yet no evidence of a single penny contributed for that purpose being diverted from it. The winterizing contract is for $150,000.00 worth of work.

Please also, Seminary Continuous Support Fund (SCSF) contributors who may have interrupted your contributions, resume! We have considerably cut the seminary's running expenses, but when term restarts in September, they climb back up to well over $20,000 a month. Here are your future priests, please God, so please look after them. And may Jesus Christ the High Priest in return look after you, and bless you. "You look after my interests," He said to St. Teresa of Ávila, "and I will look after yours."

NO. 5 | SEPTEMBER 3, 1983

SSPX Stays on Track

As THE APRIL storm within the SSPX drops back into the past, it becomes clear to all that Archbishop Lefebvre and the Society's Superior General, Fr. Schmidberger, have in no way changed their position nor compromised with the enemies of the Church, so the wisdom of the Society's position also becomes more and more clear.

If the world is today ever more confused, it is because the light of the world, Christ's one True Church, is herself in darkness. Now Christ Himself gave His Catholic Church one Head, His own Vicar upon earth, the Pope, who alone holds from God the office and authority to redress, whenever necessary, the Church. Hence to bring to an end this appalling confusion, far from refusing to recognize Pope John Paul II (JP2) as Pope, Catholics must pray for him with might and main, for only the Pope can rescue the world, and God alone can at this time rescue him from his internal and external enemies: thus "Peter was kept in prison. But prayer was made without ceasing by the Church unto God for him" (Acts 12: 5), and Peter was accordingly rescued by a miracle. Hence without wishing to be under any fond illusions, the Society

Richard N. Williamson

prays in earnest for the Supreme Pastor (Jn. 21: 15–17), for it knows that as long as he is struck, the Catholic sheep are bound to be scattered (Zac. 13: 7; Mt. 26: 31), and until he is rescued, the patience prescribed by Our Lord for us to possess our souls (Lk. 21: 19) will be much exercised.

Exercising patience then concerning its properties currently occupied by former members, and praying that those may see the error of their ways, the Society in the Northeast USA continues on its way: this month fifteen young men (at the latest count) prepare to enter or re-enter the seminary to become priests, leaving the pleasure-laden world behind them, and one more young American takes off for the Seminary at Ecône; two more from Connecticut and Texas enter the seminary to try their vocation as Brothers, and two more after a year's postulancy will soon be taking the habit as novices. The Brother's vocation is not an easy one, but the vocations are coming forward.

Now all these brave young men setting out to serve Our Lord with their whole lives must be given our support, best of all our steady support. Hence the SCSF. Our particular thanks go to the few already enrolled who have faithfully supported us over these last few months – God has not abandoned us – but we are at present living from hand to mouth with the immediate prospect of costs rising again during the school year to well over $20,000 a month. If only a large number of the seminary's friends on our mailing list would pledge themselves to give even a little each month, the seminary's operating finances would soon be on a sound basis. Please pledge what you can, however little it may be. By enrolling in the SCSF with the enclosed card and envelope, you will receive each month a letter from the seminary and an envelope facilitating a monthly contribution.

The Ridgefield Letters

The Catholic Church cannot survive without priests faithful to her divine Tradition – where else for the moment can we see these priests being formed within the USA? You too have a part to play in their formation, for which may our Lord Himself reward you!

NO. 6 | OCTOBER 3, 1983

Misleading Arguments

IN THIS HOUR of the devil "and the power of darkness," (Lk. 22: 53) as we see all around us, the seemingly unchecked advance of "all seduction of iniquity" (II Thess. 2: 10), seducing the best of men and even of priests into doing wrong while apparently convinced they are doing right, we must on Our Lord's own instructions, not judge if we would not be judged (Mt. 7) we must overcome evil with good (Mt. 5: 44) and we must be patient (Lk. 21: 9).

God has willed to allow this Passion of His Mystical Body, the Catholic Church, just as He willed to allow the Passion of the physical body of His only-begotten Son; out of the latter came our Redemption, out of the former, according to many signs, will come in God's good time an unparalleled triumph, of His Catholic Church. This we must believe, and we must wait, patiently praying for the Holy Father, the Head of the Catholic Hierarchy, who alone can redress Our Lord's Church which He Himself made. May God deign to liberate the Pope from all his enemies, internal and external!

Nevertheless, Our Lord in that same hour of darkness told us not only to pray but also to watch (Mt. 26: 41). In the anguish made universal inside the Catholic

The Ridgefield Letters

Church by these troubles at its very summit, countless Catholics are being deceived into quitting the Church. Many are falling into Protestant sects, becoming Baptists, Mormons, Jehovah's Witnesses; others repudiate Protestantism and wish to remain Catholic. By repudiating also virtually all of the present Catholic hierarchy, they too run a grave risk of cutting themselves off from the vine and of quitting the Catholic Church, notably the "sedevacantists" for whom the See of Rome is vacant, i.e., we have no Pope.

Here is the true heart of the dispute between Archbishop Lefebvre and the nine priests from the North who quit the SSPX. This dispute is continuing to cause confusion and bitter dissension amongst many faithful Catholics, and here is where we must watch. On separate sheets, readers may follow the arguments in court in August of this year of Fr. Kelly and his attorney. They can watch him arguing his way out of the Society, which is part of the Catholic Church, and into civil corporations dependent merely upon himself and his colleagues. In contrast to this version of the Society fabricated by Fr. Kelly, the footnote on those sheets which sets out what has always been the Archbishop's position, according to which all priests belonging to the Society and all who follow them are securely inside the Church and under its jurisdiction, outside of which there is no salvation. But how can the same be said for civil corporations which Fr. Kelly is now saying he deliberately placed <u>outside</u> the jurisdiction of the Church? Do followers of these corporations realize they are being led?

These courtroom arguments and the similar flow of equally misleading propaganda from Oyster Bay, show that Fr. Kelly and his colleagues and followers through failing to distinguish between the official Church, vine of Our Lord, and the Conciliar Church, gangrened with heresy, are at the very least in grave danger of schism.

Richard N. Williamson

Now the danger of heresy inherent in the Novus Ordo Missae excuses Catholics from the obligation of attending it, and once they are aware of the danger, obliges them not to attend it. It follows that Catholics aware of this ever more real danger of schism in the Masses celebrated by Fr. Kelly and his colleagues, are obliged not to attend them.

On a more positive note, there are also enclosed details of the early visit of Archbishop Lefebvre to his flock in the Northern United States. These details have been so long in suspense because only in the last few days have a brave group of Long Islanders decided to go ahead with the purchase in Farmingville of a large building for a church, highly suitable for Ordinations and Confirmations. Let traditional Catholics come in large numbers to this grand occasion where the Archbishop will also consecrate the world to the Immaculate Heart of Our Lady. By showing their loyalty and affection to the Archbishop, they will warm again his heart chilled on his last visit!

In conclusion, many thanks from all of us at the seminary to all of you who have pledged your regular support. We need still more help, but you will have a report next month when most of the pledge cards have come in.

Meanwhile may Almighty God bless you and may Our Lady protect you!

NO. 7 | NOVEMBER 1, 1983

The Archbishop's Balance

IN A FEW days' time, Archbishop Lefebvre making his first appearance in the Eastern United States since last spring, will have been able to give in a much awaited conference his own account of the state of the Church, and the state of the SSPX.

Hopefully, this time he will be understood, but it is astonishing how he is still misunderstood. If my mother catches leprosy, I am going to avoid getting too close, for fear of catching it myself, but I am not going to abandon her, for she is still my mother. Because I stay by her, some will say I love leprosy – not true, I keep at a distance. Yet just because I am careful how I approach her, others will say I do not love my mother – not true either, I refuse to abandon her.

The Catholic Church is Mother Church; leprosy in the Old Testament is a figure of heresy. By no fault of the Archbishop's, his Mother and ours has caught through the Second Vatican Council the terrible leprosy of modernism and liberalism, all over the Mystical Body. Because the Archbishop refuses to get anywhere near the Novus Ordo; Conciliar Catholics accuse him of breaking with the Pope and the Church – not true, he refuses to cut himself off from the Holy See. But then, precisely because he insists on maintaining contact with the authorities in Rome, others accuse him of being ready to compromise with the Novus Ordo or with modernism – totally false, as should be clear from a steady reading of all he has written and all he has said over the years, and as should be clear, once more, to all men of good will, from the enclosed transcript of an interview given by him in spring of this year, in France.

Yet here is an intelligent priest, not in the Society, currently proclaiming in monographs that the Archbishop has changed his position since 1976, and is compromising! Oh for the spirit of "76," is the cry of these disappointed "hard-liners" and not only in the USA! Dear Father, read the enclosed! Now, just as a well balanced man, if pushed hard from the left side, puts his weight on his right foot, but hard pushed from the right, shifts his weight to his left foot, so the Archbishop, harassed from '74 to '76 by the Conciliar Church on his left gave magnificent expression to the horror of its modernism, but then when the anti-modernists a few years later risked breaking away right into schism, he emphasized firmly his attachment to the Papacy and the Rome of all time. You might then say, Father, he changes <u>emphasis</u>, according to the needs of the moment, but to say he has changed <u>position</u> is a falsehood. The weight may shift from one foot to the other, but neither foot, love of the Mass or love of the Pope, has moved an inch. Read the Archbishop's texts.

Also enclosed is the <u>latest issue of the seminary's own newspaper</u>, *Verbum*, and also available from the seminary is the full <u>official</u> transcript from the Eastern District Court reporter of the Second Hearing on the suit between the Society and Oyster Bay Cove, because some people have wanted to check the unofficial summary they received last month. Please just send us your name and address and ten dollars to cover costs.

The Ridgefield Letters

The financial report I promised on the seminary must wait, for lack of space. Suffice it to say, <u>many have responded</u> and some of you heroically, but we are still living from hand to mouth. We are not starving, but we are delaying as long as possible turning on the heating! St. Joseph, help!

May God bless you all, and look after you, and watch over all your families!

NO. 8 | DECEMBER 12, 1983

The Archbishop Rebuilds

THE VISIT OF Archbishop Lefebvre to St. Thomas Aquinas Seminary and to Farmingville, Long Island, at the beginning of November was a great success. Ceremonies of Confirmation and Ordination crowned the admirable work of the Long Islanders and their friends who so swiftly transformed a factory floor into a prayerful church.

In *The Angelus* appears this month the text of the conference given by His Grace on the Saturday evening, and next month a picture-story on the ceremonies. One hopes the pictures will give an idea of what has been achieved. When so many church properties are being converted to the world, here is a worldly property converted into a Catholic church by what the Archbishop himself called "a minor miracle." The Faith is not dead. God's grace is still at work. It only remains for us to show our gratitude to God by the right use of His tremendous gifts.

On the Saturday night the Archbishop spoke partly on the problems of the Society, mainly on the problems (much more important) of the Catholic Church. He began by explaining why he keeps going to Rome; not in any way to compromise with the enemies of the Faith

The Ridgefield Letters

(that is obvious to anyone who has a grain of intelligence), but simply to ask for the return to Tradition. Nor, as the Archbishop made clear, does he underestimate the difficulties at Rome for he is well aware of the entrenched opposition. Last month, those on the seminary's mailing list received the Archbishop's comments on his exchange of correspondence with Rome; this month they find enclosed the continuation of that correspondence.

Firstly, Cardinal Ratzinger's letter of July 20 of this year to the Archbishop, which is doubly interesting. On the one hand the sections numbered 1 and 2 demonstrate that even if some of the Archbishop's friends (present and past!) misread his prolonged negotiations over the Council and the Liturgy, his adversaries in Rome are perfectly clear as to the uncompromisingness of the Archbishop's stand; on the other hand the section numbered 3 shows Rome treating the Archbishop as neither separated from Rome nor schismatic. As a whole the letter seems sympathetic, but in reality Catholic Tradition is as boxed in, before as after.

Hence secondly, you are receiving by way of the Archbishop's reply a historic document, marking a new stage in the saga of Catholic resistance to the modernist occupation of the Church by her liberal enemies. This is the Episcopal Manifesto, or Open Letter to the Pope, signed by two Bishops, the second being Bishop Antonio de Castro Mayer, who long battled to retain the Tridentine Mass throughout his Diocese of Campos in Brazil, until his resignation two or so years ago. Since then he has had to watch Rome doing everything possible to destroy the firm diocese he left behind him.

The contents of this letter are mostly familiar to anyone who has followed Archbishop Lefebvre's speeches and writings in his battle against the liberals. What is new is that for the first time another eminent Catholic bishop has associated himself in public with Archbishop

Richard N. Williamson

Lefebvre in his cry of alarm, such as St. Paul addressed to St. Peter, in defense of the Faith. Archbishop Lefebvre is no longer alone. *Deo Gratias*! May a third and a fourth and a fifth Catholic bishop now join them to protect the sheep of Our Lord!

Also enclosed is the latest letter to Friends and Benefactors written by the Superior General of the SSPX, and giving brief news of its progress throughout the world. This news is quietly encouraging. So too is the fact that contributions to the seminary have picked up in the last two months. Leaving aside the building costs and the Building Fund, operating costs for the seminary from July through October totaled about $84,000.00 whereas operating income for the same period was only $69,000.00. Dear friends, if Archbishop Lefebvre is defending God's cause, please continue – or begin – to support his American Seminary. And may the Sacred Heart reward you with a clear and untroubled Faith in Him through dark and troubled times!

NO. 9 | JANUARY 10, 1984

Rome in Confusion

A LITERALLY FLYING visit to Europe last week enables me to give you a little news of Mother Church, locked in her deadly struggle with the enemies of Our Lord, and a little news of the Society.

The division and disorder within the Catholic Church continue to worsen, such that unless God intervenes, the situation may in a few years' time make today's look like a holiday! The disorder and division seem to start within the Holy Father himself. It is true he went to the Lutheran church in Rome on December 11 of last year, but a front row witness (an Italian layman whom I know personally) says that he looked distinctly troubled and ill-at-ease. Maybe the letter of the two bishops (enclosed last month) helped to prevent the Pope from committing a still more terrible blunder in the name of ecumenism. As it was, the Italian people, until now slow to react, did not appreciate the Pope's appearing and speaking in a Protestant church. Nor it seems did French Catholics appreciate the Holy Father's heavily televised and mediaised meeting in prison with his would-be killer of May 1981.

Amongst the Cardinals and prelates in Rome, many are commonly known to be Free masons! *E della paroc-*

chia says one about another – "He belongs to the Parish," meaning the Masonic Lodge. Here again, deep division. Shortly before the new Code of Canon Law appeared on the First Sunday of Advent, not even explicitly mentioning, let alone condemning, Freemasonry, Cardinal Ratzinger showed the Holy Father a book recently written in German by a Freemason proving the deep implication of the late Cardinal Koenig of Vienna in the undoing of the Church's ban on Freemasonry. The result was that on the very eve of the New Code's appearing, on the Saturday, Cardinal Ratzinger's office issued another explicit exclusion of Freemasons from Catholic Communion. Does Rome itself believe in its new Code? Incredible confusion! (Archbishop Lefebvre calls the promulgation of this Code "a monstrous scandal.")

Amongst bishops in Rome the same confusion. At the Bishops' Synod of last year, one speaker praises the traditional Pope Pius XII, the very next praises in exactly the opposite sense Pope John XXIII for updating the Church!

And Rome and the Archbishop, and the two Bishops' letter? No official reaction yet, but instead such a general silence that the word must have gone out to keep silent until Rome could either recover from the Christmas season, or sort out its own confusion enough to take a position. The Archbishop (whom I saw briefly at Rickenbach and who seems in good health, *Deo Gratias*) says he does not think Rome will excommunicate him or Bishop de Castro Mayer. Meanwhile he is contacting individual bishops directly in the hope of finding a few more to take their stand, but so far in vain . . .

Against this virtually desperate backdrop, the Society makes plans with the grace of God to continue its worldwide advance. Externally, it is difficult to conceive of the two bishops' cry of alarm going indefinitely unheeded, and internally Fr. Schmidberger has for instance proj-

The Ridgefield Letters

ects for starting our first house in South Africa, and for reconstructing in the United States after the misfortunes of last April. One guiding principle will be that a priest should not be left alone if possible; which may mean the laity being disappointed in some parts, doubly delighted in others.

God willing, four new priests will be ordained by Archbishop Lefebvre Sunday morning, May 13 at the seminary in Ridgefield, Connecticut. Start planning to come in large numbers, because the Archbishop wants many people to be around their future priests at the great moment for everyone of their receiving the immense grace of the priesthood. The four of them are now Deacons, able to preach, and one of them, Rev. Tom Mroczka, helped Fr. Petit to give the Spiritual Exercises of St. Ignatius in the week following Christmas. He much enjoyed preaching the Exercises, and these were a great success, as usual, so there is, please God, one more apostle of His in the making!

Better to light a candle than curse the darkness, says the proverb, The SSPX is lighting its candle, however little, and however menacing the all-round darkness of this New Year, 1984. Many thanks to all of you that sent us Christmas cards with your good wishes, and many thanks for your support, and for your prayers above all.

The seminary is financially surviving, and spiritually thriving. May God reward you for your goodness, and keep you in His grace throughout the coming year!

NO. 10 | FEBRUARY 2, 1984

Scandal of the New Code

THE PROMULGATION OF the New Code of Canon Law at the end of November last was a grave event in the history of the Catholic Church, another milestone along the path of her present-day disintegration and destruction.

As we move into these times of which Our Lady said at La Salette that Rome would lose the Faith and become the seat of the Antichrist, so Catholics must be on their guard with regard to what comes from Rome. Sure enough, the revolutionary spirit presently overturning the Church has penetrated into the new Code, is even its guiding inspiration. Here is the Church's supreme legislator speaking in the Introduction to the Code: "Hence the fundamental novelty which . . . is to be met with in the Second Vatican Council, and especially in its teaching on the Church, also makes the novelty of the new Code."

So grave is this "fundamental novelty" that in his Long Island speech of November 5 (already circulated), Archbishop Lefebvre went so far as to say that after the Second Vatican Council and the Liturgical Reform, this new Code constitutes a third major obstacle between Rome and Catholic Tradition. Lest some nonetheless insist on misunderstanding the Archbishop's position, we

The Ridgefield Letters

enclose this month the text of an interim judgment of his upon the New Code, from a personal letter written last October.

Notice, the Archbishop in no way says the Pope is not Pope, or has no authority to make a new Code, nor does he say that nothing in the Code is to be heeded. Disciplinary regulations can positively need updating, for instance on the consulting of superiors, transformed since the last Code in 1917 by the spread of the telephone. His Grace concludes however, that overall, this Code's promulgation is "a monstrous and scandalous thing."

It is another sign of our times in which people have ever more to confuse them. Just recently I was sent a copy of a book on our apocalyptic age referring much to Scripture, but written by a Protestant, and so it is a dangerous mixture of interesting information and sheer nonsense, for instance on the Rapture in 1 Corinthians and 1 Thessalonians. Catholics should be very wary of this kind of book. Let them keep to sound doctrine and proven authors, for instance the excellent Fr. Denis Fahey. More recently appeared, Fr. Vincent Miceli's *The Antichrist* is also highly to be recommended, published by the Christopher Publishing House, and reading in-depth from a thoroughly Catholic stand-point our apocalyptic ills. This book has helped to get Fr. Miceli into much of the right kind of trouble!

Good news of the Society from Europe is that in January Archbishop Lefebvre blessed an old 17th century church in Marseilles, France, disused for many years but reopened by the Society, while Fr. Schmidberger blessed the Society's first church in Holland, bought from Protestants. Today, on the Feast of the Presentation, the Carmelite Sisters under the Society's wing opened their third Carmel near Essen in Germany. They will undoubtedly draw many vocations to pray and make sacrifices for us all.

Richard N. Williamson

Closer to home, also today, seven Americans, one Canadian and one Rhodesian received the cassock here at the seminary, making nine young men proclaiming merely by their dress death to the world and victory to Jesus Christ. Remember that on Sunday morning, May 13, also here at the seminary in Ridgefield, Connecticut, the Archbishop will, God willing, give Major Orders to ten seminarians, including the priesthood to Daniel Ahern, John Hogan, Denis McMahon, and Tom Mroczka. Pray for these brave young men. Note also the dates of the next Spiritual Exercises for men from 17 upwards, at the seminary: Monday thru Saturday, April 23 to 28. A week lost, an eternity gained! Registration forms will follow next month. There will also be exercises in the summer.

Other news? – The lawsuit against Oyster Bay Cove is at the stage of depositions, and looking hopeful. The seminary's building program is perforce in hibernation. The seminary's finances are slowly but steadily more secure, thanks, and those are grand thanks, to your generosity! May God Himself reward you!

He is doing His work – let us do ours!

NO. 11 | MARCH 1, 1984

The Archbishop Unswerving

> "Take courage therefore, and be very valiant: that thou mayst observe and do all the Law which Moses my servant hath commanded thee: turn not from it to the right hand or to the left, that thou mayst understand all things which thou dost."
>
> —Joshua 1:7

Another two documents of Archbishop Lefebvre, one never previously made public, are enclosed, and they illustrate the Archbishop fulfilling the Lord God's instructions to His great servant Joshua, to swerve neither to right nor to left. Both texts require thoughtful attention.

The first of them in time, the conversation with Fr. Kelly, goes already four years ago to the very heart of the difference between the SSPX and Oyster Bay Cove. Fr. Kelly would argue today exactly as he argued then: any kind of transaction between ourselves and the official Catholic Church would put us in communion with excommunicated heretics, so we must break off all contacts and rebuild the Church on our own. No, replies the

Richard N. Williamson

Archbishop, many modern churchmen may be weak, but they are not yet therefore heretics of such a kind as automatically to exclude themselves from the Church, so the Faith they still have, to the extent they still have it, is what we (by the grace of God) Catholics are in communion with. Hence we cannot break off. How could any church of our own be the Church of Our Lord? To break off is the road to Jonestown.

The Archbishop does not swerve right, but was he then swerving left in 1980 from the heroic stand of 1976, as Fr. Kelly and many others, not only in America, feared? For an answer, read the second text from the end of 1983, the Press Conference in which a journalist says he hears the Archbishop saying "exactly what he was saying ten years ago." Here the Catholic balance and depth of doctrine typical of so many texts of the Archbishop come out clearly, for instance in his answer to the burning question of the consecration of a bishop. On the one hand, such an act by appearing to break with Rome would further embroil the already embattled Society, so while the Archbishop still has a little health, he prefers to hold back. On the other hand, if in still more tragic circumstances than today's, the Church's very survival seemed to require such a consecration, then the break with Rome would be merely apparent, not real, so the Archbishop, while hoping it need not be, refuses to exclude such an eventuality.

Thus the Archbishop swerves neither to right nor to left, and the correctness of his course is proved by the fruits of his Society – amid the general ruin of the Church, the rebuilding of Catholic seminaries, parishes, monasteries, convents, schools and colleges. Take for instance, St. Mary's in Kansas, a parish, school and college all in one, launched within the Society by Fr. Bolduc, continued by Fr. de la Tour, but presently being menaced by a foreclosure on its mortgage. If the fruits of St. Mary's amply prove it to be the work of God, then such an attack is a

The Ridgefield Letters

handsome compliment, coming from the Devil. He likewise shows up in the Louisville Faith Baptist School Crisis, mobilizing all the powers of Nebraska State to obtain sinister control of children's education for the evil purposes of the threatening One World Government. Now if brave non-Catholic ministers and parents will go to bat and go to jail for the rights of a non-Catholic school, surely we Catholics will do all we can to help a proven Catholic school! Nourishing over 200 young Americans in the true Faith, St. Mary's College is financially healthier than it was, but even if the mortgage did not have to be repaid, it still has a monthly shortfall in income of some $5,000. Kindly direct help to "St. Mary's College", Kansas 66536, and be sure of the blessing of God upon any effort you can make for His Little ones!

Archbishop Lefebvre himself will be at St. Mary's College between Thursday, May 17 and Monday, May 21. There he will administer Confirmation, as he will have done also at Ridgefield Seminary, Connecticut on Saturday afternoon, May 12; in Pittsburgh, Pennsylvania, on Monday evening May 14, and in the Twin Cities, Minnesota, on Wednesday evening May 16. Hopefully all parents wishing to have children confirmed can reach one of these spread-out centers.

On May 13, the Archbishop is of course holding Ordinations at Ridgefield Seminary, from which should emerge four new Priests, four new deacons and two or three sub-deacons. And if each of these was divided into several parts, we could still not satisfy the demand! Patience. God's time is the very best time.

Meanwhile warm thanks from all of us at the seminary to all of you readers that have over the last few months lifted the seminary out of financial trouble. Please grant us also your prayers to keep us out of spiritual trouble, and be assured that the seminary prays for you amongst all our benefactors.

NO. 12 | APRIL 1, 1984

A Century of the Devil

One day Satan presented himself before the throne of God and asked for permission to put the Catholic Church to the trial for a certain length of time. God granted him 100 years to do so. These 100 years are under the power of the Devil, but when the secrets entrusted to you have come about, his power will be destroyed. He is already beginning now to lose his power and he has become aggressive – he is destroying marriages, sowing division amongst priests, causing diabolic obsessions and murders. You must protect yourselves from him by fasting and prayer, above all by praying together. Carry sacramentals with you. Place them in your homes, and start using Holy Water again.

NOW THIS QUOTATION from a letter written on December 2, 1983, by a Franciscan priest to JP2 may or may not be the Blessed Virgin herself speaking at Medjugorje in Yugoslavia, but it certainly fits our present situation. For instance, many people know that on October 13, 1884, Pope Leo XIII, just after celebrating Mass, had a frightening vision of the future in which he heard Jesus granting to the Devil on his request 100 years in which to attempt to destroy the

The Ridgefield Letters

Church, and in which the Pope then saw the unspeakable horror of countless devils tearing the Mystical Body of Christ to pieces, corrupting vocations, silencing bishops and priests, emptying out convents and monasteries – today's scene. That is when Pope Leo composed the Prayer to St. Michael, the Devil's great adversary, to have it said by priests at the end of every low Mass.

Certainly God may choose to give power in this way to the Devil, as we see in the Book of Job. Certainly the Devil has power today he has never had before, as we see from the evil fruits. What is not certain is that these 100 years came to an end in 1984, because for all we know the Devil may have applied for and obtained an "extension!" And so the division of priests and the destruction of marriages may continue for a while yet . . .

Concerning priests, Catholics today often ask why all the good Traditional priests cannot get together and work together. A large part of the answer is, besides their human weaknesses, the lack of authority in the Church. It is Our Divine Lord and nobody else who designed the Catholic Church, and within it He gave authority to Peter alone (Jn. 21: 17) to feed the sheep, i.e., the bishops. Hence when Peter is seen to be leading them in pastures of false ecumenism (e.g. the visits to Canterbury and to the Lutheran Church in Rome), there is nobody else who has the authority to unite and lead the bishops and priests staying with Tradition. If anyone else could unite them, then the Catholic Church would be operating differently from how our Lord Himself designed it to operate. Impossible.

Now such considerations may be only small consolation to the faithful for all the damage flowing from discord amongst their priests, but let Catholics wisely resign themselves to what cannot be cured having to be endured, and let them pray with might and main for the restoration of Peter – two priest friends of mine were more than a little depressed on a recent visit to Rome: "The order has gone out not to reply to Archbishop Lefebvre, and not to tackle the fundamental problems... We must pray a great deal for the Church."

Concerning the destruction of marriages, let husbands and wives today be especially on their guard against the Devil striving, as in his last available moments (Apoc. 12: 12), to tear apart their marriage. Were this situation before long to clear up, how a marriage partner might regret having just beforehand abandoned the struggle to keep their marriage together! How the Devil exaggerated the difficulties, and hid from view all the gifts and graces of marriage! How much harder he worked on our marriage than we did ourselves! And we gave up. And now I see it all, and it may be too late!

Patience! Let one penance for the rest of Lent be the exercise of this great virtue by which we know how to suffer and to endure whatever hardships it pleases God to send us.

News of the Seminary is contained in *The Verbum* enclosed. We continue quietly to thrive, but do not think we do not need your help! Brother Joseph has to push snow off the flat roof; otherwise it leaks in the chapel four floors below!

Presently seminarians and friends of the seminary are embarking on preparations for the Major Ordinations on May 13, when Archbishop Lefebvre will ordain here in Ridgefield four new priests, four deacons and two subdeacons (program enclosed). If you have never attended an ordination of priests, it is an extraordinary experience – into the ceremony went a young man, who is merely a deacon, out comes a priest, another Christ! We commend to your prayers the ten seminarians due to receive Major Orders, and we look forward to seeing you on this grand occasion!

NO. 13 | JUNE 5, 1984

Advance and Betrayal

ARCHBISHOP LEFEBVRE'S MAY visit to the United States unleashed another tremendous battle between Jesus Christ and Satan, His undying adversary! From this battle flowed good news and bad news. Let us start with the good news!

Firstly, the Society has a new American priest, Fr. John Hogan from Michigan. His Grace, Archbishop Lefebvre, 78 years old, arrived from Europe on May 10 and gave Tonsure or Minor Orders to twelve seminarians on Saturday morning, May 12, Confirmation to nearly fifty children and adults in the afternoon, and Major Orders to the senior seminarians on Sunday morning, May 13.

It was a beautiful ceremony in front of the very impressive High Altar put together (just in time!) inside the new church by a number of hardworking seminarians and layfolk. Outside, the sun shone brilliantly to welcome some five hundred visitors coming from all over the United States and Canada. From various comments made in person and also frequently by mail, many were deeply impressed and moved by the majesty and beauty of Catholic Traditionalism at its finest. In one of its noblest ceremonies, that of an Ordination to the

Richard N. Williamson

Priesthood, what a feast for the eyes! What an uplift for the soul! What a hope for the future!

The Society's Superior General, Fr. Franz Schmidberger, and the Society's newest District Superior, Fr. François Laisney (pronounced Lay-nay), were also present as deacon and subdeacon of the Ordination Mass, flanking the Archbishop. Immediately after the ceremony, both of them left for Michigan where I wish many of our people could have visited our church, St. Joseph's Shrine in Armada. They would have been marvelously edified by the sight of over a dozen priests, mostly, but not all, from the Society, making a silent retreat for several days under Fr. Schmidberger. They came from all over the United States and Canada, united humbly in prayer to seek God and to pursue in common the arduous work of saving souls. What a hope for the future! Those priests are not fighting on their own. Moreover, they have a father in the priesthood, a faithful and courageous bishop of the Roman Catholic Church! Archbishop Lefebvre visited them in the middle of their retreat after giving Confirmation at a non-Society Chapel in Pittsburgh, and he was able to talk at length to each of them who wished to see him. It makes an attractive and uniquely Catholic picture: the bishop amidst his priests, the priests around their bishop.

From there, the Archbishop went on to Minnesota where he administered Confirmation to nearly eighty souls. Here, although he gave a sobering picture of the dark situation in Rome, the people were obviously uplifted and tremendously encouraged by his visit. His Grace then went on to St. Mary's, Kansas, where he spent three happy days administering Confirmation, talking to various laymen who are helping Fr. de la Tour to run this major educational establishment, and holding a Pontifical High Mass on Saturday morning. A full picture-story is in this month's issue of *The Ange-*

The Ridgefield Letters

lus. He returned to New York for two more days before going back to Europe. Before leaving, the Archbishop said that he was very happy with the spirit of the Society such as he now found it flourishing at the seminary, at St. Mary's, and in the various centers of the Society which he visited.

Fr. Schmidberger, who arrived in the United States on May 10, is spending over a month here until June 11, making a long and exhausting tour all around the United States, so as to make himself directly familiar with many of the Society's endeavors, the better to build upon firm foundations the future work of the Society in this country. For half of his tour, he is being accompanied by the new superior in America, Fr. Laisney, whose youth, energy and intelligence promise to make him a great acquisition for taking the Society's work in the United States a major step forward. From the middle of June onwards, he is likely to settle (at least provisionally) in Dickinson, Texas, which becomes temporary headquarters for the whole Society in the United States.

Last – and perhaps most important – Fr. Schmidberger is anxiously making plans to establish a cloister for praying and sacrificing nuns in the United States, with the help of Mother Marie-Christiane, presently head of three Carmels which are flourishing in Europe, attached to the SSPX. He has been eager for her to come to the United States to inspect two possible locations for a fourth Carmel! Mother Marie-Christiane, a natural sister of Archbishop Lefebvre and Carmelite nun herself for 56 years has for the last year and a half been wishing for a foundation in the United States. Fr. Schmidberger's direct experience of the urgent need for holy prayer to draw down God's grace in the United States has prompted him to expedite her long-standing aspiration. Let us pray it come to fruition!

Richard N. Williamson

All this work of building and rebuilding by the Society constitutes a resistance to the Devil which he could not leave in peace. His reaction was not slow in coming!

On Sunday night, May 20, when the Archbishop arrived back at the seminary at a late hour from Kansas, somewhat tired and travel-weary, no sooner had he stepped out of the car than he was served with a civil court summons in a suit to evict the Society from the seminary property here in Connecticut, a suit filed by Fathers Cekada, Dolan, Jenkins, Kelly and Sanborn. Those standing by noticed and will not easily forget the look of pain on the face of the Archbishop, who it must be remembered was their father in the priesthood. Now according to the Old Code of Canon Law, anyone citing a Catholic bishop before a civil judge incurs automatic excommunication (Canon 2341). Hence, according to the only Code of Canon Law which they themselves recognize, these five priests are excommunicated!

Then a few days later, an event which should have taken by surprise no Catholic familiar with the Gospel story of the betrayal of Our Lord, but which has nevertheless caused deep shock and heartache and scandal to countless Catholics: of the four newly ordained priests who had freely requested and received Ordination within the SSPX at the hands of its founder, Archbishop Lefebvre, after freely taking on the evening before with their hand on the Gospels a solemn oath of fidelity to their superiors, two of the four, on the stormy afternoon of May 23, amidst flashes of lightning and torrents of rain, walked out of the seminary and went to join the nine priests who defected last year, and two days later a third, already absent, announced that he was doing the same. And it was night.

A few facts will highlight the nature of this deed. Firstly, we now know that very soon after the defection of "The Nine" one year ago, these three actually told

The Ridgefield Letters

someone that they intended to lie low in order to get the priesthood. Certainly over the course of one whole year their words and actions in the seminary were of a nature to persuade everyone, priests, seminarians and even visitors from outside, that they would be loyal to the Society. Did they for one whole year live a lie?

Secondly, on the very eve of their ordination, in accordance with the Traditional requirements of Mother Church, all three took a solemn oath of fidelity at the altar of God, with their hand touching the Gospels before the Blessed Sacrament in the opened Tabernacle, swearing amongst other things that they would respectfully obey their superiors in the SSPX. The complete text of this oath and the signatures of all three are enclosed with this letter.

The alterations made to the text by one of them suggest he was not at ease, and indeed to swear such an oath at all each of them must have found, or been given, a way of justifying or rationalizing to himself and to others what he did. However, if before God they here committed perjury, then their receiving of Holy Orders in such a state will have been, thirdly, a grave sacrilege.

Fourthly, towards the end of the Traditional Ordination ceremony, each of the three placed his hands between the hands of the Archbishop, for the Archbishop to ask him in Latin, "Do you promise to me and my successors reverence and obedience?" Each of the three answered distinctly, *Promitto*, meaning "I promise."

Fifthly, the at least apparent breaking, within ten days, of these solemn oaths and promises, taken together with all the other circumstances of this latest defection, has caused and will continue to cause a terrible scandal to Catholics; not only to those attached to Tradition who supported and assisted these three because they trusted them to follow Archbishop Lefebvre in defense of the Faith, but also to countless others not yet attached to

Tradition who will wrongly but understandably say that if Tradition fosters such disloyalty, then they want none of it.

By way of comment upon these facts, let three quotations for the moment suffice. On May 27 of this year, Fr. Sanborn said from the pulpit in Traverse City, Michigan, "I am very pleased to announce three of the four priests who were ordained by Archbishop Lefebvre on May 13 have decided to come with us. This makes me very happy because I trained them, and so not all the fruits of my labor as rector of the seminary were lost." (Does Fr. Sanborn realize what fruits he is laying claim to?).

On April 28 of last year, just after the split between the Society and "The Nine," Archbishop Lefebvre said at the seminary to all the seminarians, including the three who have just defected:

> I hope you will make the good choice. But you must choose. If you agree with the position and attitude and orientation of Fr. Kelly, then follow Fr. Kelly. If you think Mgr. Lefebvre is right, then follow the attitude of Msgr. and the Fraternity. But you must be clear . . . honest. Do not say: I will be silent until after my ordination. That is wrong! God knows that! That is a lie before God . . . not before me. I am nothing. But before God! You cannot do that! "That is precisely what Fr. Dolan said, i.e. "I knew how to keep quiet until my ordination." I cannot understand him doing that! A future priest doing that??

And on May 30 of this year, one of the three latest defectors, when reproached by a lady that such a blow as these actions of theirs might have killed the Archbishop, replied "Oh, he's 78 years old anyway. Mark you, I'm grateful to him, because without him I wouldn't be a priest."

People might ask how such a thing could happen inside a seminary, and whether the same will not happen

The Ridgefield Letters

again. The answer is that Jesus saw to the very depths of the human heart (Jn. 6: 65,71), but still chose to allow an Apostle to be unfaithful. As for Jesus' priests, we can only see into human hearts, in the words of the Ordination Rite itself, "as far as human frailty allows us to know." Also there comes a point of mistrust at which the service of God seizes up and a Catholic seminary can no longer operate, because charity "believes all things and hopes in all things" (I Cor. 13: 7). However we are keeping our eyes open, and one seminarian has already been asked to leave since the defection, who under questioning clearly shared the defectors' way of thinking.

To fortify your Faith, the seminary and St. Joseph's Shrine are again this summer offering several courses of St. Ignatius' great Spiritual Exercises. Make use of this unique opportunity to strengthen your spiritual life, which is more important than anything else. For our part, with the help of God, neither the Society nor the seminary will be shaken off course, but despite these trials or even because of them, both Society and seminary will thrive as God wills. Our next project is the opening of another mission on Long Island, where many Catholics are in distress.

May God's most Holy and Unsearchable Will be always adored, and may His Blessed Mother, Virgin most Faithful, ever obtain for us in these faithless times the graces of fidelity and loyalty!

NO. 14 | JUNE 30, 1984

Gratitude

On the feast of Corpus Christi, we celebrated at the seminary the end also of the school year. It was a perfectly beautiful midsummer's day. After Solemn High Mass we held a procession of the Blessed Sacrament through the grounds of the seminary, with an Altar of Repose in the front of the seminary, and then we lunched outside under the trees, with the sun pouring down the green slope towards the lake at the foot of the hill.

The High Mass was celebrated for the intention of thanksgiving to God for the many graces He has given to us all at the seminary over the year. One faithful seminarian He has brought to the priesthood, twenty more He has safely brought one year closer to the priesthood, and to the five of us priests, He has granted a happy year's work, divided between instructing the seminarians and ministering to our missions. May He be praised and thanked for many, many gifts!

And our thoughts at the same time turned gratefully to all of you, our benefactors, without whose regular support we could never have kept the seminary working for the greater glory of God. In April of last year the confidence of many of you had reason to be shaken, and the

The Ridgefield Letters

aggravation of those troubles in May of this year made many of you wonder what on earth is happening to the Society. It is of course by Almighty God being firmly planted in the Cross. In the long run this is a source of great blessings, but here and now the treatment handed out to Our Lord and His followers can scandalize us out of our minds. In such moments let us recall Our Lord's own words: "They will put you out of the synagogues: yea, the hour cometh, that whosoever killeth you, will think that he doth a service to God. And these things will they do to you, because they have not known the Father, nor Me. But these things I have told you, that when the hour shall come, you may remember that I told you of them... In the world you shall have distress, but have confidence, I have overcome the world" (Jn. 16: 2–4, 33).

To all of you then that have stayed with us, or rallied behind us, many thanks. With the help of God, we shall not disappoint you. He may already be bringing you another priest, a refugee from a Novus Ordo diocese, who twice visited us at the seminary in the last two months. Ordained a few years ago out of a fly-leaf Pontifical, he was at his own request conditionally re-ordained in May by Archbishop Lefebvre. While staying with us he has been learning to say the Tridentine Mass from our Master of Liturgy, Fr. Goettler. What disturbs this priest more than anything in the Novus Ordo Church is the mistreatment of the Holy Eucharist. On the other hand, saying the Tridentine Mass is, he says, "like a breath of fresh air."

Pray for this priest that he may always serve God and that he may soon be serving you. He depends upon your prayers, as do we all even more than upon your material support. Pray, and have no fear, you will have the priests of your prayers.

Enclosed is <u>the most interesting reply from Rome</u> to a Long Islander's question whether attendance at the Tridentine Mass fulfills the Sunday obligation. We always knew it did, but here is <u>Rome</u> confirming the fact. Reprint and circulate by all means.

May Almighty God grant us all the patience to bear the tribulations He designs to take us to Heaven, and may He and His Mother bless you and keep you through the summer!

NO. 15 | AUGUST 1, 1984

Assassination and Evangelization

"The time is at hand. He that hurteth, let him hurt still: and he that is filthy, let him be filthy still: and he that is just, let him be justified still: and he that is holy, let him be sanctified still."

THIS QUOTATION FROM the Apocalypse (22: 10–11), meaning the good are to get better and the bad to get worse, sums up my impressions from several days spent in June at the Seminary of the SSPX in Ecône, Switzerland, and a few days spent in July at the Society's house in Albano, near Rome.

On the one hand, the situation steadily worsens in Rome. Just one hour before boarding the plane for Europe, I picked up a book to read called *In God's Name: An Investigation into the Murder of John-Paul I* by a certain David Yallop. It is a fascinating book. It must contain many truths, because in arguing that Pope Luciani was certainly murdered, it presents a picture of him behind the scenes corresponding perfectly to the puzzling mixture of good and evil of the persona which he presented

—43—

in public at the time. For instance, we knew that as Patriarch of Venice he favored ecumenism and oppressed traditionalists; David Yallop goes further, quoting how he fully intended as Pope to reverse Pope Paul VI's stand against contraception! (Interestingly enough, David Yallop's clear approval of this intention shows that it is not Traditionalism making him criticize the Vatican). On the other hand we also knew that Pope John Paul I was reaching to the people as out of a prison in the Vatican, for on a holy card I have seen with my own eyes which he inscribed in Latin for a South African Catholic who had just written to him to congratulate him on his election, he chose the verse from Acts 12: 5: "Peter therefore was kept in prison. But prayer was made without ceasing by the church unto God for him." This interesting choice is more than explained by David Yallop's picture of the tremendous tussle shaping up between Pope Luciani and the officials around him, just when the Pope died . . . It really looks as though Pope John Paul I was on the point of straightening out the Vatican's involvement in some very crooked finances (Archbishop Marcinkus, Roberto Calvi), and of removing from office some very high-ranking Freemasons (Cardinal Villot, Cardinal Baggio), but they got to him before he could get to them . . . may his soul rest in peace.

As for Rome six years after Pope John Paul I, the situation is dramatic. To a heroic Italian priest thoroughly versed in current events in Rome, I put the question whether Rome is aware of the ruination of the Church, and if so, how can Rome possibly be allowing it to continue? He replied: "There is nothing to be done: They are all sold men. They realize they are doing wrong, but they don't want to recognize that wrong is wrong . . . Nowadays it is very easy to play a double game . . . the situation is tremendous . . . These men are egotists. They do not understand what Our Lord is about." And

The Ridgefield Letters

this alarming diagnosis was confirmed to me by others. Thus an intimate knowledge of what is happening at the very center of the Church shows that what is bad, is getting worse.

However, we who follow Catholic Tradition should not lose sight of the fact that Rome is still in some respects hampering the Modernists – these do not love Pope John Paul II, and we must be careful, in our criticisms of what Rome is doing, not to lend strength to the liberals who would throw over Roman control altogether. For our part, we look forward to the day when we can again in everything obey Rome, truly guiding us in the Faith. Meanwhile this "tremendous situation" is also a tremendous object lesson in the love and power of God, choosing to leave His Church in such frail and wicked hands and yet saving it despite the worst they can do. For even as the wicked get worse, so He is enabling the good who cooperate with His grace to become better.

For instance, in perfect early summer weather I saw twenty-five new priests being ordained at Ecône on June 29, including seventeen for the Society, and six more were ordained two days later at the Society's Seminary in Germany. Of these twenty-three new Society priests, an Australian is being sent to South Africa, a Belgian to Holland, a Canadian to England, an Italian to Portugal, a New Zealander to Australia, and a Spaniard to Mexico, but I do not know of any of these countries complaining about having "foreign" priests sent to them. The complaint is rather that they would all like more good priests, whatever their nationality, and such is the reaction of true Catholics. Did not our Lord say to his all Jewish Apostles, "Go and teach all nations" (Mt. 28: 19)? And were not countless nations duly evangelized by them, foreigners in all but the Faith? How would these nations have received the Faith, had they refused foreigners? And so it has been right down the history of the Catholic Church.

Amidst literally thousands of examples, the "Apostle of Germany" was an Englishman, St. Boniface, and my own country, England, was evangelized and re-evangelized by two Italians, St. Augustine of Canterbury and St. Dominic Barberi. Now here in the USA some of us Society priests are called foreigners, although I wonder just how many Catholic priests in America can claim as I can a great-great-great-grandfather who fought as a Patriot in the Revolutionary War. James Nelson of McConnellsburg, Pennsylvania (1757–1828) entitles me to be an authentic son of the American Revolution! But all such boasts are foolishness (II Cor. 11: 21), we will glory in the cross of Our Lord Jesus Christ alone (Gal. 6: 14). Nationality is as trivial, compared with the Faith, as earth is when compared with Heaven. England was built by Catholics who put God before all else, it was in the 16th century ruined by Protestants who pretended to be true patriots. Likewise, woe unto America from Catholics, even Traditionalists, who would bend their Faith to suit their nationality! On the contrary America has been and always will be built up by Catholics who seek first and without interference the kingdom of God (Mt. 6: 33) – was not a Spanish priest, Fr. Junipero Serra, a Founding Father of California? And was it not a Belgian priest, Fr. De Smet, who opened up large parts of the Midwest and Northwest to this nation?

Be assured, the SSPX forges ahead, the good with God's grace becoming better, and in the United States we are with your help steadily consolidating and advancing. Many thanks to all of you who faithfully send a monthly donation to support the Seminary. At the moment we have a good dozen vocations due to enter in mid-September. Pray, and that will be a dozen more good priests in May of 1990!

The Ridgefield Letters

Already your prayers may have brought you another priest. The one mentioned last month as having twice visited us from the Novus Ordo decided to write to his bishop to ask for a year's leave of absence. The answer – oral, not written – was that he must choose between submitting to psychiatric treatment or being officially suspended! He has chosen to take refuge for the time being with ourselves, and in return he looks like rendering us valuable service. *Deo Gratias*!

Another little item of good news is that the lady whose name and address we printed last month as having received from Cardinal Oddi approval of her attending on Sundays the Tridentine Mass at a Society chapel, has received positive letters from all over the country. She means to reply to them all, but begs forgiveness if it takes her a little while. She has been heartened by the positive response. So should we be. All is not lost.

May God bless you and keep you, and may Our Lady grant you a special favor on the Feastday of her Assumption.

NO. 16 | SEPTEMBER 1, 1984

May Politics Be Immoral?

AN INTERESTING DISPUTE is currently developing in New York State, as interesting as the age-old tussle between Church and State.

It began with a News Conference given on June 24 of this year by Archbishop John J. O'Connor of New York. Speaking soon after Mrs. Zaccaro's nomination as candidate for vice-presidentess – she is better known as Geraldine Ferraro, a Congresswoman with a 100% pro abortion voting record in Congress – the Archbishop made the following key statement: "I do not see how a Catholic could in conscience vote for an individual expressing himself or herself as favoring abortion." This admirable declaration said firstly that abortion is a grave sin, and secondly that Catholics should vote in politics according to the candidates' positions on the great moral issues. To stigmatize abortion like this and to affirm God's supremacy over politics is the merest Catholic common sense, but we have grown so used to supposedly Catholic bishops giving way to the world that it is admirable to see one again standing up in public for the rights of God. Archbishop O'Connor deserves in this respect all our support and prayers. Well said, Your Grace!

The Ridgefield Letters

The hit bird fluttered! Rallying to Mrs. Zaccaro's defense maybe, Governor Mario Cuomo of New York State gave an interview in which he said he is a Catholic before being a Governor or a Democrat, but he went on to marshal arguments against Archbishop O'Connor which, at any rate as reported in the *New York Times* of August 3 and the *National Catholic Register* of August 19, betray a woeful ignorance or the true Catholic Faith. On the abortion issue, the Governor argued that the Roe v. Wade decision of 1973 has made of abortion a right protected by the Constitution, and that once the law has decided in favor of abortion, the law too must be respected. Besides, the ban on abortion has no chance of passing, so to seek such a ban would merely be divisive. Also, Christ never mentioned abortion in the Gospels.

This last argument is sheer Protestantism! Any Catholic knows that Our Lord teaches through His Church many truths which He has entrusted to her through Tradition and not through Scripture. Now the true Church has always taught that abortion is what maternal instinct knows it to be, an abominable murder committed in the very sanctuary of life, the mother's womb. Hence, since God's law is the fountainhead of all law, alone giving it any authority, then no human law or court decision or Constitution can in any way make legal such a direct violation of God's law, and no law purporting to do so is any law at all. As violating God's law it has not authority or binding force and it requires no respect. Likewise, were abortion now tied to the Constitution – which one need not grant – woe unto the Constitution!

"Unless the Lord build the house, they labour in vain that build it" (Ps. 126: 1). Had any nation no more chance of banning abortion, it would have no more chance of surviving. The more Americans that can be divided from such a destruction of America, the better!

Richard N. Williamson

On the issue of religion and politics, the Governor makes even graver errors, undermining the very foundations of the Catholic Faith he professes. For instance, he credits Archbishop O'Connor with seeking to impose on everyone his private belief, as though the Catholic Faith, and what a Catholic knows to be the law of God, were merely private belief, or personal opinion! Similarly the Governor says that for him as governor to fight abortion would entitle a Jewish governor to seek to impose on everyone observance of the Jewish Sabbath, as though fighting abortion was merely a practice particular to Catholics, and not the defense of the universal natural law! The Governor goes in still deeper by saying that for him "to preserve his right to be a Catholic means preserving a Jewish right to be a Jew," a formula dangerously suggesting that Catholic truth has no more rights than Jewish untruths (e.g., the Messiah has not come)!

Governor, to rest your right to be a Catholic not upon Our Lord's direct command to believe His Truth (Mk. 16: 15–16), but upon anyone's right to believe as he likes, is to undermine the one true Faith, Catholicism, with the religion of liberty, or liberalism. And to this false religion you would harness and attach American patriotism! – "The design of this country, its greatest strength, is that people are free to believe their own thing." As though any country were great not by its obeying God, but by its liberty to obey or disobey Him! Since when did belief in a lie make a man strong? Or even free?

Our Lord said, "The truth shall make you free" (Jn. 8: 32), whereas the father of liars, the Devil, enslaves men to sin (Jn. 8: 34, 44). Freedom of worship is only good if it is rightly used, and then the good lies in the right use and not in the freedom of misuse. Truth founds true liberty, mere liberty founds many lies. The strength of America has always been in its godliness, not in its freedom to be ungodly.

The Ridgefield Letters

In brief, Governor Cuomo may say he is a Catholic first, but he is talking, walking and acting like a politician first. Fortunately Archbishop O'Connor, while being polite and diplomatic, shows no signs of backing down on essentials. If only a few more Catholic bishops would stand up clearly for the rights of God! "All power in heaven and on earth" (Mt. 28: 18) would be theirs.

News of the seminary is good. Over the summer vacation we have been delighted to share the beautiful seminary grounds and house with dozens of the laity coming in on four different retreats to make the Spiritual Exercises. They all went away spiritually much refreshed. Less welcome visitors have been a family of deer, a buck, doe and four fawns, who have found their way right around the seminary grounds to our vegetable garden, where they have coolly eaten up a good part of our economy drive! Nevertheless, thanks to your grand support of the Seminary, we have since February been able to pay back to Archbishop Lefebvre $67,000 of the $237,000 which the Seminary owed him. Maintain this generosity, and we will before long pay back the remaining $170,000! It is in all honor the least we can do for all he has done for us. Then we can attack our heavy mortgage.

Also good news is that so many new seminarians and brothers are wishing to enter the seminary this September that we are turning applicants away for lack of rooms. Pray for the perseverance of at least fifteen new seminarians, from the USA, Canada and one from New Zealand. If they all persevere, someone will have to sleep under the stairs, because the dispute over title to the property is holding up the building program. However, let us not worry unduly about lawsuits. We are not fearful of losing this property, but even if we do, God will provide. Let us avoid much confusion and dissension by praying that His justice be done, not ours, and then, while doing our duty as we see it, let us leave all in His hands.

NO. 17 | OCTOBER 1, 1984

Consecration to the Immaculate Heart

On December 8 of this year, in about two months' time, is due to take place an important event in the history of the International SSPX: the official Consecration of the Society to the Immaculate Heart of Mary.

What does such a consecration mean, and why is it of importance?

The official consecration of a society of any kind to Our Lady or to Our Lord means the whole society's pledging itself to their particular service, and putting itself in a special way under their protection. Such consecrations have taken place all down the history of the Church. As well as being a solemn act of homage in the present, they are also a solemn declaration of intent for the future those who make them are in public committing and binding themselves to fulfill the purposes set forth, with the help of God, and this help they all the more confidently expect for having made such an engagement to serve Him.

Seriously made, these engagements are certainly pleasing to God. In 1873, Garcia Moreno, faithful Cath-

The Ridgefield Letters

olic president of the little South American Republic of Ecuador, consecrated his country to the Sacred Heart; only two years later he obtained on the first Friday of the month the martyr's crown in a public square of the capital, Quito. "That is one small country which has such a great president," said Pope Pius IX. His successor as pope, Leo XIII, proceeded in 1899 to consecrate the whole world to the Sacred Heart, a consecration Mother Church has us commemorate or repeat on First Fridays or on the Feast of the Sacred Heart.

The importance today of such consecrations is underlined by Our Lady's attaching at Fatima the conversion of Russia and the salvation of the world to the consecrating of the world to her Immaculate Heart by the pope in union with all the bishops of the world. As is well known, on March 25 of this year JP2 carried out his third consecration along these lines indicated by Our Lady, but since Russia was not explicitly mentioned and since the bishops of the world were still not all united with the Pope's act, then Our Lady, according to Sister Lucy of Fatima, is still waiting for the Consecration she asked for, and so the world is still waiting to be rescued! This consecration to His Mother's Heart will finally take place, Our Lord Himself is meant to have said, "but very late."

Meanwhile the SSPX can carry out its own consecration to the Immaculate Heart of Mary, and this is what it plans to do.

On the Feast of the Immaculate Conception, in Switzerland, near to the Society's Mother-House in Ecône, either the Society's founder, Archbishop Lefebvre, or its Superior General, Fr. Franz Schmidberger, will carry out the Consecration, together with as many of the Society's district superiors, seminary rectors, and heads of autonomous houses as can be present from all over the world, and in union with all of the Society's priests, brothers, sisters, oblates and lay Third Order members everywhere.

Richard N. Williamson

At the seminary here in Ridgefield also we will be preparing for the Consecration with a solemn novena of prayer to the Immaculate Conception, leading up to December 8, starting on Thursday, November 29, and we will be inviting all members of our missions to partake. We hope to get into your hands the text of the Consecration.

In the words of the Society's new Secretary General, Fr. Tissier de Mallerais:

> What we are doing is to make a covenant with Heaven, as they often did in olden times. This covenant will be made through the Blessed Virgin Mary, in such a way that the Society becomes her domain and that from now on it is her apostolic work alone that we are doing! This will best guarantee our staying on the right path: in pursuit of sanctity, each of us remaining firmly attached to the Society, while the Society in turn remains a living branch of the Catholic Church, unlike so many congregations which have disappeared or been wrecked.

At the seminary the new school year has opened with the Spiritual Exercises for the twenty old seminarians returning from last year, and they have been joined by twelve new seminarians still in the field and running after an opening retreat given by Fr. Petit and by one of the Society's new Canadian priests, Fr. Jean-Louis Violette, at the Society's house in Shawinigan, Quebec. The six tough years of seminary training will undoubtedly sift these twelve young men further, but we think there are some fine vocations among them, and we count on your prayers to obtain from God the forging of some true Catholic priests. Count on us at the seminary to serve this purpose as best as we can, and to remember in our own prayers all our spiritual and material benefactors, for whose steady support we are steadily grateful!

NO. 18 | NOVEMBER 1, 1984

The 1984 Indult, Sign of Hope

THE VATICAN'S DECREE of October 3, released on October 15, beginning to liberate the Tridentine rite of Mass, is surely one of the very best pieces of news we have had for a long time. The full text of the Decree is enclosed, with Fr. Schmidberger's comments on the reverse side.

As Fr. Schmidberger says, the conditions attached to this permission for the Tridentine rite are unacceptable to priests of the SSPX, notably Condition "A," for while acknowledging that a Pope may legitimately introduce a new rite of Mass, (and Pope Paul VI was Pope), we can never admit that a rite departing so far from Tradition as the Novus Ordo Missae, is, as such, legitimate, or doctrinally sound. Hence common people would even see in the Decree a trap to divide Traditionalists or isolate the SSPX.

However, we must beware of getting our minds into a closed circuit whereby Christ's Vicar is damned if he helps us and damned if he doesn't. Let us suppose He sincerely wishes to liberate Tradition – what other first step would we realistically expect him to take, to set about reversing the whole direction of a massive organization like the Catholic Church? And let us suppose that this Decree is not sincere, but a false start to the rescue of the Church – will it make the Society change course? Not by one degree! And if the rescue of the Church be not now, it must come.

There are, however, various indications that this Decree really does represent the turning of the tide, the breaking of the first logs from the long locked anti-Tridentine log jam. For instance, newspapers are reporting liberals running worried, and that is a good sign: "I see this Decree as a terrible move . . . it will undermine the changes in the Liturgy," said Rev. Gerard Austin, Chairman of the Catholic University theology department, in *The Washington Post* of October 18, 1984; and in the same article "This Decree could bring out old divisions where divisions have already been healed," said Rev. John Gurriri, director of the Liturgy Secretariat of the U.S. Conference of Catholic Bishops, adding, most significantly, "By reforming the Liturgy we reformed the whole Church."

Still more encouraging than these liberals fearing the overthrow of their whole Church revolution is the manner of the Decree's signing, as told to Fr. Schmidberger last week by Cardinals at the very top of the Church: the Pope summoned the Secretary of the Congregation concerned, Archbishop Virgilio Noè, a reputed Freemason who is said to have refused previously to sign such a decree, and the Pope said: "Monsignor, I want you to sign." "Yes, your Holiness," replied Archbishop Noe, "we shall be contacting the Bishops' Conferences and we will get back to you." "Monsignor," said the Pope, "you have not understood me. I WANT YOU TO SIGN, HERE AND NOW," and Archbishop Noe signed!

If this is indeed how the decree was signed, it is of momentous importance, because it shows the rescue

The Ridgefield Letters

of Tradition coming from the very Head of the Church downwards. Charity believes and hopes all, and it believes and hopes the Holy Father is here governing as we have for so long been longing for him to govern. If he risks continuing so to govern, no wonder the liberals are running worried! As he is indeed beginning to stand firm for Tradition, that is an immense personal grace obtained for him through the Mother of God, by the persevering prayers and those true Catholics that have never given up praying for the Pope. Let our prayers now redouble, for by threatening to reverse the corruption of the Church, the Pope becomes a marked man. One or two more such decrees and he gravely risks going the way of Pope John Paul I . . . St. John Bosco had a famous vision of the pope fleeing Rome over the bodies of his dead priests, with two Cardinals . . . such a vision daily comes closer to realization.

For in no way will the Devil quietly let the Tridentine Mass be officially reinstated! His master-stroke against Mother Church, climaxing centuries of effort, was, with the promulgation of the Novus Ordo in 1970, so to split Catholic pope from Catholic Mass that seemingly no Catholic could cleave to both, and so every Catholic was split in two, and Mother Church was rent from top to bottom. With this Decree, the split begins to heal, and if Pope and Mass fully reunite, then Mother Church is out of her worst troubles, and if Mother Church recovers, then the whole world begins to lift out of the filth and confusion so eloquently portrayed by our Fr. Schmidberger in his latest Letter to Friends and Benefactors, also enclosed.

Hence we may fully expect the Devil to fight this Decree tooth and nail, with silence, ridicule, inactivity. We must hope and pray that the Pope by standing firm will force the liberals to throw off the mask so that he sees who are his true friends, and so that the schism now latent comes out into the open, not that we wish the non-Catholics ill, but that we wish they would appear for what they are. Hence if the Devil would stir up schism to head off the Pope's restoring the real Mass, so be it! And if he would stir up the Kremlin to head off the Church's restoring the West, again, so be it. "Fear not little flock, for it hath pleased your Father to give you a kingdom" (Lk. 12: 32). With this Decree, or at any rate with the next or the next that it foreshadows, Almighty God is visibly, even through poor men, steering His Church out of the difficulties into which they had brought it, and the manner and timing of the Church's rescue we shall watch Him perfectly synchronizing, for the salvation of souls, with the onset of the Third World War. "O the depth of the riches of the wisdom and of the knowledge of God! How incomprehensible are his judgments, and how unsearchable His ways!" (Rom. 11: 33)

For our part, let us first and foremost convert our whole lives to God, and worship and love Him with all our heart, with all our soul, with all our strength, with all our mind, for without this conversion, all is built on sand. Let us secondly pray and pray for the Pope to have courage, because with God's grace, we shall not abandon Tradition, whatever the Church's enemies in Rome may say, but between our defending it as a small minority without the Pope and as a small minority with the Pope, there is an immeasurable difference – the one great strength of the Novus Ordo Church has been the Pope's belonging to it.

Thirdly let us make the Decree known around us, let us write to our diocesan Bishop and let us write to Rome letters full of gratitude for this Decree and of respect for their sublime office. Addresses in Rome and good advice for such letters are enclosed beneath Fr. Schmidberger's comments. Also let us urge priests and laity, who have till now used the Novus Ordo Missae, to ask for use of

The Ridgefield Letters

the Decree, without referring too closely to the conditions attached. Let us also remember from now on in, that it is hard to admit one was wrong. We must make it as easy as possible for the misleaders and the misled to rejoin Tradition. Without a trace of bitterness or arrogance, we must convey that it was for us a gift of God to have found Tradition, and it is natural for Catholics to return to it.

Alas, we do not yet have the text of the Society's Consecration to the Blessed Mother of God, due to be made by Fr. Schmidberger at Ecône in Switzerland on December 8, but you will certainly have it with the Seminary's December letter, at the latest. You will also receive the text of the Consecration of the World to the Immaculate Heart of Mary, which Archbishop Lefebvre will carry out in Martigny, near Ecône, on the day after, Sunday, December 9. It is hoped there will be a crowd of several thousand to take part in this Consecration, as last time, in March of 1982.

The latest issue of *The Verbum* gives news of the seminary. We continue to be harassed. We continue to survive. Please think of our heating-bills as winter closes in, and may God bless you and protect all your families!

NO. 19 | DECEMBER 1, 1984

Consecration and Christmas

THIS MONTH'S LETTER is being sent to all of you by first-class mail in the hope of getting into your hands by this Saturday the text of the Society's Consecration to Mary, in particular to her Immaculate Heart.

"Modern times are dominated by Satan and will be more so in the future. The conflict with Hell cannot be engaged in by man, even the most clever. The Immaculate alone has from God promise of victory over Satan," said St. Maximilian Kolbe, who died in 1941. Hence the decisive importance of consecrating the Society to the Immaculate Heart, whose statue St. Maximilian saw, in a vision, on top of the Kremlin . . .

On the Feast of the Immaculate Conception, Society priests from all over the world are gathering in the Society's Mother-House, the seminary at Ecône in Switzerland, in order solemnly to make together with the Superior General this Consecration. The document of the Consecration will then be signed by all present, and solemnly placed within the main altar of the seminary, as a permanent pledge of the Society's Consecration. We hope

The Ridgefield Letters

and trust then that as many of you as possible will join the Society at least in spirit on that day, to help us to get beneath the only sure bomb shelter – Our Lady's mantle. I am going over to Switzerland for the ceremony, so I should be able in next month's letter to say how it went.

I could also bring back news of Rome's evolving conflict with Hell. Since the famous Decree of October on the Tridentine rite of Mass, which of course liberals everywhere are doing their best to nullify, Cardinal Ratzinger, Prefect of the Congregation for the Doctrine of the Faith, has given an interview spread over three days, extracts from which have been published in a Catholic periodical, for instance:

> The Second Vatican Council gave too much emphasis to the value of non-Catholic religions. Instead of unity and enthusiasm, the result has been division, discouragement and boredom.... Whoever thinks that Church and world can meet without conflict or can even mix with one another, has no knowledge of either. More than ever before the Christian must be conscious that he belongs to a minority, and must stand in contradiction to what <u>seems</u> good or logical. The Christian must regain the ability to withstand all kinds of cultural trends and to renounce an exaggerated closeness to the world.... Power must be given back to the bishops in their dioceses, by their being freed from the all-too-bureaucratic structures of the Bishops' Conferences. These conferences have no theological basis, but merely a practical one. We shall do well not to forget this. In many Bishops' Conferences a feeling of togetherness and maybe just keeping in line, impels passive majorities to accept the positions of freely-innovating minorities. (*Tages-Anzeiger*, November 19, 1984)

For such a highly-placed Cardinal to be taking today such positions in public, he must be receiving light and courage from God, and for him to be taking on the mighty Bishops' Conferences, Archbishop Lefebvre thinks the Cardinal must also have the backing of the Pope. Now Rome was not built in a day, so, let us be under no illusions, it will not be rebuilt in a day either. Nevertheless, a flow of letters from Catholics all over the world will help to encourage the Church's high officials to move in the right direction, for they remain human beings who will find it easier to govern the Church correctly if they sense they are being supported. Letters should be addressed to Cardinal Joseph Ratzinger, Prefect of the Congregation for the Doctrine of the Faith, Piazza del S. Uffizio, 11, 00193, Rome, Italy; or to Archbishop Augustin Mayer, Prefect of the Congregation of Divine Worship, Palazzo delle Congregazioni, Piazza Pio XII, 10, 00193, Rome, Italy; or even to the Holy Father Pope John Paul II, Vatican City, Italy.

As tender green plants can lift up and break through slabs of black asphalt laid down to stifle them, so can the humble faith of many Catholics lift up and break through the stifling modernism laid down to crush them! O we of little faith, how could we doubt in Our Lord and His Church?

> Behold the Lord will appear, and He will not fail; if He delays, await Him, because He will come and He will not be long, alleluia!
> Behold, our Lord will come with power, and He will enlighten the eyes of His servants, alleluia!
> Sing with a trumpet in Sion, because the day of the Lord is near: behold, he will come to save us, alleluia, allcluia!
> The mountains and hills will sing praise before God, and all the trees of the forests will clap their hands; for the Lord and Master will come into his eternal kingdom, alleluia, alleluia!

The Ridgefield Letters

As we enter the season of Advent, let its beautiful Antiphons revive within us our hope and <u>certainty</u> of Our Lord's coming to rescue – let the very trees teach us how to clap our hands for joy!

Just after Christmas, do not forget the Spiritual Exercises for men and young men available at the seminary. Here is one enchanted mother of an 18 year old who did the Exercises this summer:

> I've never seen such a change in a young man in all my life! Luckily, his own car broke down, so we had to drive him to the seminary and leave him there. 'Otherwise,' he told us, 'I would have come away after the first night. I couldn't face the silence. You're alone with God. The second night was a bit better. I was beginning to think how often when I'm in a bad mood I take it out on you, mom. I realized how unfair that was. You're the only one that's so good to me all the time. After the third day, I wanted to do the five-day retreat.' Since then, that boy and I have never had one single run-in! He treats me with such respect! Now his older brother is saying maybe he will go on the next retreat with him. But don't say I told you! My name will be Mudd!

Momma, need more be said? You get that darling boy of yours to do the Exercises of St. Ignatius! St. Ignatius will see to him!

Have a blessed Advent season and a happy Christmas, laden with grace, and may the Divine Child reward every one of you that has so steadily and generously supported the seminary through the year! Fresh pledge cards to join the SCSF are enclosed, in case you would like to make it easier to contribute, by receiving each month a return envelope. You also then receive the seminary's letter sooner each month, by first-class mail.

May God bless you all!

NO. 20 | JANUARY 1, 1985

Weighing the 1984 Indult

THE SSPX IS now firmly consecrated since December 8 to the Immaculate Heart of Mary. Society priests are reacting with a wary optimism to Rome's October Decree on the Tridentine Mass. Those are the headlines from my ten-day visit to Europe early in December.

It was a coincidence, or providential, that the Decree should have come out just several weeks before the gathering in Switzerland of all the Society's Seminary, District and Autonomous House Superiors for the Society's Consecration to Mary, and so at a prior meeting of the Superiors the Decree was thoroughly discussed. Archbishop Lefebvre was present, just returned from a long tour of South America, and Fr. Schmidberger invited him to speak first.

He said that in South America the people are right behind the Society. In Santiago in Chile he had in one Confirmation ceremony spent four hours confirming 1,200 children! However, nearly all the bishops are more and more strongly opposed to the Society, so few priests dare yet associate with us, and so for a while the Decree may have positive effects only amongst the people. (The Society's District Superior in France would confirm that

—64—

The Ridgefield Letters

Tridentine Mass attendance in Paris has risen considerably, since the Decree). The Archbishop added later that Church officials still holding to the principles of Vatican II, even if they deplore its excesses, are not yet truly returning to Tradition. Hence the Society should beware of asking bishops to apply the Decree who, if they do not flatly refuse, risk using it as a decoy to lure Catholics back to the Novus Ordo religion. Nevertheless, Cardinal Ratzinger's famous interview deploring the failure of Vatican II is something new in today's Rome. Even if the Decree was ill-meant (and the Archbishop does not think it was), God could still use it to bring souls to the true Mass. The Society need not and must not change by one inch, and time will more and more prove it right.

Fr. Schmidberger then asked Fr. Du Chalard, a Society priest living near Rome, to speak. Fr. Du Chalard firstly confirmed that the Decree was the personal will of the Pope, bitterly opposed by Archbishop Virgilio Noe, but the Pope will not turn back. He still does not fully grasp how the new Liturgy undermines the Faith, but he has had enough of crazy liturgies. As for Cardinal Ratzinger, his interview is making the progressives furious, and he says the Decree is just a first step; Archbishop Mayer has asked the Pope to remove the Decree's obstructive conditions; Cardinals Oddi and Ratzinger and Mayer all favor the widest possible interpretation of the Decree, to facilitate its use. The bishops on the contrary are hardening in their resistance, but when one of them sought to add to the Decree further obstructions of his own, he was summoned to Rome and forced to back down. In brief, "something is changing in Rome."

Fr. Schmidberger added details of his own meeting in October with Cardinal Ratzinger, saying how the Cardinal had definitely changed his position for the better since their meeting in Munich in 1978. Then the Cardinal contested even the most solemn of 19th century encyclicals if it opposed Vatican II; now he admitted Vatican II might be called in question. In Munich the modernists were already whistling and jeering at him; in Rome they are now positively crucifying him! In the ensuing discussion many priests were encouraged by this fury of the liberals, but many also were wary of turning for any kind of help to bishops who are still basically modernists. Nevertheless, said Fr. Schmidberger, the Decree presents the Society with an opportunity it must not miss. How? The question remained open.

The Consecration of the Society to the Immaculate Heart took place at a Solemn High Mass celebrated by Fr. Schmidberger in the Seminary two days later. After his sermon explaining its threefold purpose, the greater glory of Mary, her help in defeating the Devil who is today unleashed, and her help in renewing the Church and especially the priesthood, Fr. Schmidberger recited the Consecration in Latin, and then a long procession of Society priests from all over the world mounted the altar to sign after Archbishop Lefebvre the parchment of the Consecration. There followed Society brothers, sisters (who overflowed their allocation of parchment), oblates and finally members of the Third order, including two of the five Swiss laymen who by buying the Ecône property over fifteen years ago enabled Archbishop Lefebvre to make the name world-famous. Finally all signatures were affixed, and the parchment was laid into the main altar beneath the altar-stone, next to a large box of first-class relics of Pope St. Urban I solemnly laid in the altar the day before. Let Ecône and the Society thus be anchored to the Mother of God and to the Holy See!

That same evening began an all-night prayer vigil in the nearby town of Martigny, culminating in a Pontifical High Mass celebrated on Sunday morning, December 9, by Archbishop Lefebvre, and attended by an estimated 3,500 people from all over Europe. In his sermon the

The Ridgefield Letters

Archbishop painted a dramatic picture from the Apocalypse, of the Church battling Satan. Today's churchmen, alas, instead of, like Mary, crushing his head, are, like Eve, dialoguing with him, and so the Church is being filled with satanic errors, religious liberty, ecumenism, human rights, errors condemned again and again by earlier popes. Such dialogue is a fatal mistake.

Thus the supposedly conservative President of Columbia in South America, by dialoguing with the terrorist guerrillas, has enabled the Communists to infiltrate the universities and arm 70,000 men in five bands throughout the country, ready now at any moment, unless the army acts soon, to split the country in two and hand over to Communism the strategic gateway to the South American continent! The Archbishop proposed on the contrary the Blessed Virgin and St. Pius X as models of how to resist and fight. Then in honour of the 130th Anniversary of the definition in 1854 of the dogma of Mary's Immaculate Conception, he pronounced again Pope Pius XII's Consecration of the World to Her Immaculate Heart, but now mentioning explicitly Russia.

The Society priests from South America afterwards confirmed the Archbishop's dramatic analysis of events in South America: in Bogotá, capital of Columbia, the American ambassador in November gave Americans four months to get home, anticipating an American invasion of Nicaragua. At about the same time the French ambassador in Peru, Lima, was telling French nationals to get home within seven months, the months to come promising to be "very dangerous"...

Two days later, on December 11, another meeting of priests and laymen was held, this time in France, to discuss the Decree. Archbishop Lefebvre presided, but more than half the priests present were from outside the Society. The Archbishop reiterated his distrust of prelates clinging to liberal principles and seeking merely to moderate the most disastrous of their logical consequences, and he warned urgently against any regular cooperation with such prelates for as long as they are in the grip of such principles. However, a layman present claimed to have heard from Rome that further good changes are on the way, that the Decree's obstructive conditions will be done away with, because they highly displeased the Pope who himself wanted the Tridentine Mass to be simply set free.

The conclusion of the meeting was that priests and faithful should beware of Tridentine Masses celebrated by Novus Ordo priests, and they should not seek to benefit regularly by the Decree, because of the compromises that risk being involved. However, they should seize every occasion, e.g., marriages, funerals, etc., to ask their bishops for the use of a church for a Tridentine Mass to be celebrated by a priest they know and can trust, and all exchanges of correspondence with bishops should be forwarded to the Holy See to inform and encourage friends of the true Mass in Rome.

Back in the United States, no doubt the American bishops are mostly mobilizing against the Decree. Thus a bishop who on his own in November welcomed the Decree as giving him "a chance to extend a shepherd's care to some sincere people who need special attention," in December, one assumes after "consulting" his colleagues, was writing that the Novus Ordo should be just as capable as the Tridentine Mass of catering for such people's needs, and so he was refusing all Tridentine requests (*The Remnant*, Dec. 15)! Pray for such a bishop, and pray especially for the Pope, because he is the Church's Father, and all turns on him. The Society has received confirmation from three independent sources of the Holy Father's displeasure at the obstructions fastened onto the Decree! There is hope. St. Urban I, St. Pius X, pray for him!

The Ridgefield Letters

At the seminary, all is peaceful after the seminarians' departure on St. Stephen's Day after a long and successful school-term. We are all of us immensely grateful for the generous support of the seminary by many of you. Your Christmas gifts will neatly take out some lawyer's bills, with details of which I will not disedify you! Let me here just thank in particular every one of you that has faithfully contributed each month this year. May God bless you and keep you throughout the coming year, which promises to be interesting. May He above all reward you with an increase in sanctifying grace, faith, hope and charity!

NO. 21 | FEBRUARY 1, 1985

Petition of the SSPX to Rome

ONCE AGAIN THIS letter is coming to you all first-class to enable you to take part in time in a petition and a novena.

With the enclosed petition many of you, either through *The Angelus* or through the Society's chapels, will already be familiar (nobody should sign twice!). It is the Society's reaction to Rome's October Decree on the Tridentine Mass. A Society priest in touch with events in Rome told me in the last few days that a slow evolution continues to take place inside the Vatican in favor of Catholic Tradition. At all Cardinals' meetings the question of Tradition comes up. It is being appreciated that Traditionalists have a sense of the Church and a true spirituality, and it is expected that the October Decree will be broadened in favor of the Tridentine Mass at the end of its first year's application. Hence many in Rome are discontented with the bishops continuing to refuse the Tridentine Mass, and they like having details of such refusals. To strengthen their hand, the Society is seeking to provide concrete evidence of the widespread desire for the return of Tra-

The Ridgefield Letters

dition by collecting as many names as possible for a threefold petition:

Firstly, that the unrestricted right of any Catholic priest to celebrate Mass in the Tridentine Rite be openly recognized (notice, recognized, not granted; we are not asking that this right which has never legally been taken away, be granted).

Secondly, that the injustices committed against Archbishop Lefebvre and his priests come to an end (notice again that there is no admission that the suspension inflicted in 1976 upon Archbishop Lefebvre and his priests was ever valid; the Archbishop has steadily maintained that the absence of any grave external offence carried out with contumacy invalidated the "suspension" from the very beginning – Canon 2242 in the old Code then in force. Likewise with the dissolution inflicted in 1975 on the Society as such; at the time Bishop Mamie inflicted this "dissolution," he had no power to do so – Canon 493).

And thirdly, that the SSPX be recognized as having a status of dependency within the Church not upon the local diocesan bishops but upon the Holy See, and furthermore – that it be granted a personal prelate, in other words a bishop who is bishop by his person and not by his territory or diocese. This is the status presently enjoyed by *Opus Dei*, and it would give the SSPX still more freedom to act throughout the world, while keeping it within the hierarchical framework of Our Lord's hierarchical Church.

Of these three requests, clearly the first is the most important. It is Mother Church which matters, and her Holy Sacrifice of the Mass, of which the Archbishop and his Society are really "unworthy servants" (Lk. 17: 10). In no way can the Society replace, or presume to replace, the Church. In dark days of the Church, the Society is merely making a major contribution to preserving the sacred fire of Tradition, and holding it aloft amid the darkness for all to see, but she dreams of the day when the whole Church will again catch fire with the fire of Tradition, and when no such torchbearer will any longer be needed. Hence the Society supports all petitions for the true Mass, even independently of herself, as proposed by this Letter in November – would that this battle could and would be won without us!

Notwithstanding, that "merely" is some merely, and the Society's own view is that the vindication of her founder is an elementary demand of justice, due to a heroic servant of the Church, and that together with the open recognition of the Society, also due in justice, it will tell everyone in the most concrete and honorable way that Tradition is being restored. Hence precisely for the sake of Mother Church we are attaching the second and third requests to the first.

Note that the ideal is to collect many names on few sheets rather than few on many, but duplicate the petition sheet as much as you like to collect as many names as possible. Let each person write his own name and address. Children of seven and upwards may sign. Protestants and all but death-wish liberals may be asked to sign, whoever has the grace to recognize that all Western Civilization depends on the Catholic Church, and the Church on the rite of Mass not being falsified.

To accompany the petition, the Society's Superior General, Fr. Franz Schmidberger, is also calling for a novena of prayer to St. Joseph, preferably the recitation of the Litany of St. Joseph, to run from February 2, Feast of the Presentation, to February 10 inclusive, Eve of the Feast of Our Lady of Lourdes (but any nine successive days around this time will suffice). The joint intentions of this novena are to be the success of the petition to the Holy Father, and the resolving of the Society's remaining difficulties presently before the law courts in the United States.

The Ridgefield Letters

This monthly letter has given few details of the slow and costly litigation running now for a year and a half in Virginia, Connecticut, Pennsylvania and New York, between the Society and nine of its former priests who in April 1983 broke away from the Society and attempted to take fourteen properties with them. Few would be edified by such details. The dispute is primarily between two very different conceptions of the Catholic Church. For example Long Island's *Newsday* of December 10, 1984, quoted one of "The Nine" as saying that the Pope and his bishops would be refused Communion at the chapel of "The Nine" on Long Island. This is not the Society's view of the Church, but it is certainly "The Nine's!" – "We're maintaining this is it and everybody else is wrong. We're trying to get our message out to as many people as possible," the same priest was quoted as saying, in the Easton *Express* of January 19, 1985.

From this conception flowed a major revolt against the Archbishop ("liberalizing trends taken by the European leadership of the Society" – *ibid.*), and "The Nine's" laying claim to all properties acquired by them, under the Archbishop and in the name of the Society, or so they gave everyone at that time to think. Hence secondarily there is a dispute over properties. Now soon after the split, at the outset of the dispute over properties, the Society, to avoid heavy legal fees, offered to submit the whole question to official arbitration, which would have been rapid, inexpensive and discreet. "The Nine" refused. The matter had to go to court. By October of last year "The Nine" had, on their own admission, spent over $100,000 on lawyers, and since October they have certainly spent much more. Nor is the end anywhere near in sight. In the course of February their five leaders must give depositions, which should probe searchingly into their version of events . . . Pray during the novena that God's will shall be done!

Richard N. Williamson

More positive news from the seminary! Eleven young men who entered the seminary in September have persevered, and will be receiving the cassock in the beautiful Candlemass of the Feast of the Presentation. This will take place just after the strenuous first semester exams, heavy preparation for which has been lightened for many of them by learning to slide faster and faster down the ice-covered seminary garden out onto the frozen lake. One seminarian ran off course and tried to knock down a tree, but the tree had rather the better of it! St. Januarius, St. Securus (there is no St. Februarius, but there is a St. Securus, I have checked), keep them out of hospital!

Meanwhile and all-while, many thanks to all of you looking after us with your prayers and contributions. The building of the new chapel is still at a standstill, due to the litigation, but you have enabled us to pay off one whole third of a major debt of the Seminary to Archbishop Lefebvre. On Sunday May 19 of this year he should be ordaining four new priests here at Ridgefield. Please God may we give you the faithful priests your generosity deserves!

NO. 22 | MARCH 1, 1985

Rome – Not So Hopeful

IN THE EXCEPTIONALLY mild February weather of the last few days, there is a parable: spring is on its way, but it is not yet here (In 1983, there was a major snowfall in early March). Similarly in the Church, Cardinal Ratzinger's long and important interview of last August and the October Decree on the Tridentine Mass were such positive signs as to make many hope that the Pope's announcement in January of a Bishops' Synod in Rome at the end of this year was another decisive step on the way to the major course-correction needed by the Catholic Church. In fact, the winter of THE SECOND VATICAN COUNCIL is not yet over...

On January 10, Archbishop Lefebvre met with Cardinal Ratzinger, Prefect of the Congregation for the Doctrine of the Faith, in Rome, and he has given a few details of their meeting. The Cardinal showed himself more open than ever before. The Archbishop spoke at length: "We need a Bishop." "Ask." "We also need the Tridentine Breviary, Ritual and Pontifical as well as the Missal." "Ask." "Also, instead of the Second Vatican Council being interpreted in the light of Tradition, which is ambiguous, I would require the Council's being sifted by Tradition." "Put it in writing." Thus the Cardinal invited the Archbishop to ask without being afraid, as though he would have whatever he wanted. (In that case, said the Archbishop, how about lifting his "suspension," a grave injustice and injury? To fail to do so would be like leaving in prison someone known to be innocent).

However, despite the Cardinal's openness, the Archbishop remained anxious. The lifting of the Church's disciplinary sanctions against the Society need not mean a corresponding abandonment of the Church's doctrinal liberalism, in which case, how could the Society re-enter a sheepfold still full of doctrinal wolves? The Cardinal did not seem fully to understand the doctrinal problem.

Yet Archbishop Gagnon, President of the Pontifical Commission on the Family, visiting Archbishop Lefebvre at about the same time in the Society's house in Albano near Rome, confirmed the suspicions of a sheepfold full of wolves. He said that within the Vatican and the various national governments there is a whole mafia or network of people preventing the Pope from governing the Church. For instance, to rid himself of an unwanted subordinate, Archbishop Gagnon obtained from the Pope orders to remove him. Yet the subordinate remained in place, kept there by the network! Having once been appointed Examiner of the Curia, Archbishop Gagnon also knows details of the personal lives of Curia officials. His overall description of the Curia in Rome is enough "to make one's hair stand on end," said Archbishop Lefebvre.

Hence the Society's founder is presently in no hurry for the Society to regain Rome's good graces. He says: "It is better to wait. At some point God will intervene. The October Decree remains a very superficial improvement. Cardinal Ratzinger in our interview seemed very sure of himself, and gave me the impression that the Pope is with him, but even if they wish to govern, they cannot. Any sanctions they impose rouse such reactions

The Ridgefield Letters

as oblige them to retreat. Already the bishops of South America and Germany have taken steps to get rid of Ratzinger. He is exposed to violent counterattacks. Nor will the November Synod mean a change of direction, according to the newspapers. After all, most new bishops have been chosen by the progressives. We may fear their hardening still further."

The root of the problem is that our God is an absolute God and He makes absolute demands. The basis of our Catholic Faith is a submission which must endure, not a consent which may be taken back. We are not Catholics at our pleasure, but at God's command. However much we may wish our fellow men well, we cannot to please any of them give up a jot of God's truth, or a tittle of His commands. Cardinal Ratzinger seems at least to have grasped that the period of Vatican II has been a disaster for the Church, and for someone as highly placed as he is to admit as much is a great step forward.

Nevertheless, until the Church is once more governed by leaders who fully grasp that to trade in the least of God's rights is to deny the true God, the Church must continue to be in trouble. Until the liberal principles underpinning Vatican II, and not just their worst consequences, are repudiated, Catholics must beware of most churchmen – they still have leprosy. The good leaders needed, God can give to His Church when He likes, indeed they can only come, like all good gifts, from above. We must pray for the Cardinals and increase our prayers for the Pope.

Oddly enough – but then extremes do meet – the same error of submission by consent underpins the breakaway of the former Society priests in the USA who accuse Archbishop Lefebvre of being too liberal! Questioned in depositions in mid-February, they gave such evasive answers that the New York Federal magistrate is obliging them to continue their depositions in front of him! And they had reason to be evasive. After all, how can they deny the documents, demonstrating from the early 70's through to April of 1983, their recognition of Archbishop Lefebvre's authority? On the other hand, how can they admit his authority without losing all right to the properties they acquired under him? In front of the magistrate they will have to answer one way or the other.

The end of January ruling of a Federal Court in Pennsylvania has also favoured the Society. In moving for Summary Judgment, in October the breakaway priests leaned heavily on their favorite argument that ever since the Society's "dissolution" by the Swiss diocesan bishop in 1975, it has not had any hierarchical structure or authority. In refusing the motion, the court ruled that what happened in 1975 was irrelevant, since the property in question was only acquired in 1980. Moreover, even leaving aside questions of hierarchy, the corporate documents of the property clearly tied it to the Society. All that the Society now need do is prove that in 1980 it had a clear hierarchical structure. Were the breakaway priests not themselves at pains at that time to say so to the people? This litigation is very sad, and expensive. However, it was the only alternative to letting a gross injustice pass, and the American courts do seem to be tightening the noose around the neck of the fraud. Just let us know if you would like a copy of the Pennsylvania judge's ruling.

Also let us know (and let us have $25, for costs) if you would like a copy of a Video-cassette tape-recording of a Seminary priest explaining how to celebrate the Tridentine Mass. We made this tape at Christmas, having in mind Novus Ordo priests who might turn or return to the Tridentine Mass, if they knew how. This tape should certainly help teach them or remind them of the priestly mechanics of celebrating the Tridentine Mass, but it is

The Ridgefield Letters

not designed to be a devotional tape. For a limited supply of free devotional videotapes of the Tridentine Mass write to "Keep the Faith."

Enclosed is the Minimum Knowledge sheet for Confirmation, in case any readers know of children to be confirmed in the course of Archbishop Lefebvre's April-May visit to the United States. His Grace will be confirming as follows:

Also at Ridgefield he will be ordaining, *Deo volente*, two subdeacons on Friday, May 17, twenty-two seminarians to Minor Orders and Tonsure on the morning of May 18, three deacons and four priests on Sunday morning of May 19. Priests will be very welcome to visit the seminary at that time, and to take part in the ordinations to the priesthood, if they can disengage themselves on the Sunday. Let us hope the weather is as good as it was last year. We look forward to seeing as many of you as possible.

NO. 23 | APRIL 1, 1985

Corks and Nets

THE NAMES AND signatures of many of you, together with over 100,000 others, were presented personally last week to Cardinal Ratzinger in Rome by the Society's Superior General, Fr. Franz Schmidberger.

The Society's triple petition on behalf of the Tridentine Mass, Archbishop Lefebvre and the SSPX, collected in the United States about 12,000 names, including 5,000 from the seminary and the missions it serves; from France some 40,000 names; from Germany 22,000, from Switzerland 14,000, from Austria 9,000, from Great Britain 5,000, from Italy 4,000; from India, mired in "Indianisation," meaning in effect Hinduisation, of the Catholic Church, an admirable 3,000; from Ireland 2,000, and a scattering of further signatures from literally all parts of the world.

Altogether well over 100,000 signatures, quite an achievement in the space of a few weeks. Let us hope this evidence of a considerable weight of properly Catholic opinion will help the best prelates in Rome to defend Catholic Tradition. Notice in the Superior General's enclosed letter where he says that we are battling not just for the relatively modest SSPX, but for the whole Cath-

The Ridgefield Letters

olic Church. Said the nets to the corks: "What are you doing, lazing in the sun, while we down below catch all the fish?" Replied the corks to the net: "Without us, you would all long ago have been lying useless at the bottom of the sea." Say many Catholics to the Society, "What are you doing there outside the Church while we fight within?" Replies the Society: "Without our stand outside the CONCILIAR Church, countless Catholics within it would have lost all sense of the Faith and the fight long ago."

Notice also from the same letter the eloquent plea from Bishop Sarto of Mantua, later Pope Pius X, on behalf of his diocesan seminary. You have, dear Friends, most certainly loved the seminary in Ridgefield. Since April of 1983, you have, besides covering all running costs of the seminary, enabled us to repay $85,000 of debts, and to pay so far over $45,000 in legal fees. This is, if I am thinking straight, admirable generosity on the part of you all. I am very sorry that much of what you give us must be spent for the moment on litigation, but the fight was not of our choosing. We were, by excessive trust, victims of a skilful and deceitful aggression. "Revenge is mine, I will repay, saith the Lord," (Rom. 12: 19). But in the meantime please maintain your generosity, because seminary reserves are severely depleted, and more lawyers' bills are on the way. Remember, if you wish to know how the courts are reacting, we can send you a judge's ruling in January from Pennsylvania, highly favorable to the Society.

For the Archbishop's program of ordinations at Ridgefield in May – all are invited – for lodgings around Ridgefield, and for spring and summer Spiritual Exercises, see over. An added incentive to do the Exercises at Ridgefield is that the clearing away of brushwood is uncovering the beauty of our grounds. Three or five beautiful days, in the peace of God!

Richard N. Williamson

Concerning Confirmation, be careful of a mistake in the Minimum Knowledge sheet we sent out last month. The Holy Ghost is of course the third, and not the second, Person of the Holy Trinity. As the love of God, in Person, may He fill our hearts and minds to the exclusion of all foolish cares and preoccupations!

Happy Eastertide!

NO. 24 | MAY 1, 1985

April 1983 – A Doctrinal Split

ARCHBISHOP LEFEBVRE IS back in America! In his 80th year he is undertaking a 20-stop tour, spread over thirty-four days, of the United States and Canada, the climax of which will undoubtedly be his ordaining of one Canadian and three Americans to the holy priesthood here in Ridgefield on May 19. He will return to Europe four days later.

"Ecce sacerdos magnus," says the Gradual for the Mass for a Bishop, quoting from Ecclesiasticus, "Behold a great priest who in his days pleased God. There was not found like to him, who kept the law of the Most High." Not that the SSPX goes in for any personality cult, nor that it holds Archbishop Lefebvre to be infallible or impeccable, but that the Society venerates him as a great defender of the Faith and loves him as its founder. "Yes, but when he dies?" people ask, and it is a serious question, to which the surest answer is that it is intrinsically impossible for God to leave the humble sheep of His one and only Church without a true shepherd. "You shall seek me, and shall find me: when you shall seek me with all your heart." (Jer. 29: 13) Within or without the SSPX,

God is bound to provide a visible beacon to show sincere souls the way to Heaven. Meanwhile, welcome, Your Grace, and may this not be the last of your visits!

May it also not be disturbed, as were your last two visits, by the spirit of defection. For indeed the defections of April '83 and May '84 still cast their shadow after them. Parents for instance, following the priests who left the Archbishop two years ago, are hurt that the Society should no longer be perfectly willing for their children to receive from him the Sacrament of Confirmation. Like many Catholics since the split in 1983, they hold that it was merely a scandalous quarrel between priests in which the laity should not get involved. They say they insist on having respect for all the priests involved because to condemn any one priest is a grievous sin, and after all, all they wish is to attend Mass and receive the sacraments, so that to refuse Confirmation to their children is simply to penalize the innocent.

Such arguments would apply had the split of 1983 not been grave, but it was grave, engaging the true Catholic Faith, and so for the sake of the Faith, avoiding all idle abuse or recriminations, let us recall what was – and still is – at stake. Holy Scripture says in two places (I Cor. 11: 19; I Jn. 2: 18–19) that the use of such divisions is to manifest who are the true believers.

For the Archbishop, the key issues in dispute were the Liturgy, the Pope, and the new sacramental rites, all of which issues, he once interestingly said, come back to the question of the Pope. For the priests who decided to disobey the Archbishop, the Archbishop was wrong principally on the Liturgy and the sacraments of Holy Orders and Holy Matrimony. Either way, surely grave issues of doctrine, as the actions confirmed: the Archbishop declared that by taking their harsh positions the priests had taken themselves out of the SSPX that he had founded, whereupon the priests gave everyone to under-

The Ridgefield Letters

stand that, the Society was accepting the Novus Ordo Mass because the Archbishop wanted to compromise with Rome.

Two years' events have since shown the inaccuracy of the priests' allegations, but in any case the priests then set in motion the mechanism they had long prepared in civil law to go independent if necessary. Spending hundreds of thousands of dollars in litigation, they lay claim to all fourteen Society properties of that time, including for instance the seminary property to which in the Archbishop's opinion their only title was "plain theft." To back their independence they are now in depositions under oath repeatedly contradicting their written and spoken word for years prior to the split, and they have in public praised three seminarians for lying low for a year in the Archbishop's seminary and walking out on him ten days after ordination, as though they were "the three young men in the burning fiery furnace!"

On any reckoning, such actions are grave and betoken a grave dispute, founded, as we saw, in doctrine, and merely spelled out in action. Hence the normal rule that priests must not battle one another in public and that the laity should not get involved, does not apply. Luther, like many leading heretics, was a Catholic priest, yet every true priest was bound (then and now!) to battle him, and the laity, at the risk of their eternal salvation, had to take sides, and take their innocent children with them. Where basic Catholic doctrine is involved, there can be no neutrality – "He who is not for me, is against me," says Our Lord. (Mt. 12: 30)

Now in 1983, immediately after the split, a layman might still have said, out of misguided loyalty to the dissident priests, or out of lack of discernment, that he could see nothing anti-Catholic beneath all their trappings of Tradition, but since the triple walkout of May, 1984, who cannot see that these priests, whatever they say, act on the totally un-Catholic principle that the end justifies the means? What Catholics ever defended Tradition by actions resembling in all points lying, stealing, perjury and betrayal?

Hence the Society which was in 1983 maybe slow to warn Catholics against regularly exposing themselves to the presence or influence of these priests, now at any rate tells such Catholics that they must choose. If they really wish their children to be confirmed by the Archbishop, well and good, then they must show that they are not infected by what the Archbishop holds to be the doctrinal errors of these priests. Otherwise, not having the mind of his subjects, how can they claim any of the benefits of having him as their superior?

If on the other hand they seriously judge that the priests are right and the Archbishop or the Society is going wrong, so be it, but let them turn to the priests for Confirmation, because one of them is quoted as saying that he would give it. If however they wish to have it both ways, or if they insist that they cannot judge or condemn, despite Our Lord's own warning to beware of wolves in sheeps' skins (Mt. 7: 15), then they must take the consequences of their refusal to distinguish between shepherd and wolf, and they must realize that they cannot be both insubordinate by following dissidents and subordinates who may claim Confirmation. Of course the Society can always be deceived, as it was in May of 1984, but for its part, so far as in it lies, it will do what it can henceforth to ensure that those who claim its special benefits essentially have its mind, which is meant not to penalize but to protect the innocent.

The Society meanwhile goes its way. It was not 100,000, but finally 134,000 signatures that were collected for the triple petition to the Holy Father, including 13,759 from the United States, and 5,310 from Canada. The Society's new District Superior in Canada, Fr. Jacques Emily,

The Ridgefield Letters

based in Shawinigan, Province of Quebec, has recently purchased two new churches, one in Sherbrooke, and one in the center of Montreal. These churches should considerably extend the Society's work in Canada – they risk also extending the work of the seminary priests, if Fr. Emily has his way!

Visitors to the seminary for the ordinations will notice a large (second-hand) fence going up around the vegetable garden to keep out the deer who last year treated it as a salad bar, but they will notice little change in the new chapel, still at a building standstill until the litigation clears. Our adversaries employ expensive lawyers (what might be called a "stein" of lawyers!), but we continue to place high hopes in the common sense and equity of the courts.

In any case thank you all very much for another burst of support in the month of April. Our burdens are heavy, so our reserves are still non-existent, and the seminary's brown Impala (Chevrolet) has just thrown a rod-bearing (it was entitled to do so after 238,000 miles), but St. Joseph continues to look after us. Warm thanks to all his agents! With a subsequent letter I mean to send you a color photograph of the ordinations you are supporting. Watch out also for details of three tapes we shall be making available of conversations between a young Canadian and myself on the Crisis in the Church, the Mass, and the Society. I am told they have come out well, but I have no time to listen to them!

With all good wishes for Our Lady's blessed month of May, month of life, month of beauty, month of mothers.

NO. 25 | JUNE 1, 1985

The Archbishop Comforted by US Visit

ONE PICTURE, THEY say, is worth a thousand words, and so we are getting to you this month as soon as we could a picture of the Ordinations Ceremony held here at the seminary on Sunday, May 19. Framed within the tall wooden pillars of the unfinished interior of the new seminary chapel is the beautiful altar erected last year, immediately in front of which can be seen from left to right, standing, the Society's American seminary rector, and sitting, the Society's Superior General, Fr. Franz Schmidberger; its Founder, Archbishop Lefebvre; and its American District Superior, Fr. François Laisney, who is watching the Pontifical from which the Archbishop is about to read the first admonition to the seven ordinands to the diaconate and priesthood kneeling in a semicircle before him.

A full picture-story on the ordinations should be coming to you in the next issue of *The Verbum*, but in the meantime the picture gives a little idea of the colorful dignity and serene majesty of the nearly four-hour ceremony which brought into being three new deacons and four new priests for eternity, according to the order

The Ridgefield Letters

of Melchisedech: Fr. Christopher Brandler from Texas, Fr. Gregory Foley from California, Fr. Loren Gerspacher from British Columbia and Fr. John Rizzo from Massachusetts. Of these four, Fr. Gerspacher returns to Canada, Fr. Brandler is being posted to the Society's International Seminary in Switzerland and Fr. Rizzo goes to Great Britain, maybe because it was thought that New England should have a chance to get its own back on old England! However, the Society will be bringing in two priests from abroad to replace Frs. Brandler and Rizzo, so the United States will still have three new priests. Fr. Foley is due to go to Philadelphia, to ensure the chaplaincy of the new Carmel. It goes without saying that had the Archbishop been able to ordain many times more new priests, they could all have found work looking after your needs throughout the English-speaking world, but we must be patient.

Meanwhile send us vocations, and the means to defend and, when necessary, to build up the seminary. The handsome pillars and rafters in the picture are all your work, as are also the glorious vestments. Let the picture be a small token of our thanks for all your grand support of the seminary!

Arriving in Ridgefield after nearly a month of continual traveling and ministry in the New World, Archbishop Lefebvre should have been completely exhausted by the time he reached Ridgefield on Ascension Day, but with his customary devotion and resilience he carried out in four days at the seminary a ceremony of Confirmation and three ceremonies of Ordination, enriching us, besides the new priests and deacons, with one new subdeacon, nine clerics and nine seminarians advanced in Minor Orders, the patient framework of future priestly ordinations. How much patience the Archbishop needs can be imagined from his own description of how it was "with his heart in his mouth" that he laid on hands this year in the same time and place as last year! Yet this is the heroic work which is saving the Church.

For indeed actions, like pictures, speak louder than words. The Archbishop may give conferences, sermons and speeches on the devastating effects of liberalism within the Church, on the subversion of all authority by liberty, equality and fraternity, errors of which he told the seminarians again this year that the principal source is the first and most important liberty of the Freemasons – religious liberty. Hence a situation in the Church of which the Archbishop said the Pope himself is now very afraid. However, such words carry limited weight in our world so steeped in the same Masonic ideals. It is only when the words are spelled out in actions that most people seem able to understand – "Sticks and stones will break my bones, but words will never hurt me."

On the one side Catholics see the Conciliar bishops tearing down the Catholic Church they knew and loved, emptying out the seminaries, pulling down the churches, putting lay ministers and ministresses on the altar; on the other side they see a Catholic bishop laboring the world over to ordain and rebuild in beauty. This year Archbishop Lefebvre has attained by his labors the point of being due to ordain in the Society's four seminaries altogether forty new priests. How many other bishops, he asks, are due to ordain forty priests in their diocese? In the Catholic Church, error devastates, and devastation betokens error; on the contrary the Truth builds in beauty, and Catholic beauty is one sure sign of Catholic truth. Inspired and uplifted by the splendor of the ordinations of May 19, every visitor must have clearly known, here is the Catholic Church!

In the Church at large, Archbishop Lefebvre said on this visit that as against the October Indult's being used for instance in France merely to attempt to draw people

The Ridgefield Letters

away from the centers of the SSPX, a definitely positive sign was the inclusion of Bishops Gagnon and Stickler among the new cardinals. Both men, he said, are intimately in sympathy with the Society, still more firmly so than the Society's best friends to date among the cardinals, e.g., Cardinals Palazzini and Oddi. The Archbishop hopes that these four and maybe a few others will form a kernel of Cardinals to group together at the Synod in November and stand up and tell the truth about the last twenty years in the Church. If they do, then something may yet come of the Synod, but if they do not, if they keep quiet, then the Second Vatican Council will merely continue on its present path of ruin and destruction. However, said his Grace, if Bishops Gagnon and Stickler can become Cardinals, then even he may have a chance, although his Cardinal's hat has proved up till now to be somewhat of a flying saucer!

Altogether the Archbishop was most comforted by this visit to the United States. He said he found the Society rebuilding on a much more normal basis, more truly priestly and in accordance with the spirit of the Society. Before leaving for Europe he made a brief visit to Philadelphia to admire the grand efforts being made by the Society's coordinator in Philadelphia (better known as Editor of the SJN Newsletter) to transform in time for the Carmelite nuns' arrival, hopefully in August, a country-house in a location near the village of Charlestown which should make it the most beautiful of the four Carmels attached to the Society so far. Pray, however, because the devil will in no way let the praying nuns arrive in peace, if he can help it.

Also, the Archbishop was due on the eve of his departure for Europe to give evidence to be videotaped for one of the lawsuits between the Society and its former members. By a misfortune quite out of his control, the testimony had to start all over again on the day itself of his departure from New York to Switzerland. He testified, with one break, from 8:45 a.m. until 3:30 p.m., six hours of answering lawyers' questions, and with a plane to catch for New York at 4 pm! A taxi dash for the plane – too late. On standby for the next at 5:15, take-off for Switzerland being at 6:45! His Grace made his plane for Europe, but what a grueling conclusion to an already arduous tour!

> O, let him pass! He hates him
> That would upon the rack of this tough world
> Stretch him out longer

says Kent of the old and stricken King Lear, but the Catholic bishop quotes not Shakespeare but the aged St. Martin: "Non recuso laborem," "I do not refuse the work," and we can be sure that for the love of souls and so long as God gives him health he will be back again in the USA next year, even this year if work required. What an extraordinary man! His 80th birthday falls on November 29 of this year, and yet his latest missionary journey has once more left behind him a fresh and youthful trail of supernatural grace, sparkling courage and uplifting memories literally all around the United States and Canada. For our part let us make sure that our admiration and gratitude do not stop at mere sentiments which could betray us (and him) tomorrow, but let us during the month of June pray especially to the Sacred Heart for his intentions, and let us thank the Sacred Heart and His Blessed Mother for giving us such a champion of the Faith, and let us strive to love and to defend and to build, as he does, Catholic Tradition.

NO. 26 | JULY 1, 1985

The Archbishop Not Hopeful of Rome

IF ONE PICTURE is worth a thousand words, then eighteen pictures should be worth eighteen thousand words! Here, a little late, is the promised commemorative edition of *The Verbum* on the ordinations of May. No doubt we should have bought a new car instead, because our second and third cars, both having run over 200,000 miles, risk being hospitalized and coming out disabled like the first, but we could not resist the extravagance if it would put before your eyes a little of the color and joy which warmed our own souls two months ago.

After all, these technically brilliant color printing presses serve to place before us so many and seductive occasions of sin – why should they not be put to serve Our Lord instead? Our special thanks must go to the photographer Keith Forrest who came all the way from Virginia with his wife, took with her aid over two days a series of beautiful pictures, gave us the prints, and will not take a cent in return! What a world it would be if we were all bound each to each by the bonds of charity instead of by the slip-knots of commercialism! "Freely have you received, freely give," says Our Lord (Mt. 10: 8), but if you enjoy Keith Forrest's pictures and Mrs. Graham's story, pay them in Catholic currency and say a prayer for each of them!

Such a scene of peace and joy as we see in these pictures we might have seen had we been with Our Lord when He gave the Sermon on the Mount, and we would have asked ourselves or one another, "How should such a man ever get into a fight?" Yet had we followed him into Jerusalem, we would have found the Pharisees and others locking horns with him (Jn. 5: 9) in doughty verbal battles, firm on his side, on theirs bitter unto death. Why must he who is "meek and humble of heart," who comes only to give "rest to our souls" (Mt. 11: 29), who gives "peace, his peace, not as the world giveth" (Jn. 14: 27), who always photographs so well – ! – why must he get into these fights with people who, after all, share his religion? Why the regular polemics? Why can't the sweet Archbishop be sweet all the time? Why can't he bring all the positive good of his Society into the bosom of the official Church where it belongs and where it is so needed? Especially why, when that Church is surely coming halfway to meet him? While the Roman officials seem so reasonable, is not Archbishop Lefebvre constantly "upping the ante," i.e., proposing terms only to raise them before settling?

The answer is as unchanging as is, alas, the problem. Our Lord's own religion gives true peace, as no other religion can do; the Pharisees pretend to share this religion, but in fact they require him out of the way in order to replace it with theirs which is not the same. They pretend to have Abraham for their father (Jn. 8: 39), but their real father is the father of lies (Jn. 8: 44). Hence the Lamb of God must on occasion roar like the Lion of Judah, and His bishop who asks no better than to share the true religion with everyone in Rome, cannot accept,

The Ridgefield Letters

and has never proposed to accept, the mere appearances of that religion resting upon its basic denial!

Addressing this very question of why he cannot come to an agreement even with traditionalizing Rome, the Archbishop himself said in Paris on March 17 of this year that despite a few encouraging surface signs, all the evidence till now is that beneath the surface the false ideas – not to say heresies – of the Second Vatican Council still remain anchored in the Roman prelates' minds. The Council launched religious liberty, ecumenism, human rights and collegiality, and these ideas are still being upheld. Here is where it matters, and here nothing has changed.

From his own direct experience of the Council, corroborated by a recent article in the *L'Osservatore Romano*, the Archbishop went on to attribute to the Secretariat for the Unity of Christians, founded in 1960 and headed up by Cardinal Bea and then Cardinal Willebrands, the infecting of the entire Vatican Council with the poison of religious liberty (man has the moral right to choose what religion he likes) and ecumenism (all religions are to be put on an equal footing). Hence there took place at that time three contacts fatal for the Church: firstly of Cardinal Bea with the Freemasons, notably through the B'nai Brith in New York, who obtained the Church's acceptance of religious liberty; secondly of Cardinal Willebrands with the Protestants through the Ecumenical Council of Churches, working for the dissolution by democratization of Catholic authority (notably the Pope's, by "collegiality"), and for the protestantising of the Catholic Liturgy; thirdly of Cardinal Willebrands with the Communists through the Russian Orthodox bishops, leading to the Catholic Church's disarming in the face of Communism, with the Council refusing to condemn it, and, graver still, with Rome appointing "Pax" priests and bishops to collaborate with it!

Richard N. Williamson

What we must grasp, continued the Archbishop, is that the disastrous situation for the Church flowing from these contacts is continuing, and there will be no real change until Rome backtracks on religious liberty. But how? For twenty years priests have been appointed bishops for their acceptance of these errors! Hence even while recognizing Cardinal Ratzinger's genuine desire to come to an understanding, the Archbishop was obliged to say to him when they met in January that the Cardinal's self-confessed attachment to liberal values would make of any such proposed understanding an unacceptable mixed marriage between Catholicism and Liberalism.

Thus, he went on, "We are arriving at a very dangerous turning point. Between now and the end of the year, there is going to be a synod. Do you think the synod will decide to return to Tradition? That religious liberty will be set aside? That the errors of false ecumenism will be done away with, which puts all religions on an equal footing? I wish it were so. We all wish it were so. But I don't believe it. We must expect this synod to confirm the guidelines laid down by the Council. All the bishops chosen are conciliar bishops. They make up this new Conciliar Church, as Msgr. Bugnini amongst others has called it. They will quite simply confirm the direction they are now taking. They may say this or that abuse must be avoided or suppressed, yet such abuses are just the natural consequence of their false principles."

The Archbishop wished he could be more optimistic, but everything gave him to think the contrary: the Pope's praising Luther and preaching in a Lutheran temple; the Concordat de-catholicising the State of Italy and the Vatican's approving the construction of a mosque in Rome (just try building a Catholic church in Mecca, commented the Archbishop!); lastly the "appalling" new Code of Canon Law, appalling by its errors for instance

The Ridgefield Letters

on the Church, Eucharistic hospitality and marriage . . . such a Code could only be signed by a Pope convinced, as the speeches of his recent tour of Canada showed, that there are two churches, the pre-Vatican II Church now disappearing, and the new Church which began in 1960. What to do?

The Archbishop concluded that we must continue to maintain Catholic Tradition and accept no truce with the destroyers of the Church. We must witness to the Faith, even if in Greek, witness and martyr are the same word. Eve dialogued with the devil, the Blessed Virgin did not, nor should we. "It may be hard to tell the truth, it may be good to know what is going on, in any case let me tell you, I remain confident because everything is in the hands of God." On a strong upbeat of hope, the Archbishop said that "miracle" would not be too strong a word for the worldwide achievements, humanly impossible, of the SSPX over the last fifteen years. Surely, by these and by the numerous traditional Catholic communities and schools thriving in Europe and France in particular, God is showing His Will to maintain the Church's Tradition at all costs, and not to allow her self-destruction.

Thus at Ridgefield we look like having another dozen young men try their vocation in the autumn. Mr. Forrest, I absolutely insist that next year we pay your expenses, and Mrs. Forrest's!

With many thanks to all of you who most generously support the seminary month by month, and with all good wishes for restful and truly Christian vacations.

NO. 27 | AUGUST 14, 1985

The Ongoing Standoff

ENCLOSED YOU SHOULD find the latest exchange of letters between Rome and Archbishop Lefebvre, which the Archbishop himself has wished to make public so that Catholics may see once more where things stand between himself and Rome.

There is really nothing new in the two letters. The Archbishop's central position is that the documents of Vatican II are acceptable on condition that they are sifted according to Tradition (what text would not be acceptable, on such a condition?), and the Novus Ordo Mass, at any rate in the original Latin text, is not automatically invalid (which is not to say that it is a good or acceptable rite of Mass, merely that transubstantiation does not automatically fail to take place).

This position Cardinal Ratzinger says he might accept, and indeed the whole of his respectful letter demonstrates once more that no rupture between Rome and the Society has taken place. However, the Archbishop adds to his position a clarification which makes the Cardinal refuse to take any steps favorable to the Society, so that relations between the Society and Rome remain where they have been for ten years: the Archbishop will not relinquish Tradition, whereas Rome insists on obedience to the Reform.

The Ridgefield Letters

What did the Archbishop add? That the criterion of Tradition would, amongst other things, require major revisions of several Council texts, notably the *Declaration on Religious Liberty*; it would reject several key points in the new Code of Canon Law; it would require an entire revision of the Liturgical Reform, and a public condemnation of Communism.

While objecting that these precise demands on behalf of Catholic Tradition make unacceptable the Archbishop's request for regularization of the Society within the Church, the Cardinal gives no precise arguments of reason why the Archbishop is wrong, he merely gives arguments of authority, which, unless that authority is divine, are intrinsically the weakest of arguments. Thus the Cardinal argues, in 1985 as in 1983, that the Council documents are the Church's Magisterium, therefore they are in line with the Church's Traditional Magisterium. In other words the documents, simply because they were approved by Pope and Council, must be alright. But the Church's true Magisterium is either Extraordinary or Ordinary. Now in the case of all the Council's documents, the Extraordinary Magisterium is ruled out because the two Popes of the Council, John XXIII and Paul VI, both expressly renounced the use of their extraordinary authority; whereas to come under the Church's Ordinary Magisterium these documents would have to be wholly in line with Tradition, which is exactly what the Archbishop is denying, and what Cardinal Ratzinger makes here no attempt to prove. "Dear Cardinal, these are ERRORS!" "Dear Archbishop, they come from Pope and Bishops." (Period!).

Likewise, whereas the Archbishop has elsewhere shown reasons for saying that the new Code of Canon Law is on several points gravely out of line with Tradition (e.g., Canons 336, 204 #1, 844 #4, 1055), all that the

Cardinal replies is that the Code was published "with the full authority of the Pope." But again, the Pope's extraordinary authority can only be behind pronouncements on faith and morals, not behind a Code of Law as such, and his ordinary authority supposes the alignment on Tradition, which in the case of the New Code the Archbishop has given reasons to deny, and which the Cardinal gives no reasons to prove. "Dear Cardinal, these Canons are NOT CATHOLIC!" "Dear Archbishop, they come from the highest authority." (Period!)

Similarly, the only argument given in 1985 as in 1983 by the Cardinal for refusing Archbishop Lefebvre's well-known reasons for criticizing the Liturgical Reform (Archbishop Lefebvre was actually behind the *Ottaviani Intervention* in 1969), is that such criticism hinders or destroys obedience, and questions the legitimacy of the liturgy everyone else is using. "Dear Cardinal, the New Mass makes Catholics into Protestants!" "Dear Archbishop, OBEY!" (Period!)

Of course the argument of authority is the only argument against the Archbishop that Rome has, which is why Rome has never dared put the Archbishop on trial, and why it has rarely tried to argue with him from Tradition. But the argument of authority alone is, in true Catholicism, not enough. Always, in any dispute, the Catholic Church has the natural and supernatural reasons on her side, behind which she puts her authority. Against Luther, Rome had all the arguments of Tradition on her side. Against the Archbishop, she has none. As Our Lady of La Salette said in 1846, Rome will lose the Faith and become the seat of the Antichrist.

Yet the Society will not abandon Rome unless Rome cuts her off, and so as a next step the Society means to ask Rome a series of questions. Let Rome answer, but a thousand to one she will not, for the simple reason she cannot. Rome must convert, back to the only position

The Ridgefield Letters

defendable with solid Catholic reasons – the Archbishop's position.

And this is the same Archbishop of whom we were gravely warned over two years ago that his actions "seem to be directed toward arriving at some sort of "deal" with those who rule the Vatican." As Churchill would have said: some "seeming"! Some "deal"! Now I hear, the line has changed, because even the simplest of souls can no longer be made to swallow that the Archbishop is planning to give way to Rome, so instead we who follow him are now accused of crediting him with infallibility, and so on! Great heavens! The simplest proof of his fallibility is the trust he placed in those who so betrayed him! The first full-scale trial between them and the Society took place in Philadelphia early in July. The Society's lawyers think it went well. The decision is pending with the judge. Let us pray that his verdict be just. God's will be done.

Most encouraging news is the marked increase this summer in the number of retreatants at the men's and women's Ignatian Exercises given by seminary priests. In Ridgefield and Armada the Ladies' Three-Day Retreats in June and July were so overbooked that both had to split into two retreats, back to back, and the Men's Three-Day Retreat here in August filled the Seminary to capacity. *Deo Gratias!* Heroic work was put in by the skeleton staff, old seminarians and young visitors here on vacation. As Churchill would say, some vacation! But all had the immense satisfaction of knowing how spiritually uplifted and refreshed the retreatants went on their way, to pick up their burdens in the world again and spread the Kingship of Christ.

A most successful two-week boys' camp in New Hampshire and three-week Exercises in Armada have also enabled many seminarians to profit by their summer vacation to progress in knowledge of their

Richard N. Williamson

Divine Lord, as Master of youth and Master of the interior life.

Also enclosed this month is a flyer on a triptych of tapes made by the seminary rector as an introduction to Tradition. I can't say I care for his British accent, but I must say I find myself agreeing with a remarkable amount of what he says! Further tapes on obedience and other topics are on their way.

Many, many thanks to all of you who responded with such generous donations to the latest *Verbum*. May Our Lady in the month of her Assumption bless you all. Support us also with your prayers, without which there is no reason why our Priestly Society should not go the way so many poor priests have gone, and in return, be assured we pray at the seminary for all your intentions, every day.

NO. 28 | SEPTEMBER 10, 1985

Conciliar Church Mentally Stricken

From the Seminary comes good news, from the up-coming Synod the probability only of bad news. Let us start with the good news.

Nineteen young men are due to enter the seminary in two weeks' time to try their vocation. In a world so corrupt as to make Archbishop Lefebvre say that a religious vocation coming out of it is almost a miracle, this is an impressive number. At the same time about forty more young men are due to enter the Society's French and German speaking seminaries in Switzerland and Germany respectively, making a prospective total of fifty-nine new vocations. Of course not all of them will persevere, but the stories that many of them can tell of the origin and circumstances of their vocation most amply prove that God's grace is at work. Pray for these young men.

The seminary is also gaining an English speaking priest, Fr. James Peek, from New Zealand, newly ordained last June at the Society's main seminary in Ecône. His brother Frank was ordained a priest at Ecône one year before him, and has been serving the Society under Fr. Gerard Hogan in Australia, from where come three of Ridgefield's nineteen new seminarians. These three prove how the Society's ministry Down Under is thriving, and they will certainly add to the seminary's intercontinental flavor, so long as they do not lose their home-grown accent. Hence they are being given instructions to continue speaking Strine (better known as Australian!).

Most interesting is that the seminary is receiving the visits of several young American priests from the Novus Ordo dioceses. Some of them come with a serious desire to learn how to say the Tridentine Mass. To attend once more Mass in the rite of which they were deprived before they even entered their Major Seminary, inspires in them nostalgia, and their fervent hope is one day to be able themselves to celebrate Mass in the tried and true rite. Here is a sign indeed that souls of good will can keep the true Faith despite surroundings largely apt to take it away. We thank God for the opportunity to serve priests from outside the Society, and we wonder where He means to lead them. We think we see green shoots springing up in the blackened wasteland of modernism, and we sense that as soon as Almighty God chooses to turn the situation around, then where in Ezechiel's image there seemed to be only multitudes of dry bones, the Faith on the contrary will spring to life again in the most surprising way.

So God has not handed in His resignation, as some might be tempted to think, nor is He inactive, but He is working in hidden ways. Let us not however delude ourselves that He is yet turning the situation around in the way we would like, for instance with the up-coming Synod of Bishops, due to take place in Rome from November 25 to December 8:

> There is every reason to think that the Synod will confirm the new Conciliar Church, with all its errors

> and false orientations, to enable it to continue enjoying the favour of the world, meaning the Zionists, Freemasonry, false religions and international socialism which is receiving the Pope with open arms in all countries of the world.
>
> In the Vatican, all those who accept these orientations while keeping up the appearances of Tradition will be well looked on, for instance *Opus Dei*, the charismatics, Una Voce and so on . . . ; I mean all those who do not oppose these orientations. The only ones that have to be pursued are those who publicly refuse the new Church. Such is clearly our own case.
>
> Blessed persecution which keeps us in the Church and in the Truth and in grace!

This is what Archbishop Lefebvre wrote about the Synod on August 21, and he spoke in similar vein at Fruehli in Switzerland a few days later in a sermon, the text of which we may hope will be published in *The Angelus*. A Novus Ordo priest, in the "Dear Padre" section of the Liguori Bulletin of August 25, coming out of Missouri, makes essentially the same forecast of a conciliar Synod, only in different words: "The Holy Father will seek advice and recommendations from the bishops on how best to continue the spirit of Vatican Council II in a balanced and orderly fashion . . . "

What is happening is that the Novus Ordo prelates in Rome are being forced by the facts to recognize that a disaster is taking place in the Church, but they still do not want to admit that Vatican II, the Council itself with the novelties it brought into the Church, is the cause of that disaster. Hence they wish to check the wild consequences while continuing the cause of the wildness! They cling to the principle of religious freedom yet they do not want the Catholic religion to be too free; they upgrade all other religions with ecumenism, but they do not want Catholicism to be too downgraded. They will not let go of their Council, but they do wish that the demons it unleashed would behave like nice little boys. Thus they dream of putting a biretta on religious liberty and a cassock on ecumenism, and all the groups and organizations promising to do just that are greeted with open arms in Rome, whereas the Archbishop and all those who like him insist that such a dream is impossible, continue to be frozen out in the cold.

But why is a "balanced and orderly" continuation of "the spirit of Vatican Council II" an impossible dream? Because Vatican II was a revolution (both its friends and its enemies say so – see Michael Davies' *Pope John's Council*), and a revolution means by definition the upsetting of an established order. Hence to project the orderly continuation of the Vatican II revolution is like projecting a warm ice-cube, or tranquil uproar. It is a contradiction in terms, and in realities. For wherever there is established the principle of religious liberty, there is supposed the right of men to choose their own religion, and so to refuse the one true religion of God. This means either that God put no force of command behind His own religion, which is false, for He threatened with condemnation all who would not believe it (Mk. 16: 16), or that His commands have no binding force. Therefore religious liberty means that men may disobey God if they like. There could not be a surer principle for throwing everything into imbalance and disorder.

Thus it is impossible that order should be restored to the Catholic Church until the prelates in Rome give up their dream of combining the outward fruits of the Faith with the inward principles of the modern world.

Just as a healthy organism will spit out a poison or die, so those parts of the Catholic Church which are not yet spitting out Vatican II and the Novus Ordo Mass, are slowly but surely dying. The Faith cannot assimilate these products of its bitterest enemies, notably the Freemasons.

The Ridgefield Letters

Now nobody is popular who snatches away someone's cherished dream, and so inscribed in the logic of this pursuit of orderly disorder is only the continuing persecution of the Society and its traveling companions. So be it. We wish the Roman prelates well, we hope they will understand their radical mistake, we earnestly pray they will turn from the errors of their ways, we look for and are ready – even to a fault! – to greet the least signs of such a conversion, we ask no better than to obey them as soon as they are back in their right minds, but we are under no illusion that minds easily awake from the dreams of liberalism, and so we gird our loins. With God's grace, we are not willing to compromise His Faith.

Enclosed is a flyer on the Mass laying out the contrast between the old and the new. We have had thousands of copies printed, so ask us for as many as you like. Donations are welcome. We are sorry for the delay on video tapes of the May Ordinations, but they are on their way. The three audiotapes on *The Faith in Crisis* we have had to reorder and reorder again, but we expect no delay in supplying them. Remember we also have available a video tape designed for priests to show them the mechanics of saying the Tridentine Mass. Suggestions on how such a tape could be improved are always welcome – we are only beginners. Enclosed next month will be details of the usual men's five-day retreats at the seminary after Christmas and Easter.

Lastly, as usual and as always, many thanks to all of you who continue to support the seminary, especially to those who come through month by month. A little given, but regularly and by many, goes a long way, even towards paying lawyers' bills! (We still await the judge's decision on the case in Philadelphia). All of us at the seminary thank you. May the Sacred Heart reward you!

NO. 29 | OCTOBER 1, 1985

Cardinal Ratzinger Stricken by Council

THE WEEKS AND the months flash past, another school year has started, autumn has come and the trees in New England are turning brilliant red, yellow and gold – and souls are saved and souls are being lost, and the Mother of God weeps for so many of her children, all meant for heaven, going astray and going to perdition...

I have just received an advance copy of the English translation soon to be published in the USA of the complete text of the famous interview, given by Cardinal Ratzinger to an Italian journalist in his summer vacation a year ago. Extracts published last November showed the Cardinal Prefect of the Congregation for the Doctrine of the Faith making such a devastating analysis of the present ravaged state of the Church, as inspired many traditional Catholics with hopes of Rome coming straight at last. These hopes were confirmed by the Cardinal's coming under heavy attack ever since by the leading liberals and progressives in the Church. They were further confirmed when Archbishop Lefebvre was kindly received by Cardinal Ratzinger

The Ridgefield Letters

in January of this year, and spoke of a warmer atmosphere in Rome. Indeed the Cardinal's book contains many things that traditional Catholics can agree with, and that should make a good tape to come out from *Keep the Faith*.

Yet the meeting of the Cardinal and the Archbishop bore no fruit, except an exchange of letters in the early summer which showed that the situation was basically unchanged from 1975! What was happening? The complete interview tells us.

The basic principle of the Cardinal's thinking is fidelity to the Second Vatican Council. For him, it has the same authority as the Council of Trent and the first Vatican Council, and like them, it cannot be questioned. What the Cardinal objects to is the crazy "excesses" perpetrated afterwards in the name of the Council, but which in his view have nothing to do with the true Council. Hence, he holds the Archbishop has no right to refuse the Council. Here is a passage (not included in the November extracts) in which the Cardinal talks about the Archbishop's movement:

> I see no future for a position that, out of principle, stubbornly renounces Vatican II. In fact in itself it is an illogical position. The point of departure for this tendency is, in fact, the strictest fidelity to the teaching particularly of Pius IX and Pius X and, still more fundamentally, of Vatican I and its definition of papal primacy. But why only the popes up to Pius XII and not beyond? Is perhaps obedience to the Holy See divisible according to years or according to the nearness of a teaching to one's own already-established convictions?

One sees here that the Cardinal has no true concept of Catholic Tradition, and hence no understanding of the Archbishop's position. For instance, the Archbishop rejects Vatican II not "out of principle" but as being out of line with Tradition. He is faithful not "particularly" to Vatican I or Pius IX and Pius X, but to the whole of Catholic Tradition, of which these two Popes (the second a miracle-worker) were merely outstanding defenders amongst others. The Archbishop "divides" his obedience to the Holy See neither by years nor by his own subjective "convictions," but by the Holy See's major fidelity or infidelity to the objective truths of Catholic Tradition. For the Cardinal, every Pope would seem to have to be obeyed in all things, regardless of Tradition. Yet Christ Himself repeatedly gave to the Jews as reason why He should be heeded and obeyed, that He was only doing and saying what His Father had handed down (tradition) to Him to say and to do. "My doctrine is not mine, but His Who sent me" (Jn. 7: 16), "I always do what pleases Him" (Jn. 8: 29), etc. Thus Catholicism was a Tradition from Father to Son even before Jesus founded His Church or instituted the Papacy! The Catholic religion is essentially a handing down, outside of which even the Holy Father has no authority. The Archbishop sees this, the Cardinal does not – they are in two different ballparks, virtually in two different religions.

Why then does Cardinal Ratzinger show any kindness to the Archbishop? Because, the Cardinal goes on "Clearly everything possible must be done to prevent Archbishop Lefebvre's movement from giving rise to a schism peculiar to it that would come into being whenever Msgr. Lefebvre should decide to consecrate a bishop which, thank God, in the hope of a reconciliation he has not yet done." Ecumenical thinking today, says the Cardinal, regrets divisions arisen in the Church through an insufficient openness to reconciliation. Hence the kindness of January. Yet even while listening sweetly to the Archbishop, the Cardinal apparently never had the intention of making any real concession to the stubborn

The Ridgefield Letters

enemy of Vatican II, and so the kindness bore no fruit, because, as the Cardinal goes on to say: "Absurd situations (like that of the Archbishop's movement) have been able to endure up to now precisely by nourishing themselves on the arbitrariness and thoughtlessness of many post-conciliar interpretations. This places a further obligation upon us to show the true face of the Council: thus one will be able to cut the ground from under these false protests."

In other words, the Archbishop only follows Tradition as a false protest! And it will be cured by more doses of the true Vatican II! Yet when the two bishops in November of '83 indicted at length the very documents of the Council itself – surely the true Council! – what answer or refutation did Rome give? None!

In fact Rome's answer is surely the upcoming Synod. Cardinal Ratzinger's book shows clearly Rome's intention behind the Synod, namely to re-establish the "true" Vatican II, because that is supposed to be the solution to the extremism on the left and on the right. In fact the Synod gravely risks merely confirming the Church in her liberal errors, in a nightmare world without any fixed bearing in Tradition or objective truth.

"In my opinion," said the Archbishop in Canada last May, "this is exceedingly grave, because it approaches what the law calls pertinacity in error. This pertinacity in error or heresy truly leads to formal heresy.

That poses another grave problem of conscience with regard to the Roman authorities if in a public and official manner they once more hold to errors condemned by the popes of the 19th and first half of the 20th centuries."

Confronted by this risk of the Synod's marching us all – even with the best of intentions – into the mental madhouse of modernism, the Archbishop must be thinking at the very least of issuing another grave warning. Let us pray with might and main that the bishops of the Synod so stand for Tradition and truth that the Archbishop is not driven to extremes, but let us also remember that if men abandon the Truth, Our Lord said the very stones in the street would cry out (Lk. 19: 40).

Enclosed you will find the promised details of the two retreats for men at the seminary after Christmas and Easter. Sign up! How many inhabitants of Mexico City might now wish they had done a good retreat? At least three Society parishioners perished there. May their souls rest in peace.

Also enclosed is the annual card for you to list the departed souls whose names you would wish to be on the altar to be prayed for in the Masses of All Souls' Day, and in a Requiem Mass each month of the year. You need not list again names already submitted. We are happy to enclose also excerpts from the judge's decision in the Pennsylvania law suit in case any of you would like to see why he decided in favor of the Society (the full text is available from the seminary). If we are doing God's work, let us make sure we thank Him for this decision (which does not look like it will be appealed), but in your prayers do not forget the souls of the priests who broke away, more precious than a thousand properties. May God have mercy upon them and upon us all, for "Let he that thinketh himself to stand, take heed lest he fall." (1 Cor. 10: 12)

We shall in any case be praying for all of your intentions each day of October, with the Holy Rosary. May Our Lady of the Most Holy Rosary guide and protect you.

NO. 30 | NOVEMBER 1, 1985

The Archbishop's 80th Birthday

On the 29th of this month, November 1985, Archbishop Marcel Lefebvre celebrates his 80th birthday. Let us take the occasion to commemorate a truly great man, not to promote any cult of personality, but to "know the gift of God" (Jn. 4: 10).

What, after all, makes a man great? Surely the hallmarks of greatness are vision and courage: the vision of what man can and fully should be, and the courage and fortitude to overcome all obstacles in the way of inspiring one's fellow-men with that vision. Great artists are great rather by their vision, great warriors and statesmen more by their fortitude. Either way our own age is singularly deficient in great men because of modern man's brutish and materialistic view of man – "the law is no more, and the prophets have found no vision from the Lord" (Lam. 2: 9). All that remains to admire is a certain brutish, more or less aimless, fortitude.

Yet every Catholic, by his Faith alone, should have a deep and true vision of what man can and should be, namely destined for Heaven; and the mere practice of his Faith necessarily requires a fortitude more or less

—113—

heroic to overcome the Faith's powerful enemies, the world, the flesh and the devil. Thus any Catholic practicing his Faith is in line for greatness from the moment Providence gives him to inspire his fellow-men, and so the Martyrology is filled with truly great men and women drawn from all walks of life.

As for Archbishop Lefebvre, he has firstly a clear and deep vision of the Catholic Faith. Contrary to what some people think, his grasp of theology is profound and accurate, as a true peritus of Vatican II magnificently testifies in the Introduction to *I Accuse the Council*. For consistency, learning and good judgment the Archbishop is in my opinion head and shoulders above all other living analysts of the Church's present crisis. In each situation more confusing than the last, his fruits prove he has picked out the line of the true Faith, and he has done it virtually alone. We ask how one bishop can be right against two thousand, but imagine what it must be like to be that bishop! It is lonely at the top, especially so when the overwhelming mass of your colleagues decries you. Not even from pride comes that kind of strength, but only from the humility of being completely possessed by one's Catholic Faith.

Which brings us naturally to the Archbishop's fortitude and courage. Marked out even before the Council by the body of French bishops as a conservative to be shunned, the Archbishop was fated during the Council to have to watch the realization of the blueprint of the self-destruction of his beloved Church. He saw it all quite clearly, as *I Accuse the Council* proves, but his warning voice went unheeded by the euphoric Council Fathers. A few years later, he organized the *Ottaviani Intervention*, accurately foreboding disaster from the Novus Ordo Mass, only to see the utopian Pope Paul VI impose it on the Church with a will of iron! Just imagine the temptation to anger, bitterness, despair, recriminations! But instead of cursing the darkness, he lit the candle of Ecône, and built single-handed, against all opposition, the only large and cohesive body of traditional priests worldwide, because he is the only consistently Catholic bishop. Humanly alone, always alone.

And inspiration?

> How far that little candle throw his beams!
> So shines a good deed in a naughty world.

(*The Merchant of Venice.*)

No need to say how many thousands of Catholics all over the world would in the last fifteen years have given up the Faith in despair had they not seen it being still defended by one venerable bishop from his bastion in the Swiss Alps. And how many more thousands could have been confused and deceived, would have lost their way amid the clash of arguments, would have believed this bishop was rebel, schismatic or heretic, had not his person been such that one contact with the sanctity of his presence sufficed to inspire in them the lasting conviction that here is quite simply a man of God! So much so that the villains in Rome are no doubt trusting in his death to put an end to Catholic Tradition. Vain trust, but not a vain testimony to the inspiration flowing from him!

"Let us now praise famous men" says Scripture (Ecclus. 44: 1), and for our own part let us commemorate greatness even amongst the living, in order that we should show ourselves not ungrateful to God for the gift of those leaders without whom we should perish (Prov. 11: 14, 29: 18). Happy 80th birthday, your Grace, and may God give you to see your heart's desire, the saving of the Church!

The Archbishop will on that day, typically, be on another long apostolic journey bringing him for a few days through the United States in the middle of this month, mainly to give a deposition in another lawsuit, but also to hold the opening Ceremony and Mass for the Society's new Carmel in Phoenixville near Philadelphia at 12 noon on Wednesday, November 13. This is late notice for an event only recently organized, but visitors are welcome.

The Carmelites' prayers should be a great help to us in our tremendous battle for the Faith. Seminarians had a taste of battle when they all went down to New York City to take part in the protest procession held on the Feast of the Holy Rosary outside the Manhattan cinema first showing in the USA the blasphemous film from Europe entitled *Hail Mary*. Friends of ours already there when we arrived said that the appearance of all the black cassocks felt like the arrival of the rescuing cowboys to relieve the beleaguered stockade! It was battle in Our Lady's style, with rosary for weapon and that particular atmosphere of charity and serenity somehow characteristic of her occasions. Several thousand Catholics by taking part did at least something to avenge their Mother's honor. But woe unto the makers of such a film. It is safer to insult God Himself than to dishonor His Mother.

We have also had to reorder the flyers on the Mass, a great success. Almost all 40,000 copies have gone, we are ordering as many again, so order as many as you like and if you wish to make a donation, reckon from the cost, price to us, for the reprinted flyer, of about 9 cents a copy.

We must also apologize for an error on last month's retreats flyer. December 26 is of course a Thursday, not a Monday. It may seem hard to give up five days of the holiday season, but wise is the man who turns holidays into such holy days!

No flyers this month, but the latest letter from the Society's Superior General, and the autumn *Verbum*

The Ridgefield Letters

giving seminarians' summer news. Thirteen of the new seminarians are still with us, including all three Australians. My remarks about Strine puzzled one Australian who wrote to me from Down Under that he had always thought "it was only Englishmen and Americans who spoke English with an accent." Well . . .

Many thanks for your continuing and generous support of the seminary. The lists of Holy Souls you sent us will be on the altar through November and for one Mass every month of the year. May these souls all rest in peace, and may their prayers help us to the safe harbor of salvation after our voyage on the stormy sea of this world.

NO. 31 | DECEMBER 1, 1985

Romans Fiddling While Rome Burns

"There is a brutal, merciless, spiritual war being waged inside the Catholic Church, and the Society of St. Pius X is the First Aid Station the weary soldier drags himself into, to bandage his gaping wounds."

So writes one of our readers, and another: "My most fervent prayers are for a fruitful Synod, but I think that if there is not a turnabout, the risk of a schism-like situation involving the Society is very real, thereby making the lot of the devout in the clutches of the Novus Ordo even harder and also, quite possibly, making us traditionalists less outgoing, less joyfully charitable, liable to fall back into a siege mentality." And: "Nevertheless the truth which we hold dear is absolute, and 'if push comes to shove,' I'll continue to be guided by the Society of St. Pius X."

These two readers are grasping many truths. The true Faith, the Catholic Faith, is fighting for its life against a false substitute religion that has gotten inside the Catholic Church and is determined to exterminate the "old" Faith, deliberately destroying anything connected with it. It is unbelievable. It is happening.

The Ridgefield Letters

As for the chances of "a fruitful Synod," we are, at the risk of being repetitive, enclosing Archbishop Lefebvre's official and public statement, dated October 31, on what we might expect from the Synod. His Grace is pessimistic. We all wish he was wrong. No doubt he wishes so himself. The fact remains that two priests, both friends, neither of them members, of the SSPX, each brought back separately to the United States from a recent visit to Rome the identical impression of Rome fiddling while Rome, or the Faith, burns. These priests know at firsthand how the fire of modernism is blazing unchecked in the household of the Faith, yet very high prelates that each priest met in Rome seem unaware of it, and are certainly unconcerned.

In any case, since the Synod is soon over, the Archbishop's text makes possible an on-the-spot check of whether he is correctly diagnosing events in the Church. At one point we hoped that Cardinal Mayer, Prefect of the Congregation for Divine Worship, stood for what Archbishop Lefebvre stands for, but here is what the Cardinal wrote to an American laywoman two months ago: "In answering your question about Archbishop Lefebvre unfortunately it has to be said, that he is practically in schism, although it has not been declared explicitly: he does not obey the directives of the Holy Father. It is a pity that fervent young men and priests following him are no longer in full communion with the Church."

Yet many leaders of Catholic opinion, honored and respected men ("for they are all honorable men," said Mark Anthony), present to us a Rome turning around for the better. The Archbishop presents to us a Rome set upon destroying itself. The essential point is that these "honorable" men and the Archbishop cannot both be right.

Now if the Archbishop is right, what are the consequences? – The household of the Faith is burning down, and the firemen are all having a party. A Catholic may well say, let us not cross our bridges before we come to them, let us charitably wait until the prelates of the Synod have proven themselves unwilling to defend the Faith. Very well. Let us pray, as did the whole Society and this seminary with a vigil of prayers for the Synod through the night of November 23 – 24, and let us wait. But can we wait indefinitely while the house burns down?

The Archbishop was in North America again briefly last month. On November 9th, he ordained in Montreal one new priest for the Society, Fr. Dominique de Vriendt, who has already begun work in French Canada. A van full of seminarians drove north to help with the ceremony. On Monday and Tuesday, November 10 and 11, for six and seven and a half hours respectively, the Archbishop gave a deposition in Connecticut required by the Society's adversaries in their Connecticut State lawsuit against the seminary.

News of the lawsuits? After the Philadelphia Federal Court ruled in July that the breakaway priests had to give the property back because they had "abused a confidential relationship," a second Federal Court verdict went against them in October when the first of their two libel suits against the Archbishop and the Society was dismissed without trial. (This suit claimed ten million dollars in damages, but their New York State suit went one better and demands twenty million!) The judge said they had failed "to state a claim on which relief can be granted," but they are appealing against the dismissal, just as they are also appealing against the Philadelphia verdict. Everything indicates they will continue their fantastical campaign for as long as they can find someone to pay their lawyers.

Returning to sanity, on Wednesday, November 13, the Archbishop drove south to Phoenixville, near Philadelphia, followed again by a number of seminarians to help

The Ridgefield Letters

with the ceremony of opening of the Society-attached American Carmel. Actually, it is a ceremony of closing, or enclosing, as it concludes with the bishop's handing over to the Mother Superior the keys of her Carmel, and then the last visitors bid farewell to the nuns within, come back outside, the door of the cloister is closed and the nuns are enclosed, to pray for themselves, to pray for us, and draw down by their sacrificial lives God's mercy upon our poor world. Mother Marie-Christiane, sister of the Archbishop by blood and Superior of the Carmelites, said that the American Carmel was the best situated and the best prepared of the four Carmels she has opened with her brother.

The Archbishop will be back for his regular springtime visit to the USA in April of 1986. He will be ordaining two or three deacons to the priesthood at Ridgefield on Saturday, April 19 (to enable priests to attend who are otherwise engaged on Sundays) and on Sunday morning April 20 he will be holding at the Society's chapel in Farmingville on Long Island the one main Confirmation ceremony of this year in the Northeast, followed by Solemn High Mass. More details in due course.

Meanwhile Advent is here. One month before the calamitous earthquake in Mexico (and a colleague close to Mexico says that many, many more died than the media reported), the President of Catholic Mexico is reported to have said, "We need no imported God," meaning the God of Catholicism! This God did not delay to remind Mexicans that He chastises those whom He loves (Heb. 12: 6) and to whom He has given such gifts of the Faith. In Columbia, also once a most Catholic country, now a main producer of drug plants, God chastised with a devastating mudslide, and over 20,000 people perished, apparently in a drug-producing region. Let us profit by Advent to do penance, or we "shall all likewise perish" (Lk. 13: 5). Penance on the other hand will prepare our souls for the religious joys of the Christmas season.

To all of you that have faithfully and generously supported the seminary throughout this year, sincere thanks from all of us at the seminary. If the Archbishop is right, it is his seminaries we must support. To any of you that might like to begin regularly supporting us, just fill in and send back the enclosed card, and besides getting this letter sooner by first-class mail, you will also get a monthly envelope to facilitate a monthly contribution. May Our Lady reward you by bringing to you at Christmas fresh graces of her Divine Son! "Behold, the Lord shall appear, and shall not lie: if He make delay, wait for Him, for He shall come and shall not tarry, alleluia!"

NO. 32 | JANUARY 3, 1986

First SSPX Ordinations in the Argentine

THE FIRST ORDINATIONS to the priesthood at the Society's seminary in the Argentine one month ago were a beautiful occasion. Your correspondent, leaving New York at the end of November in snow and cold, arrived to find the seminary at La Reja, about thirty miles west-north-west of downtown Buenos Aires, bathed in the warm and brilliant sunshine of the end of the Southern Hemisphere's May. Where only four and a half years ago I had seen Archbishop Lefebvre in gum-boots planting a foundation-stone in the middle of a muddy field, now I saw sprung up a beautiful white cloister, in the Spanish colonial style of architecture, housing some forty seminarians under half a dozen young professors, most of whom I had helped to teach at Ecône.

What a flowering in the wilderness! Praying the breviary in the early morning around the cloister, amidst the flowers, bird-song and sunshine, I would be forcibly reminded of those moving monuments of the Faith in California, the Spanish missions on the Camino Real, or King's Highway. Built in the 18th century up from Catho-

ichard N. Williamson

lic Mexico the old mission-stations are now surrounded by the …n and materialism of the most un-Catholic 20th century, but still their stones speak, eloquently to an attentive ear, of a more tranquil and God-centered age: "The sun is the same," they say, "but the soil you tread on was once trod by men with a different tongue and very different concerns from those you see all around you" – and if stones could sigh – "What a beauty is gone from the world!" But the beauty is not gone, says La Reja. Here is that same tongue, of the descendants of those virile yet docile Spaniards, and the same concerns, the glory of God and the salvation of souls, and still Mother Church is fostering her sons, and still her sons are building up their Mother. The very essence of that beauty is not dead and gone, but alive and building...

On November 29 after a night spent in airplanes bringing him south from Columbia, Archbishop Lefebvre arrived at La Reja, just in time for the luncheon celebration of his 80th birthday. A number of his sons in the priesthood were gathered around him from afar for the occasion: the District Superiors of France, England, Switzerland; the Seminary Rectors of Germany and the USA and a professor from Ecône; Fr. Groche soon to open a house in black Africa, Fr. Babinet from El Paso, Texas (who has sent four vocations to La Reja), and many others. There were also distinguished French and Swiss priests, friends of the Society (one of them outstanding in his biretta with a brilliant purple pom-pom), and there were from France and Switzerland a dozen faithful friends to represent the laity, not to mention all the priests and laity present from the Argentine.

When his turn came to speak, the Archbishop said that such a gathering in the Argentine was a great consolation and satisfaction for his 80 years. He recalled the words 16 years ago of one of a group of Swiss laymen to whom the Archbishop had just laid out his reasons

The Ridgefield Letters

for buying what would become the seminary of Ecône: "My dear friends, Ecône will be talked of throughout the world." His Grace urged the young seminarians present to become holy Catholic priests, expressed his hopes also for a novitiate of Argentinean Sisters, and concluded that those who wished him another 80 years of life exaggerated a little, "but whatever God gives me, I will continue the combat."

The Superior General, Fr. Franz Schmidberger, wishing His Grace a happy birthday, declined to determine how many more years he should have. The pastor of Riddes, Fr. Epinay, after evoking the memory of the Archbishop's parents, faithful to their country and to their Faith, said, "Providence will give you the time you need. We have an absolute confidence in the future."

On Saturday morning, November 30, His Grace ordained seven seminarians to the diaconate, four to the subdiaconate, and in the afternoon there arrived the guest of honor for Sunday's Ordinations, Bishop Antonio de Castro Mayer. Let me help you to make the acquaintance of a truly venerable bishop. He is maybe 5 ft 6 inches tall, cannot weigh much over 100 pounds, is most simple, humble and cheerful in his bearing, but he speaks like a lion in matters of the Faith. When visiting on this occasion the shrine of Our Lady of Lujan, not far from La Reja, some Novus Ordo priests, on learning he was visiting with Archbishop Lefebvre, said, "Oh, then you belong to our separated brethren!" "Separated, yes," shot back the reply, "brethren, no!"

The Ordinations to the priesthood took place on Sunday, December 1, in the open air under a tent, a week earlier than originally scheduled, to enable Bishop de Castro Mayer to attend. The Archbishop began his sermon by warmly thanking his fellow bishop for being there to encourage the candidates and the whole seminary by his presence and participation in the ceremony of Ordinations. He went on to urge the eight ordinands to become men of prayer, men detached, with a spirit of Faith and of sacrifice, a true spirit of missionaries. The Archbishop, the Bishop, and some two dozen priests then laid on hands, and by the end of the ceremony the Society had eight new priests, including three Americans, two of whom, Frs. Gavin Bitzer and Alberto Gonzales, are working in the United States.

On the Monday the new priests celebrated their first Masses in the seminary, and then on the Tuesday the Archbishop had an extra joy: Bishop de Castro Mayer consented to perform the ceremony of conferring Tonsure and Minor Orders. This he did, resplendent in the purple pom-pommed biretta, because the Archbishop's mitre was too big to fit him. For the first time in many a year the Archbishop was able to watch an ordination ceremony! At the end of the ceremony Bishop de Castro Mayer said he was very happy to have spent these days at the Seminary of La Reja. They had been "a most promising and encouraging herald of the future of the Church." The bishop left for Brazil the same afternoon, to the applause and farewells of the Archbishop, priests and seminarians he had himself so encouraged. The Archbishop in turn left for New Zealand a few days later.

Meanwhile in Europe the much-heralded Synod was taking its anticipated course of singing the praises of the Second Vatican Council. Enclosed is the second letter of the same two bishops addressed to the Holy Father, for to their loving construction of the Church described above corresponds their firm hatred for the errors that destroy her. They warn the Holy Father that if the Synod merely confirms the Council, as indeed happened, then "we shall be entitled to think that the members of the Synod no longer profess the Catholic Faith." And if the Synod under the Holy Father's authority persists in the line of the Council, then he "will no longer be the Good Shepherd."

The Ridgefield Letters

Whether or not, as the European newspapers apparently say he did, the Pope made laughing reference to this last remark, it is in all truth infinitely grave. For if such remarks are backed with arguments, as they are in this letter, then either their falsity must be proved, or their truth must be taken seriously, but they cannot be laughed off.

So grave is the situation become that the two Bishops conclude that they can only persevere in the Church's holy Tradition and take "whatever steps are necessary for the Church to still have a clergy faithful to the Catholic Church." What they are certainly envisaging is the consecration of another bishop or bishops to ensure the continuation of the Traditional sacraments of Confirmation and Ordination. Rome for its part is preparing to cry "schism!" But who will have done the breaking with Tradition? The two bishops of La Reja, or the two thousand represented at the Synod? To ask the question is to answer it.

Back at the seminary, the Christmas to New Year Exercises have just announced more vocations for next year, and for this year another has just got in under the gate, a young Texan, bloody but unbowed from a trimester spent in a Maryknoll Novus Ordo seminary. These youngsters' sense of the Novus Ordo's falsity can be coming from God alone. Pray we give them the priestly formation God wishes.

And we are immensely grateful for your ongoing generosity. Christmas brought in a great number of gifts which enable us to cover most of our short-term debts. Thank you! May God bless you all, and guide and protect you through the New Year.

NO. 33 | FEBRUARY 1, 1986

Infallibility and the New Mass

INFALLIBILITY IS A difficult question, but it is one in which we should try to see clearly. For instance a friend of mine who is normally no friend of the Novus Ordo, has recently been half-way convinced, by the argument from the Church's infallibility, that the Novus Ordo is Catholic and acceptable. Of course we know – and he knows – that even in its Latin text the Novus Ordo is ambiguous, ecumenical, un-Catholic and unacceptable, but how did the infallibility argument deceive him for a moment?

In truth, Mother Church's teaching on her own infallibility is a delicate balance, easy to upset. Her infallibility, or inability to err, is easily underestimated or overestimated. In the last century, faced by the Masons and liberals undermining her authority and underestimating her infallibility, Pope Pius IX defined in 1870 the Pope's "ex cathedra" infallibility, and that definition acted as a sheet-anchor for Catholics being swayed around in the gales of liberalism. In this century however, history may tell that overestimation of Papal infallibility by Catholics blindly following the Pope has

The Ridgefield Letters

damaged the Church as much as underestimation of it by her enemies.

The Church's infallibility is delicately balanced between two grand principles. Like her Master, the Church is both divine and human. On the one hand, enjoying divine protection and the divine promises, she cannot fail. On the other hand, she is composed of sinful human members whose liberty God respects, and so churchmen can gravely fail, as when the pope in 359 AD excommunicated St. Athanasius. This freedom of churchmen to almost ruin the Church is a great proof of God's respect for His creatures, but God can never allow it to reach the point where the ruin of His Church is complete, if He did, He would be breaking His own promise to be with His Church to the end of the world (Mt.28: 20). Thus at the end of the world, the persecution by the Antichrist will almost have wiped out the Faith (Lk. 18: 8) but the Church will still be there. The Catholic Church cannot altogether fail. This is called her gift of indefectibility.

Now before the Catholic Church can have members to sanctify by her sacraments and to govern by her hierarchy, she must teach them the Faith with which to be baptized and enter the Church. In this sense her prime function is to teach, and so if she failed in her teaching, she would have failed altogether. But she is indefectible, as we have seen. Therefore she cannot altogether fail in her teaching. The Catholic Church cannot altogether lose the Truth and those who come to her are bound to be able to find it. This is her gift of infallibility, which she has always had and always will have, but it does not stop parts of the Church, even large parts of the Church, from falling into error through their own fault, as in the Arian crisis.

There is only one churchman absolutely protected from error, and that is the Pope, as we know from the definition of his infallibility in 1870, but note that even he is only protected if he fulfils all four conditions of the definition, by (1) defining (2) as Pope (3) a point of faith or morals (4) binding on the whole Church. If he fails to engage any one of the four conditions, the Holy Ghost is no longer bound to protect him from any possible error. Note however also that the Church's gift of infallibility is not limited to this special or "extraordinary" privilege of the Pope. The great mass of the Church's unfailing transmission of the deposit of Faith, or Tradition, her infallibility, goes on through "ordinary" means. Only occasionally does the Pope need to use his "extraordinary" infallibility. Thus the Church's ordinary gift is like a mountain of which the Pope's extraordinary privilege is merely the summit, snow-capped by the four conditions defined in 1870 so that it can be clearly seen, but still only the summit. And as summit rests on mountain, and not the reverse, so the Pope's "ex cathedra" privilege rests on the Church's gift, and not the Church's gift on the Pope's privilege, immensely useful though that privilege is to the whole Church because it is so clearly seen, and fixes where the mountain is.

Now how does all this apply to the present crisis of the Church? Firstly, as to the documents of the Second Vatican Council, both Pope John XXIII and Paul VI disavowed any intent to define any point of faith or morals at the Council, and thereby excluded any extraordinary infallibility. As for ordinary infallibility, it is discerned by the alignment with the Church's enduring Tradition, and so wherever Vatican II says what the Church has always said, it is infallible, and we must believe it if it is put before us to be believed. Where, however Vatican II went in for novelties out of line with Tradition, any ordinary infallibility was also excluded, and so such novelties as the Council's doctrine on ecumenism and religious liberty, we are in no way bound to accept.

The Ridgefield Letters

Similarly with the Novus Ordo Missae. At his general audience of November 19, 1969, Pope Paul VI said about the Novus Ordo that its rite and rubrics "are not by themselves a dogmatic definition; they are susceptible of varied theological gradings, according to the liturgical context in which they are to be found." With such words he excluded any extraordinary infallibility by excluding any definition. And ordinary infallibility will apply only to what is still traditional in that mixed up Missal, not to any of the dangerous novelties.

But, my friend argues, the theologians say that universal Church disciplinary (not doctrinal) laws must also be infallible in doctrine, otherwise Mother Church would have failed by imposing upon Catholics a corruption of their Faith; and the Novus Ordo Missae is just such a universal disciplinary law. Hence it cannot be bad.

Answer – the key-word is "imposed." These theologians hold a universal disciplinary law of the Church to be necessarily free of error if it is mandatory or obligatory, but not if it is a mere proposal, recommendation, suggestion or permission, because in that case the Catholics are not having error forced upon them. Now the best canon lawyers say about the Novus Ordo legislation that while it may have succeeded in establishing the New Mass as an alternative rite, it was certainly never of sufficient legal force to abolish the Tridentine rite. Hence it was the modernist authorities' sleight of hand, and never true force of Church law, which "imposed" the New Mass. Hence the New Mass, howsoever it was made to appear, has never in fact been mandatory, and so it cannot claim infallibility as being a universal Church law either.

No. The New Mass is indefensible, and infallibility is an argument which requires careful handling.

For easier reading, turn to the enclosed *Verbum* where you can read what some Novus Ordo priests think of the Novus Ordo.

Richard N. Williamson

Also enclosed is a card with the Archbishop's picture and a prayer of the Church for bishops. It was meant to commemorate his 80th birthday in November. We have had thousands printed. Ask for as many as you like.

On a personal note, may I ask your prayers for my dear parents who celebrate their 50th wedding anniversary on February 4. They do not have the Faith. Pray they may die with the Catholic Faith, and I will be eternally grateful to you. Meanwhile be sure that we pray daily at the seminary for the intentions of all of you who support us so generously. Bless you and thank you!

NO. 34 | MARCH 1, 1986

Replace Bishops Who Betray?

OVER THE LAST month or so, a few of you have written to express your anxiety over the prospect of Archbishop Lefebvre consecrating a bishop or bishops, and what a few of you write, probably a number of you feel.

First of all, let us see what the Archbishop himself has most recently said on this question. On October 27 of last year, a few weeks before the Synod, he said:

> I am often asked: 'Your Grace, are you going to consecrate a bishop?' And I reply: 'Stop bothering me with this question of a bishop! I myself have no idea, and that's all I can tell you.' But they insist: 'But your Grace, you are getting old . . . ' Yes, I am very well aware I am getting old. As I am fond of saying, I follow Providence, I do not lead it. I am confident that the good Lord is going to give us still clearer signs of where our duty lies. If it has to be done, I will do it. However, only if I am convinced by events that the good Lord will Himself have let happen. I can't out-do the Almighty. I am not a prophet. I do not know what is to happen in the future. I mean to wait for the good Lord to speak through

events which will show us what we have to do. So let no-one ask me what events are going to take place in one month, two months, three months, I know no more than anyone else does. If such events take place, some things will become very clear, and at that moment we will do what the good Lord requires of us.

These words are clear. Archbishop Lefebvre does not exclude consecrating a bishop without Rome's permission, but he is waiting for a clearer sign than he has yet received from Providence that such is truly God's will. Now the lamentable Synod, with its resolute failure to address the true problems of the Church, is certainly one more sign, and a major sign, but still maybe not enough souls yet see the full gravity of the Church's situation justifying such a drastic step.

Yet Heaven knows, the situation is grave. In the same October of last year, Archbishop Lefebvre gave a conference in Nantes, France, in which he quoted appalling examples of three European Episcopal Conferences betraying in public the Catholic Faith.

Firstly, the bishops of England and Wales last summer made a declaration to the Pope separating themselves at least in spirit from Rome. They said, in effect, they wished to remain in union with the Pope, but not in submission to him. In effect they wanted the Pope to give them their independence, just like the Anglicans took theirs 450 years ago. The English Catholic bishops have returned to Anglicanism.

Secondly, on January 1, 1985 the German Catholic bishops made a joint declaration with the German Evangelical Church Council on the subject of mixed marriages. This declaration, amongst other things, urgently advises engaged couples to decide before they marry in which church (i.e., Catholic or Protestant) the children are to be baptised and educated! In other words the bish-

The Ridgefield Letters

ops are saying what matters is not the Catholic Faith, but a faith! Under Pius XII, said the Archbishop, any bishop signing such a declaration would have been excommunicated on the spot!

Thirdly, on June 6 of last year at Einsiedeln the Swiss Bishops' Conference gave their approval to a revision of Swiss marriage law then pending before the Swiss Parliament whereby the traditional and Christian model of marriage (as laid down by God in Ephesians 5) would be largely replaced by a free and equal "partnership," in which for instance disputes will be settled not by the head of the family, but by recourse to a local magistrate! In September the law passed with a narrow majority, making the Archbishop say that by their approval these bishops bore the responsibility for this major advance in the destruction of Christian marriage, family and society.

And these episcopal betrayals are still not the gravest. Graver still are these words quoted in the *L'Osservatore Romano* of August 21, 1985, the Vatican's official newspaper, from a speech made in Morocco to a meeting of young Mohammedans: "We (Catholics and Mohammedans) believe in the same God, the one and only God, the living God." The Archbishop recalled that the Mohammedans refuse the divinity of Our Lord Jesus Christ. Now "Whosoever denieth the Son, the same hath not the Father" (I Jn. 2:23). How then can any Catholic say Mohammedans have the same God as Catholics? Yet the speech as quoted in the *L'Osservatore Romano* contained half a dozen quotes of similar import. "Is it possible the Holy Father does not realize the full meaning of what he is saying?," asked the Archbishop in October.

More recently still, on January 25 of this year, the Pope, closing the Week of Prayer for Christian Unity in Rome, said (*L'Osservatore Romano*, English edition, February 10, 1986, page 19):

— 135 —

Richard N. Williamson

> The ... Synod ... has shown how alive today is the desire ... to relive the Church's own experience on Pentecost morning in the Cenacle of Jerusalem. The indivisible fullness received then by the Church was destined to be developed, during the course of the centuries, in a multiplicity of diverse and complementary historical forms. The task of ecumenism has this very goal: to bring the Church to fulfillment as the sacrament of the harmonious unity of the multiple forms of a unique fullness ...

More simply, ecumenism is to reunite the diverse forms of the fullness received at Pentecost from the Holy Ghost. Now obviously the Pope is not talking of an "ecumenism" addressed to Catholics alone. In that case his words are saying that the sects and heresies which have broken away from Catholic unity are just as much from the Holy Ghost as is the Catholic Church which has preserved that unity! In other words the Holy Ghost authored the heresies like He authored Catholicism! Reread the Holy Father's own words. Do they not carry this blasphemy within them? And do not these words correspond to his actions as when a few years ago he walked down the aisle side by side with the Archlayman of Canterbury?

Whether or not our Holy Father realizes all that he is saying and doing, it must in fairness be asked: can the German bishops be blamed for their ecumenism when the Bishop of Bishops utters ecumenical words of such – at the very least – confusion?

Here is only a little idea of the gravity of Mother Church's situation, but present signs are that the Archbishop is still waiting before taking the step of consecrating a bishop to preserve the Catholic priesthood and the Catholic Church. For myself, I would hate to be in the Archbishop's shoes, but I cannot think of anyone I would be happier to see in them! As far as I am concerned, I hope he does not have to go ahead, and if he does not, I shall be happy, but if he does I shall be equally happy. It is all in God's hands, and this crisis has some great graces in store for whoever is willing to go whichever way God wants.

At the seminary, Lent is upon us and the priestly Ordinations before us, this year a Saturday, 9 am April 19, to enable priests to attend. Let all priests consider themselves hereby invited. Some we can put up at the seminary for a night or two if they will kindly give us notice.

Thank you, all of you, for your moral and material support. God will repay your sacrifices, especially during the Lenten season. Bless the benefactor who sent us "just a little something that I can afford once in a while, that the whole seminary could use better than I might on some type of foolish luxury, especially now during the Lenten season." And bless you all.

NO. 35 | APRIL 1, 1986

The Joys of Spring

EASTER IS A season for the poets. Here is a timely poem, especially for readers from Washington D.C. and up-state Michigan, both laden with cherry-trees, by A. E. Housman:

> Loveliest of trees, the cherry now
> Is hung with bloom along the bough,
> And stands about the woodland ride
> Wearing white for Eastertide.
>
> Now of my threescore years and ten,
> Twenty will not come again,
> And take from seventy springs a score,
> It only leaves me fifty more.
>
> And since to look at things in bloom
> Fifty springs are little room,
> About the woodlands I will go
> To see the cherry hung with snow.

It takes a poet to capture in words a fragment from the outburst of freshness and beauty with which nature presents us each spring. The poet has the eye, the heart and the way with words to put on paper a

The Ridgefield Letters

message from the volumes and volumes which God reads aloud to us through nature in the springtime. And yet how sad the poets can be, running up against mortality! The daffodils of April are a pure delight for Wordsworth:

> I wandered lonely as a cloud
> that floats on high o'er vales and hills,
> When all at once I saw a crowd,
> A host, of golden daffodils:
> Beside the lake, beneath the trees,
> Fluttering and dancing in the breeze . . .

Yet the same daffodils draw a tear from Robert Herrick:

> Fair daffodils, we weep to see
> You haste away so soon;
> As yet the early-rising sun
> Hath not attained his noon . . .

For Herrick cannot help himself reflecting:

> We have short time to stay as you;
> We have as short a spring;
> As quick a growth to meet decay
> As you or anything.
> We die
> As your hours do, and dry
> Away,
> Like to the summer's rain;
> Or as the pearls of morning's dew,
> Ne'er to be found again.

It is a seemingly insoluble problem as the human heart's "immortal longings" beat against the mortal framework of this life. Virgil gave stately voice to this grief in his famous line:

Richard N. Williamson

Sunt lacrimae rerum et mentem mortalia tangunt

to which the nearest equivalent in English might be a line again from Wordsworth:

The still sad music of humanity . . .

Is there no solution? Are the joys reawakened by spring in our heart fated merely to perish? Is this life all?

St. Thomas Aquinas did not think so. In fact upon the soul's immortal longings he built a solid argument for the soul's own immortality. The rational soul naturally knows of and so desires immortality, he says, and the poets amply prove that. But nature does nothing in vain. Hence the rational soul must have an immortal life.

Now to the modern mind such an argument can seem wishful thinking. How can we claim that nature does nothing in vain? The romantics come perversely to enjoy the frustration of their own longings, and blasphemous existentialists scrawl "Absurd" across the very charter of the universe. Not so the sane and robust Catholic mind! Nature is not in vain. Spring truly tells of joy. However swiftly it passes, it speaks of a beauty conquering death. No wonder God chose this season in which to die, so that nature's yearly breaking into life should commemorate His own breaking out of death. Resurrexit, sicut dixit. He hath risen again, as He said. And so here is an answer to A. E. Housman:

> The cherry-bloom's lovely tale of joy
> Well have you read, dear poet,
> Which fifty springs spent to enjoy
> Would be well-spent, you know it.
>
> But fifty springs, you seem to think,
> Your heart from all will sever;

The Ridgefield Letters

> You fear, as 'neath the grave you sink,
> Your eyes will close for ever.
>
> Poor man! You missed the better part
> Of the tale told by the cherry –
> It said: "Who made me, made your heart
> And made it to be merry.
>
> "Such beauty as mine, it cannot die
> And if on earth it wither,
> Then there's a heaven to which must fly
> Your heart! Go, hasten thither!"

How do we hasten thither? By dying to this life and straining towards the next:

> Therefore if you be risen with Christ, seek the things that are above; where Christ is sitting at the right hand of God; mind the things that are above, not the things that are upon the earth. For you are dead; and your life is hid with Christ in God. When Christ shall appear, who is your life, then you shall also appear with him in glory. Mortify therefore your members which are upon the earth; fornication, uncleanness, lust, evil concupiscence, and covetousness, which is the service of idols... Put ye on therefore, as the elect of God, holy, and beloved, the bowels of mercy, benignity, humility, modesty, patience: bearing with one another and forgiving one another, if any have a complaint against another: even as the Lord has forgiven you, so do you also. But above all these things have charity, which is the bond of perfection: and let the peace of Christ, rejoice in your hearts, wherein also you are called in one body: and be ye thankful.

Thus Colossians III starts out from the Resurrection.

Dear friends, pardon this letter for having broken into verse, but the sombre chain of reflections upon

Richard N. Williamson

Mother Church's situation (ably laid out once more by Fr. Schmidberger and Fr. Wickens in the enclosed Superior General's Letter and *Verbum*) was interrupted by the arrival of spring. Of course the Catholic Church will rise again after her present crucifixion. Let us merely do our duty day by day, in our different stations of life, and let us not forget the prime duty of charity amongst ourselves.

And thank you for the so generous charity of so many of you towards the seminary. Promising vocations are continuing to apply. Right now I don't know where we would put them, but I would know who to appeal to as soon as we had to start building again! Meanwhile, has anyone some spare daffodil bulbs?

May God bless you, and His Mother protect you and all your families.

NO. 36 | MAY 1, 1986

The Archbishop's Mounting Fears

THE ORDINATIONS OF April 1 went very well. God blessed us with beautiful weather. The SSPX and Mother Church have three new priests, all three of them Americans and all three posted to work in the United States. Two of them are already at work, the third sets his hand to the plough in mid-August.

Archbishop Lefebvre has just left for Europe again, after his annual springtime visit to the United States. It lasted two weeks, including three full days at the seminary. Here he gave Tonsure to twelve seminarians, Minor Orders to another thirteen and the diaconate to one, besides the priesthood to three. This means in the coming two years few priests to be ordained at Ridgefield because the classes of '81 and '82 were devastated by the desertion of several professors in '83. In 1989 however, there should begin to arrive at the priesthood a flow of seminarians now receiving Minor Orders. Such priests, formed (with the grace of God) traditionally, are indispensable to the survival of the Catholic Church. Where today, outside of the seminaries of Archbishop Lefebvre, can they be seen to be receiving the integrally Catho-

— 143 —

lic formation they need? For an eloquent description of the Major Ordinations ceremony, see next month's color *Verbum*! We hope also to get out a high class videotape recording of the Major Ordinations ceremony, on which faith-starved hearts and eyes can still feast, even after the gulag has moved in!

Even after the gulag has moved in? – Read this month's enclosures. They are daunting. Even while the Archbishop creates ceremonies of heavenly beauty and joy, the gravity of his warning voice escalates as the gravity of the crisis of the Church escalates. If your courage is failing you, wait for next month's *Verbum*. If you have courage, read on . . .

Read firstly Cardinal Ratzinger's reply of January 20 to the Solemn Warning addressed by the two bishops to the Holy Father in August of last year. In the Pope's name he answers that the Second Vatican Council's teaching, notably on religious liberty and ecumenism, is merely a continuous development of the Church's age-old doctrine on these points. In fact, the Council's friends and enemies alike recognize in this teaching a revolutionary break with Tradition, as is clear from the fruits. In any case the Cardinal excludes any calling in question of "the authentic doctrine of the ecumenical Second Vatican Council, the texts of which are magisterial and enjoy the highest doctrinal authority." And so the Cardinal is making Vatican II into a dogmatic Council!

Archbishop Lefebvre remembers how, when the Council opened, everyone said it was "pastoral," i.e., not concerned with doctrine but only with how pastors should more successfully reach the people with the Faith. In this way, says the Archbishop, everyone felt liberated from the burden of the past whose doctrine weighs down on a dogmatic Council. "Anything goes" was the heady feeling of those halcyon days. However, once the novelties had been brought into the Church, the tune

The Ridgefield Letters

changed. Now they say it was a dogmatic Council, and every Catholic must believe every word it says! Read next in Archbishop Lefebvre's letter to Mr. Madiran, his reaction to Cardinal Ratzinger's reply: "We are dealing with people who have no notion of Truth." By their perseverance in pretending that Catholic Tradition and Vatican II do not contradict one another, the Cardinal and the Pope prove that they have no idea what contradiction or falsehood or truth means, or they do not care. In the minds of men at the very summit of the Catholic Church, such dissolvent notions of an evolving truth are unbelievably grave. So the Pope says it is impossible to accuse the Council? Then it is impossible any longer to excuse the Pope, or to seek to blame only those around him. It has been understandable enough for Catholics to seek to cover over the failings of their Holy Father, but to do so any longer, says the Archbishop, would be for him a "grave failure in truth or charity." Nor can anyone accuse the Archbishop of enjoying this situation, of relishing this criticism of the Pope, of not having waited long and patiently for Rome to correct itself before so criticizing the Holy Father himself.

The third item enclosed is an adaptation of the Archbishop's sermon at Ecône on Easter Day and his conference to seminarians at Ridgefield on the day before Major Ordinations. Read how Bishop de Castro Mayer and the Archbishop have waited long and prudently before saying such grave things about the person of the Pope as the Archbishop here says. No doubt, for some people the Archbishop is speaking too late; for many others, he is still speaking too soon, and indeed it is not forbidden to hope and pray that God may yet avert the worst in Rome. The truth of the matter is that when the daylight of the Faith as it were began to fail at the Second Vatican Council, the two bishops said so; as the dusk grew ever darker in the '70's, they said so; now that well into the

'80's the night is almost upon us, they say so, but it will be soon enough to say that night has fallen when these two bishops say so.

Read also in the third item the Archbishop's fears even for Traditional Catholics. He is afraid that the ceaseless presentation by the media of the Pope's befriending of non-Catholic religions is, even in Catholics that love and attend the old Mass, blunting their sense that Catholicism is the one and only true religion. After all, people feel, what is so bad with befriending all men, men in all religions? Answer: yes, but that is not the same as befriending them in their false religions, which is to befriend falsehood.

Now the Holy Father is presently and publicly seeking out men of all religions, in, and as representing, these false religions. That is a publicized fact, and a terrible scandal if we think clearly as Catholics. And note how the Archbishop fears that even so-called Traditional Catholics are in danger of losing the Faith by seeing little or nothing wrong in this Faith-denying ecumenism! It is not enough to love the smells and bells of the old Mass, we must love our Lord, and to love Our Lord, we must hate His enemies, not as men, but insofar as they are His enemies. There is no true love of good without a proportionate hate of evil.

There is no true Catholic without a hatred of all false religions as such: "Honourable and dear Protestant, I love you, but I hate your false religion."

And if after reading all three items you need courage, then turn to the fourth, and inscribe for a retreat! Here is what one young man wrote after the Easter Week Ignatian Exercises: "What made me decide to do the Exercises was some words in a flyer publicizing them which appealed to all who were in the darkness of doubt and confusion to come to the Exercises, and promised them light and peace if they did. I answered the appeal

The Ridgefield Letters

and the promise was kept. After the five days of silence, prayer and solid spiritual direction my soul had a clarity and peace I had not known for a long time. I heartily recommend to anyone experiencing spiritual darkness and anguish (especially if they are tempted to discouragement) in these dark days, to take the Exercises. They will not be disappointed if they do."

Dear readers, one million thanks for your unending generosity towards the seminary. The regular contributors amongst you are the lifeline of the seminary. That is why we guard jealously our mailing list, and we have lent it out only once outside the Society, for a one-off mailing from the "Fatima Crusader," so that you could then subscribe on your own if you wished. However, our mailing list will soon be shared with the Society's U.S. District Headquarters in Dickinson, Texas, so that you can receive information about much more of the work of the Society in the USA.

Bless you for all the support you have given us so far. Please be generous also with your prayers for us, which are so important, and be sure that we pray for you as our friends and benefactors each day at the seminary. And let us be especially faithful to the Rosary of the Blessed Virgin Mary during her beautiful month of May.

NO. 37 | JUNE 6, 1986

Faith's Ebb and Flow

ENCLOSED IS THE *Verbum* in color of this year's ordinations. It has been a little slow in getting through the printers, but we trust you will enjoy it. As I said last year, so much state-of-the-art technology and brilliant color is spent in the service of the devil today, why should not a little be spent for the honour and glory of God, in gratitude for three new priests He has given us?

You will notice that the sequence of the photographs corresponds to the sequence of the text. You may not be used to reading verse in our prosaic times, but poetry is one of those arts which is bound to flourish again whenever the Catholic Faith revives. With the Faith, come beauty, discipline and order back into a man's thoughts and feelings, and to express these in his language, he naturally turns to rhyme and rhythm to give his words more power and dignity.

On the contrary, when the tide of the Faith ebbs, as when Matthew Arnold (Dover Beach) could write in the last century:

> The Sea of Faith
> Was once, too, at the full, and round earth's shore

The Ridgefield Letters

    Lay like the folds of a bright girdle furled.
    But now I only hear
    Its melancholy, long, withdrawing roar,
    Retreating, to the breath
    Of the night-wind, down the vast edges drear
    And naked shingles of the world,

Then chaos is come again, to express which man progressively shuns any order of rhythm or elegance of rhyme, until in our own day the poets and artists can deliberately make their products as ugly as possible in order to cry havoc, the havoc which is in their own souls and in most souls around them.

Yet poetry is so natural to man, it does not disappear. Scorned as an art, it is still appreciated to make money. See how the advertisers make their commercial jingles bounce and rhyme to give them more penetration! It is truly sad that the only poetry and song known to many little children today are those of the television advertisements. So here is a poem instead about the making of priests.

We have also put together the videotape of this year's ordinations. It is a better tape than last year's. Thanks to Mr. Lou Tucker of Pennsylvania, it was made with four cameras, including two within the sanctuary, and it enables the viewer to follow the sequence of the ordination ceremony as he never could, sitting in the congregation.

Concerning the summer retreats, hurry, if you wish to be sure of a place, and pray for the retreatants, that they all draw the full measure of God's grace from these blessed retreats, which can turn that "melancholy long withdrawing roar" into the roar of triumph of "the victory which overcometh the world, our faith" (1 Jn. 5: 4).

All is well at the seminary. Studies picked up again after the Ordinations, and are now drawing towards the close of the school year. Second semester exams take place within the next two weeks, then most seminarians head for home on mid-summer's day, June 24.

How many more semesters and vacations will follow one another in relative tranquility? One may well ask. In the seminary refectory this year was read the book *Martyrs of the Coliseum* including the story of St. Vitus. Threatened with death by his father for his miracle-working Faith, he was led down to the sea by an angel to a specially prepared ship which took him to a quite different part of the country where he preached, baptized and worked miracles for the people. Meanwhile, back in Rome a devil possessing the Emperor's son said that he could only be driven out of the boy by St. Vitus, whose exact whereabouts the devil gave! St. Vitus was duly fetched back to Rome, drove out the devil and was martyred.

It is a remarkable example of God's guiding events. Rarely does one see God intervening so clearly by an angel and by the use of a devil to direct a man's life and death, but it does us good to be reminded that God is always and everywhere in control of events. Everything he knows; nothing happens that He does not at least permit; anything He positively wills is certain to come about. "We know that to them that love God, all things work together unto good." (Rom. 8: 28)

Let us then for the month of June renew our trust in His Sacred Heart.

NO. 38 | JULY 1, 1986

Happy Servants, Unhappy Trials

THIS LETTER COMES to you just after the close of another school year, in which the seminary has surely been blessed. Since September of last year – and need it be said how quickly ten months have flown! – nothing seems to have disturbed the calm even flow of seminary life, centering around the prayer, study and recreation of some thirty young men aiming to become Catholic priests.

Theirs is an "alternative life-style" if ever there was one! No drinking (except on feast-days), no smoking (that we know of!) no television (except the occasional carefully chosen(!) VCR on a holiday evening), no movies, no dances, no rides to the beaches, etc. – what sense can it make to a red-blooded young man? Yet these seminarians do not have pale blood, and one might well wager they are one of the happiest groups of young men in the country. How is that possible?

Answer, the same way it has always been possible down all the centuries. Tightly disciplined, forced to learn Latin with tears (no attempt whatsoever being made to teach it without tears!), cudgeling their bemused brains to rise to the first, let alone the third, degree of abstraction of Church philosophy, maybe not even persevering to the last three years of theology, still a large number of them, persevering or not persevering, will look back on their seminary years as amongst the happiest of their lives – once more, why?

The answer is not complicated: the love of Our Lord Jesus Christ. It is the Divine Master who has drawn them to the seminary, and He is revealing himself in a quite special way to the chosen souls who will hear Him speaking through the liturgy on the day of their ordination: "Now I will no longer call you servants, but friends." Imagine Jesus forming someone to be His friend! That is the seminary. Now Our Lord never promised anyone an easy way to Heaven. On the contrary, He required daily renunciation of self and carrying of the cross, and so the cross is stamped on every moment of seminary studies and discipline – but – but – what can compare with the beginning of that divine game of hide-and-seek, as the Divine Master reveals Himself, hides Himself, reveals Himself again, to draw the chosen soul onto a path specially close to His own, on the way to Heaven? Recall the Sacred Heart having John lean on his breast at the Last Supper. Did John understand? No. Did he love? Yes. What a mystery! – God drawing His creatures to love Him. What a heartbreak, our infidelity! What a privilege, a vocation! Help us give thanks to God for a happy year, and always pray the seminarians be, with Our Lady, faithful pupils and scholars of the Sacred Heart – then you will have the priests you need.

Good news from the law courts, where the Society has again won. In September of last year in the Federal Court for Eastern Pennsylvania (case #83-6030), Judge McGlynn ruled after a three-day trial that the occupiers had to return the Philadelphia church property to the Society. "It is clear from the documents and actions of

The Ridgefield Letters

the people involved (in setting up St. Cyprian's Chapel) that the parties intended to create a trust for the benefit of the Society," he said, and "Even if an express trust had not been established, the evidence shows that a constructive trust should be imposed," because the occupiers' control of the property was, in the judge's own words, "the result of an abuse of a confidential relationship."

The Society's opponents appealed against this judgment which undermines their claim to thirteen other properties as well. A fully-fledged appeal was set in motion, and on June 5 of this year, a month or so ago, Circuit Judges Gibbons, Becker and Stapleton of the US Court of Appeals for the Third Circuit heard both sides argue for and against Judge McGlynn's judgment (case #85-1726). On June 12, just one week later, they gave their 25-word decision – Judge McGlynn's judgment upheld.

There is ample evidence that the Society's opponents expected to lose both the original case and the appeal, as in fact happened. Yet their lawyers announced that if they lost the appeal, they would appeal again to the Supreme Court. Fighting spirit is one thing, but before poor Catholics have to see tens or even hundreds of thousands more dollars of theirs spent on lawyers, can someone make sanity prevail?

Enough. If you would like photocopies of the first and second Philadelphia verdicts, just ask. You have the reference numbers if you prefer to write to the courts direct. Meanwhile let us thank God for justice being administered in the courts, which discourages evil and encourages the doers of good.

Alas, justice is not prevailing at the highest levels of the Church. For one view of just why the proposed Meeting of World Religions in Assisi in October will be as welcome to the world as it must be abhorrent to Catholics, read Archbishop Lefebvre's enclosed words on the "Religious United Nations." He has long said that Catholic bishops and priests are presently the most potent promoters of Communism. A Nicaraguan refugee doctor has made an excellent tape for the Cardinal Mindszenty Foundation explaining how the Communist Revolution in Nicaragua was defeated until the Catholic Church swung behind it. Now Cardinal Bravo understands, but it is too late . . .

There is only one way to stop Communism, and that is to make reparation to the Immaculate Heart of Mary, such as she asked for at Fatima. Meanwhile the SSPX will promote the Rosary and humbly strive to help guard the Sacred Priesthood and the Mass and the true sacraments for better days. Do not give up supporting us. We have already fifteen more young men due to enter the seminary in September. Some may have to sleep under the stairs, but they will all need to eat!

If the last *Verbum* nourished your Faith, may I also ask for a prayer for the three benefactors who put it together? – Mrs. Horton, Mrs. Graham and the photographer Keith Forrest. They took no other remuneration.

Bless you, and may Almighty God guard and guide you. July is the month of the Precious Blood. Let us recall it is no less powerful to redeem us today than when Our Lord first shed it upon the Cross. We men are wicked, but God is not weak.

NO. 39 | AUGUST 6, 1986

Insider Describes Horrendous "Rome"

THE WEATHER FOR the outdoor ordinations at the Society's seminaries in Ecône and Zaitzkofen this year was beautiful. Twenty new priests were ordained in Ecône, thirteen for the Society and seven for traditional Catholic communities operating alongside, but not within the Society, five Benedictines and two Franciscans. And then five more Society priests were ordained in Zaitzkofen, in Southern Germany.

I was fortunate enough to attend these ordinations because they coincided with the tenth anniversary of my own ordination at Ecône. On June 29, twelve of us were ordained priests of the Society. Of these, six were present at the ordinations in Ecône this year to celebrate together God's gift to us of ten years of priesthood and of fidelity to the Bishop and the Society of our ordination. We promised to meet again at Ecône in 15 years' time to celebrate our 25th Anniversary. Rendezvous for 2001, if God wills.

Then I went down to Rome to ask again the question I asked two years ago: how can the trained and dedicated high officials of the Catholic Church in Rome be doing

Richard N. Williamson

exactly what is necessary to destroy the Roman Church? How can the prelates in Rome not know what is happening to the Church? And if they know it, how can they let it continue? Two years ago I put the question to the valiant editor of the famous anti-modernist fortnightly paper *Si Si, No No*, Dom Putti. He died a few months later, but his answer still rang in my ears:

> There is nothing to be done with Rome. They have all sold themselves to the devil, for stupid reasons. They know they are doing wrong but they don't want to recognize that wrong is wrong. There may be a handful of exceptions. It is very easy now to play a double game. The situation is horrendous. They are egotists. They have no notion of the interests of Our Lord Jesus Christ.

Then came the Indult of October '84 which raised hopes that something good could still come out of Rome, but the only good effect seemed to be the proof that the Tridentine Mass was not completely forbidden. So this time I put the same questions to two Italian laymen, old friends of Dom Putti and of mine, who watch everything going on in the Holy City. Their answers help to fill in the picture. For those who want the truth, let me sketch in their answer:

> Ever since the death of Pope Pius X in 1914, the Catholic Church has been sliding into the abyss, through one decade after another of compromises and betrayals. The point has now been reached where an invisible master gives anti-Catholic orders, and the whole Vatican obeys. For instance, until recently all non-catholic sects were meant to be "expressions of creativity, etc.", but recently the order must have gone out to discredit the anti-ecumenical and anti-communist sects, because suddenly we saw an orchestrated series of

The Ridgefield Letters

meetings, articles, books, pronouncements of the Holy See etc., all following the same line: an attack on the Witnesses of Jehovah, the Mormons, the Moon, certain Anglicans and charismatics, all the sects claiming there is an exclusive truth and which refuse Liberation theology and the progressive political struggle. It is easy to follow such public maneuvers of the modernists simply by reading their publications, for instance the *Agenzia Adista*.

What is much more difficult to uncover is their secret manipulations, for which of course we do not have the documentation. We know that Msgrs. Casaroli, Silvestrini and Noe are three of the leading enemies of the Church that appear in public, but behind them are no doubt far more influential manipulators who may appear as moderates or even conservatives. There is a whole inextricable network, a semi-secret society, of delinquents, a Mafia far worse than the Mafia associated with Sicily and New York.

Here are two examples: in the 1950's a major biblical scholar in Italy,, now dead, Msgr. Antonino Romero, set up a strong opposition to the heresies of modernism being spread inside the Pontifical Biblical Institute. He underwent a severe Mafia-style persecution, anonymous letters, threats, night-calls, etc, and was dropped by his colleagues (such men are easily isolated). In 1960 he nonetheless wrote a famous article, denouncing the infiltration of modernism and masonry in the pontifical seminaries and universities. From then on he had no peace. He slept away from home, in friends' houses, as though he was being pursued by the KGB. He trusted no one any more, always fearing an informer, and was driven almost out of his mind. There is in fact a highly efficient psychological terror machine at work in Rome, to keep anti-modernists in line.

Second example: Msgr. Silvestrini (cf. *Si Si, No No*, November 15, 1985) is known to have a file in the Vatican with information on all members of the hierarchy, all present and future bishops, but then he also

Richard N. Williamson

has a secret parallel file containing details from their past enabling them to be blackmailed. These details will frequently consist of crooked financial dealings or gravely immoral personal actions in which the bishops or candidate-bishops have let themselves get involved. Thus the "best" of churchmen in Rome today are liable to be silent, for some reason from their past. In public they give out the hierarchy's official line, namely that all is well except for the exaggerations of a few progressives, and that "the traditionalists are disobedient." In private, however, in their very rare moments of truth, they say, "Don't ask us to do anything, our hands are tied."

Humanly speaking, there is no way out. The problem is that Catholics are misinformed, but worse still, they do not want to know the truth, because if they knew it, they would be obliged to react. Anything for the quiet life. The modernists have corrupted the Faith of Catholics with a utopian dream of a charismatic church without hierarchy, property or structure, to provide spiritual animation for the modern world and bring it to the Teilhardian Omega Point of Man's identification with God upon earth.

The modernists themselves at least partly believe in this nonsense. The rest of their motivation is pride – they feel themselves called to build a new church, a new world. The old world and the old religion must go. Hence they have dissolved the latter with a weak and sentimental spirituality of ecumenism, pacifism and dialogue, and even the "best" of Romans have given up the struggle. They have no will-power or fight left in them.

However, Catholics are not powerless, because the simple presentation of the truth gets the modernists in a tangle. Were public opinion against them, they would lose their power. They ensnare people in illusions like, all we need do is properly apply the Council. They live on illusions, they live in darkness, like a heap of horrible insects beneath a stone. Brought out into the light

The Ridgefield Letters

of day, they are paralyzed. They fear public exposure more than anything. As it is, their secret service of information is such that they know everything and can program and influence even their enemies' actions, but they are not omnipotent, and one day Our Lord will tear away the veil hiding their machinations...

From this daunting description of the situation in Rome, clear and positive conclusions follow. Firstly, we must pray that God preserve and strengthen our own Catholic Faith, pure and free of any taint of heresy, because Catholics' weakness is the modernists' great strength. Secondly we must pray that He save His Church, because He Himself said that He sends us as lambs and not as wolves, among wolves. He does not want us to fight His enemies with their weapons, but if we will only pray, He can overthrow them in a moment. Thirdly, we do not have nothing to do, we must stand up for the pure Catholic Faith and tear apart the modernists' falsehoods and deceits. "Heaven is not for cowards," said St. Philip Neri. Catholics must want to know the truth and must be ready to give battle. Ours is a time not for eating lotus-flowers, but for heroism, like that of the informers who most likely paid with their lives for revealing the list of 121 Masons inside the Vatican a few years back (*Die Freimaurer und der Vatikan*, Manfred Adler, p.13).

Well, neither the eighteen young men presently applying to try their priestly vocation here next month, nor the two hundred odd retreatants filling the seminary's seven summer retreats, are lotus-flower Catholics! "O love the Lord, all ye his saints, for the Lord will require truth and will repay them abundantly that act proudly. Do ye manfully, and let your heart be strengthened, all ye that hope in the Lord." (Ps. 30: 24–25)

We are grateful as ever for your support. We shall soon have to build again at Ridgefield, unless someone

Richard N. Williamson

can swiftly find us a bargain 100-room seminary ready-built, within easy reach of a major airport, and which the Seminary could buy, for remember that the Novus Ordo would usually rather pay to destroy a building than let it serve Tradition. Lord, have mercy upon us!

NO. 40 | SEPTEMBER 3, 1986

Assisi Meeting – False Ecumenism

It has been a happy summer at the seminary. Priests, brothers and seminarians have rotated here to enable a larger number than ever of retreatants, men and women, to reinvigorate their spiritual life with the grace of St. Ignatius' famous Exercises. There have been plenty of serious faces, as souls grappled with the grand truths of our existence, but I have seen no sad or long faces – "Blessed is he that cometh in the name of the Lord."

Now however comes the fall, with the October meeting in Assisi of the Holy Father with representatives of many other religions . . . At a Cardinals' meeting, Cardinal Gagnon is reported to have asked the Pope, "What god are you going to pray to?" to which the Pope's reported reply was, "What is wrong with praying for peace?" With a parable and with Pius XI, let us attempt to think clearly about ecumenism. Firstly, the parable.

Two children fell into the middle of a fast-flowing river and were being swept downstream to certain death. Running alongside them on the bank were a man and his son with a rope. "Help!" shouted the children. "Grab hold of the rope and we'll pull you on shore," cried out the man throwing the rope to them. One child caught hold of it, and father and son pulled him to safety. The other child, being willful, shouted back, "No, you jump in too." The father knew that the current was too fast and dangerous for him, but the imprudent son, thinking only of reaching the drowning child, jumped in to join him, and both were swept away to be drowned.

The fast-flowing stream is this world, with its many whirlpools and delusions, sweeping men towards eternal death. The children represent mankind, the rope is the doctrine and sacraments of the Catholic Church, the bank is the Church itself. The father who does not stand still but runs along the bank to keep up with the world and throw out to it the means of salvation, is the wise ecumenist who stays on the bank. The foolish ecumenist forgets the need of the Church and its doctrine, thinks only of reaching out to the world, jumps off, and perishes with it.

The word "ecumenism" comes from the Greek "oikoumene", meaning "inhabited", referring to the whole inhabited earth. Thus an ecumenical council has participants from all over the earth, in other words it is a council of the universal Church. Hence "ecumenism" means the universal outreach of the Church.

Now there is no question whether the Catholic Church should reach out to all men – Our Lord himself commanded her to do so – "Go, teach all nations" (Mt. 28: 19). The question is, how she should do it. Pius XI gave the Catholic answer in his encyclical of 1928, *Mortalium Animos*.

He says that as men today are seeking more than ever to unite the nations, so they hope to unite all men of many different religions in the common profession of a few basic beliefs. After all, did not Christ pray that his disciples might be one? Did not Christ insist on charity towards all men? And should not all men of any religion unite forces to combat the rise of irreligious Marxism?

No, says Pius XI, for beneath these enticing words lies a great error. The error consists in denying one or another great truth, namely: the one true God once took flesh and revealed the one true religion He laid down for men, and He founded one Church to perpetuate that religion. This Church He designed to be visible and to last to the end of time, with unity of faith and of government.

To claim that that one Church is now indistinguishable amongst many others like it, is to say that what Christ promised to assist (Mt. 28: 20) has failed, or, what the Holy Ghost enlightens (Jn. 16: 13) has grown dark, which is tantamount to blasphemy. Also, how could God require of men, on pain of damnation (Mk. 16: 16), to believe in a Church they could not distinguish from many others like it?

As for the argument from charity, the Pope points out that it is the very Apostle of Charity, St. John, who forbids to even say "good-bye" to a heretic (II Jn. 10). Also, as love presupposes knowledge of the beloved, so true charity, loving neighbors for God's sake, presupposes a true faith in God. Hence the chief bond of unity amongst believers or Christians must be their unity in the faith. But what unity of faith can exist between Catholics who believe, and non-Catholics who disbelieve, in Tradition, in a divinely instituted hierarchy, in the sacrifice of the Mass, in transubstantiation, in the veneration of the Mother of God, and so on? These are not small matters.

Hence the true unity of Christians can only be achieved by individuals separated from the Catholic Church reuniting with her. To represent her as being composed of separate and scattered members is absurd, because she is the Mystical Body of Christ, compactly fitted together like a human body (Eph. 4: 16). And

Richard N. Williamson

Pius XI gives a beautiful quotation from St. Cyprian on the oneness of the Church: "The Spouse of Christ cannot commit adultery; she is incorrupt and modest, she knows one house, she guards with chaste modesty the holiness of one room." How then could anyone think that "the unity which proceeds from the stability of God and is bound together by the sacraments of heaven could be torn asunder in the Church or separated by the wills of the discordant?" Thus Christ's prayer for unity (Jn. 17) has never been waiting upon men for fulfillment, but has always been fulfilled, by that unity which God gives to true Catholics, which is observable even today, and into which all men are invited, nay commanded, by God to enter – Mt. 7: 13 and Jn. 10: 9.

As for combating atheistic Marxism with humanistic solidarity, one might as well try to put out a fire by pouring gasoline on it! The humanistic mindset is in fact the very seed-bed of Marxism. That is why the West, by pursuing "human rights", is committing suicide, betraying one anti-communist ally after another into the gulag, the barbarous concentration camp, of communism – Nicaragua yesterday, the Philippines tomorrow, South Africa the day after, and so on.

The same humanistic mindset within the Church is at the very root of today's false ecumenism. If I leave out God, there is only human solidarity left. If I lose from view the Way, the Truth and the Life, Jesus Christ, then of course unity and charity can only mean mutual benevolence meetings. After all, what is wrong with praying for peace?

But anyone who has the Catholic Faith has a quite different frame of reference: God exists, and all things are ordered to Him. He intervened in history, and by and in Jesus all things were created and consist (Col. 1: 16–17), "One Lord, one faith, one baptism" (Eph. 4: 5), and down all the centuries that one faith has been told

The Ridgefield Letters

by the one Church which Jesus founded. All the rest is human dreams and errors.

Alas, the media are powerful promoters of the humanistic mindset, and so let no Catholic who frequents the media be surprised to find himself confused or tempted by their version of ecumenism. Hence the praises lavished in modern times by one Pope after another upon Ignatian retreats, because they so vigorously renew in a man his Catholic mindset, and dissipate that confusion arising from two mindsets struggling for supremacy within one and the same mind.

The retreats at the seminary each year afford us the particular pleasure of seeing some of our friends and benefactors themselves profiting by the beauty of the grounds and facilities of the seminary which they support. Even if the seminary had to move (and we have not yet found anywhere to move to), the Society would keep Ridgefield if it could, as a retreat house.

However, keep us in your prayers, because the Devil cannot leave alone a happy seminary and a successful retreat house! Remember in particular our battle in the law courts. We won a resounding double victory in Philadelphia, but the Connecticut and New York property cases have still to be fought, and may come on soon. God's will be done.

In return we will pray for yourselves, being ever mindful of your generous support without which the seminary could not exist, and we will pray through November at every Mass on the main altar for Holy Souls dear to you that you will inscribe on the card enclosed and return to us. (No need to reinscribe souls inscribed with us in previous years).

May God bless you and guard you.

NO. 41 | OCTOBER 2, 1986

The Archbishop Resorts to Cartoons

THERE IS A flyer enclosed with this letter which many of you may find shocking. It is the flyer on ecumenism with pictures [printed at the end of this letter] firstly of the Pope refusing Our Lord entry to the Ecumenical Prayer meeting at Assisi at the end of this month, secondly of Our Lord in turn refusing the Pope entry to heaven. These pictures were conceived by Archbishop Lefebvre. A little explanation may not be out of place:

You might in the first picture be shocked by the words being put in the Pope's mouth: "No! No! There is no room for you here. You are not ecumenical." You might think that this Pope would never actually say such a thing, that, on the contrary he would welcome Our Lord to the Meeting with open arms, merely asking Him to keep quiet His awkward claim to be the only true God. But how could Our Lord, who is the one true God, possibly accept such an invitation? And how could a Catholic who has the Catholic Faith ever issue such an invitation? Actions speak louder than words, and the very act of putting together such a meeting tells Our Lord to

The Ridgefield Letters

stay out. True, Pope John Paul II would put it in gentler terms, he would have words to clothe his act in sheep's clothing, but the <u>act</u> of calling the Meeting remains, in reality, the act of a wolf who wants the sheep but does not want their Shepherd. Must you not agree that if the Pope's words in the first picture do not correspond to his language, they at least correspond to his acts?

But, you might reply, the Pope means well – how dare the Archbishop in the second picture damn him to Hell? Firstly, the Archbishop is not judging intentions, which God alone can do – "Man seeth those things that appear, but the Lord beholdeth the heart" (I Sam. 16: 7). However, just after telling us not to judge (Mt. 7), Our Lord Himself also tells us to beware of false prophets who come to us in sheep's clothing, "but inwardly they are ravening wolves" (Mt. 7: 15), so obviously Our Lord was not telling us to abandon our critical faculties. In the sane and robust Middle Ages, the greatest Catholic poet of all time, Dante Alighieri, put plenty of bishops and popes in his inferno, or hell. The trouble is that since the Counter-Reformation, the good Lord has almost spoiled us with so many relatively good Popes that we have difficulty in readjusting to the fact of a bad Pope. These two pictures do not call in question this Pope's intentions, nor damn his inner soul, but they do remind us that his present outer acts are damnable, and lead to hell. It is an unpleasant truth, but nonetheless true, that Catholicism was never designed to please the world and never has done so.

Yes, you might reply, but even if the two pictures correspond to the reality of today's situation, the Archbishop risks alienating a lot of his followers who will not find such an attack on the Pope acceptable. Reply: if millions of souls, Catholic and non-Catholic, are in danger of receiving mortal scandal from the ecumenical acts of this Pope, then such souls must be warned by whatever means will reach them (and many souls are reached today by pictures). And if many souls will be turned away by such an overdose of reality, the Archbishop may have judged that at this late stage those that have ears to hear should hear, even if many others take offence. Our Lord knew that when he told people to eat His flesh and drink His blood, the great majority (Jn. 6: 67–68) would abandon Him as a crazy preacher of cannibalism – but He announced the Holy Eucharist all the same. The truth must be preached in season, out of season, says St. Paul. Is, or is not, today's ecumenism a mortal danger? The Archbishop thinks that even some Traditional Catholics are growing to accept this viper into their bosom. No wonder he is resorting even to shock tactics! How else can he get through to this television generation?

Nor are the pictures in themselves undignified. They caricature neither the person nor the standpoint of the Pope. I happen to know that the Archbishop has long ruminated on these two pictures. I am convinced that after maybe an initial shock, time and events will prove he was right to resort to this means to tell the essential truth – ecumenism as practiced today is damning, damnable and to be damned!

Less controversial is the flyer on the Mass, sent to all of you a year ago. In its English edition, we have printed 140,000 copies, and will no doubt have to go to a fourth printing. The German edition is doing equally well in Germany. Recently I had to send the original pictures to Japan for a Japanese edition about to be published. Moreover the Japanese student who asked for them was the first to make a learned and accurate correction to the phrasing of Reason no. 48! – he points out it was Pius IV and not Pius V who condemned vernacularism, etc., at the Council of Trent! Finally we ourselves, at the request of a colleague in Portugal, had printed in Connecticut a Portuguese version of the flyer, and we

The Ridgefield Letters

have already shipped – by your generosity, dear Benefactors – 20,000 copies to the land of Fatima. On each was printed in Portuguese, "pray for the American Catholics who offer you this flyer." If you would like any copies for yourselves, just let us know, and you also will have them for free.

Meanwhile we are about to ship some 15,000 of them to Portuguese-speaking Brazil. Your apostolate extends, dear Benefactors, and in return Catholics from these poorer countries will be praying for you.

That is the interaction of the various members of the Mystical Body of Christ, His Church. We are shipping these flyers to Don Fernando Rifan, priest and secretary to Bishop Antonio de Castro Mayer. You will no doubt be interested in Don Fernando's letter to me:

> We very much like the Mass flyer in Portuguese. Very attractive and popular, the sort of thing Americans know how to do so well. I would very much like you to send the 15,000 copies you promised. We will distribute them throughout the Diocese. We promise to pray for the Americans who printed the flyer.
>
> Here in Campos the situation continues to be one of combat. The new bishop (a modernist, who succeeded Msgr. de Castro Mayer) has just driven me out of my parish – the motives were the same as usual: refusal to accept Vatican II and the New Mass. However, thanks be to God, the entire parish has remained faithful. The Masses I celebrate here in exile are heavily attended, about 1,000 people every Sunday . . .
>
> We mean to go to the Argentine for the Ordinations again this year. I think there will be some pleasant surprises. I conclude by thanking you for, and awaiting the arrival of, the flyers, etc.

What he means by "pleasant surprises" I do not know, but he is clearly in the front line of just the same combat as ourselves. The Campos priests could also most certainly use our prayers.

Back at Ridgefield, this is the time of year when the seminary is most crowded. This year it is more crowded than ever, with eighteen new seminarians freshly arrived from their Entry Retreat in Canada, and with two more still to come. Before next year the seminary must either build or move. Most likely we shall build, and we shall not be unhappy to stay in these beautiful surroundings, but I think we must leave Providence the chance to find us the bargain ready-built seminary elsewhere which would enable us to make of Ridgefield the retreat house for which it is ideal and which the Society in America could clearly use. Keep looking for Providence's bargain!

Do not however think we are worried by the litigation continuing over the Ridgefield property. We are very confident of winning. In the essentially similar case in Philadelphia, our adversaries spent (said Fr. Hesson) $200,000 on lawyers only to lose twice, in the Federal Court and in the Federal Court of Appeals. Now they have just spent another estimated $10,000 on a motion to appeal again, to the U.S. Supreme Court. Our lawyer calls this latest motion "disgraceful, containing not even a passing effort to show an issue in which the Supreme Court should be interested." He is not even troubling to file a brief in reply. Yet our adversaries are keeping up a great pretence that all goes well for them. Pray that their blindness be not terminal. It is already a terrible punishment.

A breath of sanity – thanks to Mrs. Emily Johnston's old-fashioned thrift, the seminary's kitchen bill for July '85 to June '86 inclusive was only $36,076, or, little over $2 per person per day, an astonishingly low figure when one knows how well seminarians – and retreatants – ate under her care. May she have a happy retirement. Also the seminary's heating bill for the same period was only

The Ridgefield Letters

$9,683, but that is not a figure to which seminarians take so warmly! Be that as it may, dear friends and benefactors, your admirable generosity (also proved by the year's audit) does not go to waste in Ridgefield, if we can help it.

So, many thanks to you all, and may God reward you. Be especially faithful to His Mother's rosary through the month of October.

Richard N. Williamson

NO. 42 | NOVEMBER 1, 1986

Assisi: Save the Wolves?

TWO MORE HISTORIC documents of the crisis of the Church, besides the Superior General's Letter no. 31 and the latest *Verbum*, are reaching you with this letter. The first is the Archbishop's covering letter sent to the Pope together with the double picture you received last month concerning the International Prayer Meeting held a few days ago in Assisi.

Here it is:

> Holy Father,
> Be so good as to meditate on these two pictures, since you are deaf to the anguished appeals which we have filially addressed to you. Deign at least not to offend gravely and in public against God's First Commandment: the salvation of your soul is at stake! Preach Jesus Christ, as did the Apostles, even at the cost of their lives. That is the fervent and filial wish of those who still remain Catholic.
> Marcel Lefebvre,
> Bishop Emeritus of Tulle.

This letter shows that the double picture really did come from the sweet and gentle Archbishop. Anyone surprised should remember that good shepherds would not be half so sweet to the sheep were they half as fierce with the wolves. Wise sheep do not complain of the nasty noise when their shepherds shoot at wolves. By being "nice" to the wolves, your liberal churchmen fill Our Lord's sheepfold with the carcasses of lambs whose Catholic Faith has been utterly mangled.

The second document is the Archbishop's noble and dramatic appeal addressed to eight different Cardinals in August, which you will find on the same sheets as the Superior General's Letter no. 31. In the matter also of the Assisi Prayer Meeting the Archbishop begs these Cardinals singly or jointly to intervene to save the honor of the Church, "being humiliated as she has never before in all her history been humiliated."

Very soon after giving birth to her second son, Marcel, in 1905, the Archbishop's saintly mother (see *The Angelus*, May and June, 1984) is reported to have said: "Dear Marcel, he will one day render such service to the Church! One day he will be alone in battling with the Pope to save the Church."

That day has surely come.

For of the eight Cardinals appealed to, chosen for their sympathy with Catholic Tradition (Cardinals Gagnon, Gonzalez, Oddi, Palazzini, Siri, Stickler, Thiandoum and Zoungrana), was one heard to raise his voice in public protest? Yet, as the Archbishop predicted, the scandal was immeasurable. For instance, from the *New York Times*, October 28, 1986:

> The Buddhists, led by the Dali Lama, quickly converted the altar of the church of San Pietro by placing a small statue of the Buddha atop the tabernacle and setting prayer scrolls and incense burners around it.
>
> Two American Indians, John and Burton Pretty-On-Top, of the Crow tribe, caused a stir wherever they went in their plumed headdresses. And when they

The Ridgefield Letters

smoked a peace pipe at the final ceremony, the crowd responded with a great clicking of pocket cameras and then applause.

Naturally the journalists of such newspapers will miss no chance to make the Catholic Church look ridiculous, but how can they be blamed for reprinting excerpts from the various prayers prayed on this occasion if – as they – no doubt truly say – these were supplied by the Vatican itself?

"(African Animist) Almighty God, the Great Thumb we cannot evade to tie any knot . . . " "(Shinto) . . . I only earnestly wish that the wind will soon puff away all the clouds which are hanging over the tops of the mountains." And ranked alongside such inanities and absurdities, under the title of "Christian", words from the Sermon on the Mount of the Incarnate God. In the long history of the Church the Vicar of Christ has often like Christ been humiliated, but when did he ever himself organize and preside – whatever his intentions – over such a humiliating of his divine Master? But the Cardinals lay low. Truly the Archbishop is alone in battling to save the Church.

And let no one's sentiments mislead him that in battling with the Pope the Archbishop is bandying insults with him or making a personal attack upon him. This is in no way a personal question. It is the survival of the Catholic Faith which is at stake. For who ever will believe in the God of Catholics when their leader lets this God rank alongside "the Great Thumb?" The Catholic Faith is in mortal danger.

The problem is that over many years the enemies of God have succeeded in blurring out of our minds any sharp sense of an exclusive and demanding truth. Our sentiments go out to our fellow men – what is so wrong in fraternizing with false religions? Indeed nothing, and to do so would be the most normal and natural thing in the world, IF – if there was not one true religion. But there is.

We should continually meditate on the Word of God concerning these end-times: the Antichrist will come "in all seduction of iniquity to them that perish; because they receive not the love of truth, that they might be saved. Therefore God shall send them the operation of error, to believe lying: that all may be judged who have not believed the truth, but have consented to iniquity" (II Thess. 2: 10–11). Following our mere sentiments, we are easily misled. With our reason we must beg God to give us an overriding love of truth in this hour of all-engulfing lies and "the power of darkness" (Lk. 22: 53), when, as in the Garden of Gethsemane, the leading-most servants of God, in almost total confusion, are running away from the defense of Our Lord.

How ashamed must the Apostles have been when first they met Him again, risen from the dead! How ashamed of our own present weakness and confusion will many of us have to be, when the Catholic Church, shining in singular glory, re-emerges from her present hour of darkness! Watch and pray, said our Lord to His beloved Apostles in Gethsemane, for the spirit is willing but the flesh is weak. Let us pray for our love of truth, and pray for Archbishop Lefebvre, carrying on his shoulders the honor of the Church, and let us not descend to ascribing to him any personal animosity or disrespect towards the occupant of the See of Peter, for the time is coming when we shall look back and say, "Thank God, one Bishop raised his voice to save the honor of our Church."

Compared with this titanic battle for the mind and soul of the Church, how insignificant seem the Society's law suits in the USA! You have, however, the right to know that the U.S. Supreme Court has, as expected, refused to hear the appeal of the Society's adversaries

The Ridgefield Letters

against the smashing double verdict given against them in Philadelphia. This is the fourth time an American Court has judged a law suit between the Society and these adversaries, and the fourth time the Society has won. Alas, the Connecticut and New York cases still have no trial date set, but how many more defeats do these adversaries need? How many more tens of thousands of dollars must they spend on lawyers? And to think that they broke with the Archbishop because – they said – he risked compromising with Rome! What poor creatures we men are!

However, all is well at the Seminary. The year's studies are well underway; we still have a housing problem because very few seminarians have quit; we are easily most of us in God-given good health; Christmas is coming up at break-neck speed (Men, remember the Spiritual Exercises, available December 26 to 31); we soon start planning for the summer . . .

Dear Lord and God, this life is short and eternity is long. Grant us not to waste your precious gift of time, but let us spend all our brief lives in the honor, praise and love of your everlasting truth and glory, Amen.

And many thanks always, dear readers, for your absolutely necessary prayers and support. We shall be praying specially for your beloved departed during the month of November.

NO. 43 | DECEMBER 1, 1986

The Blessed Virgin Describes Christmas

THE MONTH OF Christmas is already here, and with it a little present for all of you. We enclose a tape recording of Christmas music sung by seminarians under the direction of their choirmaster, Fr. Dominique Bourmaud. We trust you will enjoy it. Extra copies are available if you would like to order more at a nominal fee.

It is thoroughly normal for Catholics to break into song, especially at Christmas time. Let us for a moment leave behind us the clash of arguments, and, to remember why we Catholics so fiercely argue in defense of our incarnate religion, let us evoke how the Mother of God herself may have experienced that extraordinary blend of divine and human which was the birth of the Incarnate God:

> It was getting late and Joseph was very concerned . . . A biting wind was constantly rising . . . People were hurrying towards Bethlehem, bumping into one another, and many of them poured abuse on my little donkey which was going so slowly, looking down to

The Ridgefield Letters

see where to put his hooves . . . It seemed he knew you (Jesus) were inside me . . . , sleeping your last sleep in the cradle of my womb. It was cold . . . but I was all on fire. I could feel you coming. Coming? You might say, "Mother, for nine months I had been with you." It's true. But now it was as if you were coming down from the heavens. The heavens were descending, descending upon me, and I could see their splendours within . . . I saw the Godhead ablaze with the joy of your imminent birth, and those fires penetrated within me, set me on fire, lifted me on high, high above everything – cold, wind, crowds were as nothing! I was seeing God . . . every now and again, with an effort, I managed to bring my mind down to earth and I smiled at Joseph who was afraid of my getting cold or weary, and who was guiding the donkey to stop it from stumbling, and who was keeping me wrapped in a blanket to prevent me catching cold . . . But nothing could go wrong. I didn't even feel the jolting. It seemed I was advancing on a path of stars, amidst white clouds borne up by angels . . . and I smiled . . . firstly at you . . . I watched you, through the barrier of flesh, sleeping with your tiny fists clenched in your cot of live roses, my lily bud . . . Then I smiled at my spouse who was so distressed, so distressed, to encourage him . . . and then at the people unaware they were already breathing in the atmosphere of the Saviour."

We stopped by Rachel's tomb to give a few moments' rest to the donkey and to eat a little bread and olives, our provisions of the poor. But I was not hungry. I could not be hungry . . . I fed on my joy . . . We started off again for Bethlehem.

Bethlehem! Dear, dear land of my fathers, that gave me the first kiss of my Son! You opened wide to give to the world dying of hunger the True Bread from heaven! You opened wide your arms to me like a mother, O holy land of David's city, first temple to the Saviour, to the Morning Star born of Jacob to show the way to heaven for all mankind. How beautiful is Bethlehem, even when the fields and the vines were bare as then! A

Richard N. Williamson

light veil of hoar-frost glinted on the leafless branches, which were like dusted over with diamonds, wrapped as it were in a diaphanous veil of paradise. Smoke rose from each household's fire for the supper at hand, and the smoke rising from one level to the next till it reached this crest, showed the whole town like under a veil . . . Everything was chaste, recollected, in expectation . . . of you, of you, my Son! The earth sensed you coming . . .

The people of Bethlehem too would have sensed you coming, but they could not take us in. The houses of the good honest people of Bethlehem were already crowded; the scribes, pharisees and others, deaf and proud, then as now, could not sense you coming, they turned away their poor sister that evening, and their hearts have remained closed ever since. Refusing to love neighbor, from then on they pushed away God.

Night had fallen when we reached the shepherd's cave . . . Joseph made a light for me to enter. Then, and only then, getting down from the donkey, did I realize how tired and frozen I was. An ox greeted us, I went up to it, to feel a little warmth, to rest on the hay. Joseph laid out the hay so as to make me a bed, and dried it out for me and for you, my Son, at the wood-fire lit in the corner . . . because my virginal husband had for us both all the tenderness of a loving father . . . Holding one another by the hand, like brother and sister lost in the darkness of the night, we ate our bread and cheese, and then he went to build up the fire, taking off his cloak to shut off the opening of the cave . . . In reality he was lowering a veil to cover the glory of God coming down from Heaven, you, O my Jesus . . . and I remained on the hay, by the warmth of the two animals, wrapped in my cloak and with the woolen blanket . . . My dear husband! . . . In that moment of fear when I was alone before the mystery of being mother for the first time, moment always laden with the unknown for a woman, and laden for me in my one and only motherhood with the mystery also of what it would be to see the Son of

The Ridgefield Letters

God emerging from human flesh, in that moment, he, Joseph, was like a mother to me, like an angel . . . he was my comfort, then and always . . .

And then silence and sleep came down to envelop the Just One . . . so that he should not see what for me was each day the kiss of God . . . And for me, after the interval of rest we humans need, behold the measureless waves of ecstasy, flowing from the sea of paradise, lifting me once more on ever higher crests of light, higher and higher, rising, lifting me with them into an ocean of brilliance and light, joy, peace and love, until I was immersed in the sea of God, in the bosom of God . . . A voice from the earth I still heard – "Mary, are you asleep?" How far away it was! – An echo, a distant memory of earth! . . . So far away that the soul does not bestir itself, I don't know what part of me replies, I am climbing, still climbing in this chasm of fire, of infinite bliss, of fore-knowledge of God, unto Him, unto Him . . . Oh! But were you born of me on that night, or was I born of the Trinity flashing forth? Was it I who gave birth to you, or you who drew me up to give birth to me? I do not know . . .

And then coming down to earth again, from choir to choir, from star to star, slipping gradually downwards, gently, slowly, in contented bliss, like a flower-petal lifted on high by an eagle and then let fall, dropping slowly on the wings of the air, bejewelled with the pearl of a rain-drop, with the splinter of a rain-bow snatched from heaven, coming to land on its native earth . . . My diadem: You! You lying on my heart . . .

After adoring you on my knees, I loved you in my arms. At last I could love you without a barrier of flesh between us, and then I stood up to carry you over to Joseph, worthy with me to be among the first to love you. Between two rough pillars of the cave we offered you up to the Father. Then you lay for the first time on Joseph's heart – and then we wrapped you in swaddling clothes and I rocked you in my arms while Joseph dried the hay by the fire and kept it warm by put-

Richard N. Williamson

ting it in his breast, and then laying you in the manger we adored you together, bending over you to drink in your breath, to marvel at the self-annihilation of love, to weep the tears certainly wept in heaven for the inexhaustible joy of seeing God.

And then the shepherds came inside to adore with their good hearts and with the strong odor of earth which came in with them, an odor of men and sheep and hay; outside, and everywhere, the angels adoring you with their love and their chant far above all human chant, with their love from heaven, with the air of heaven that came with them, that they brought with them in their brilliance . . . , that is how you were born, my blessed son!

Glory be to God on high for the true religion brought by His Son of a human mother, which so defends, honors and exalts motherhood as no other religion remotely does. Let the world go mad as it will, it cannot, so long as I stand guard, break into the corner of my heart where I know this Mother rocked this Little Child.

Happy Christmas, dear readers, and may Our Lord give you back in blessings all the prayers and support you have so generously given us throughout the year!

NO. 44 | JANUARY 6, 1987

Another Joint Statement of Two Bishops

FIRST AND FOREMOST, an immense thank you for so many Christmas and New Year greetings, cards and contributions sent by you to the seminary and to all of us here. We could never acknowledge them all, so would readers who have had from us no acknowledgement for their card or gift please take this letter as the expression of our sincere gratitude.

Many of you wrote to say how much you enjoyed the tape of seminarians singing Christmas music. We are delighted you so enjoyed it. The enclosed *Verbum* describes some of the hard work involved, but it was obviously more than well worth it. Thanks be to God.

Some of you also wrote to say how much you enjoyed the evocation of Christmas as it might have been experienced by the Mother of God. This was drawn from the third volume of the ten-volume series on the life of our Lord, called *Il Poema dell' Uomo-Dio* (The Poem of the Man-God), by Maria Valtorta, who may well be the 20th century equivalent of the Venerable Anne-Catherine Emmerich. Maria Valtorta was a nurse from Italy, born in 1897, died in 1961, confined to a sick-bed from 1933

Richard N. Williamson

onwards by great sufferings providentially fitting her to become the privileged receiver from 1944 to 1947 of a series of visions of the whole life of Our Lord. I could write a long letter about *The Poem of the Man-God*, and maybe one day I will, but you have – much better – been able to sample it for yourselves. Suffice it here to say that if the books of Anne-Catherine Emmerich's visions could be looked on as our Lord's alternative to the 19th century romantic novel, surely Maria Valtorta's visions of the Gospel story might be seen as Our Lord's answer to the 20th century TV soap opera!

And so the Christmas season has slipped past, and we are into another New Year with all the old problems, alas. Enclosed is a copy of the December 2 Statement of Archbishop Lefebvre and Bishop de Castro Mayer, following on John Paul II's visit to the Synagogue in Rome and the Religious Congress in Assisi. The Statement was occasioned by an unofficial inquiry from Rome being addressed in November to the Archbishop in the Argentine as he was about to ordain eleven more priests (nine for the SSPX, two for Bishop de Castro Mayer's group of Traditional priests in Campos, Brazil): was the Archbishop also about to proclaim his rupture with Rome? Thus Rome cunningly sought (and seeks) to pin on the Archbishop all responsibility for any imminent break – in their statement the two bishops parry by putting the responsibility where it belongs, back on Rome. It is Rome which is breaking with the past, breaking with Tradition, breaking with the Church.

The Statement is historic by its dramatic content but not by its novelty, for it adds nothing new to the Archbishop's twenty-year old diagnosis of the Catholic Church's crisis, except the tenth paragraph's brief reference to the horrendous facts of Assisi, October 27, 1986. Here are a few examples quoted from the Italian newspapers of the following day in *Si Si, No No* of Dec. 15, 1986: in St.

The Ridgefield Letters

Peter's Church the bonzes adored the Dalai Lama (re-incarnation for them of the Buddha), with his back turned to the Tabernacle where a sanctuary lamp signaled the Real Presence; in St. Peter's also, a statue of the Buddha was placed atop the Tabernacle on the main altar; in St. Gregory's, the Red Indians prepared their pipe of peace on the altar; in Santa Maria Maggiore's, Hindus sitting around the altar invoked the whole range of Hindu gods; in Santa Maria degli Angeli's, the Vicar of Christ sat in a semi-circle of wholly identical seats amidst the heads of the other religions so that there should be "neither first nor last," etc . . . Newspaper titles read, amongst others: "Our Fathers who are in Heaven" . . . "In the name of all gods" . . . "The peace of the gods" . . . "All mankind's gods' Assisi meeting", etc.

Yet in no Mass was Our Lord Himself made present at the Meeting, the Pope having taken care to celebrate Mass earlier in Perugia. Nor was Our Lady allowed entrance, a statue of hers from Fatima, brought by pilgrims from Calabria, having been stopped at the gates of Assisi by the Meeting's ushers (*Si Si, No No*, December 15, p.8 – does it remind you of anyone's drawing of our Lord and Our Lady being kept out?) .

Si Si, No No concludes that never has Our Lord been so outraged, never have His holy places been so profaned, His Vicar so humiliated, His people so scandalized, by His own ministers, as at Assisi. The superstitions of all the false religions practised there pale in comparison with the betrayal of our Lord by these ministers. How can they have reached this point?

There is a most interesting article in *The Angelus* of last month in which a well-informed Italian layman, living in Rome, addresses himself to exactly that question. His answer is, firstly, a lack of supernatural Faith, followed by a lack of solid Catholic doctrine. To the powerful ideas of the Revolution even the best of today's churchmen oppose mere sentiments of religion and ideas fatally contaminated with liberalism, which is like fighting tanks with pea-shooters. It is this lack of Faith and of the bazooka of integrally Catholic doctrine which has enabled the enemy to install in the Vatican a machinery of terrorization, bribery and blackmail which is humanly insuperable.

Notice on this analysis that the Catholics have the initiative. It is only their weakness which enables the enemies of Our Lord to thrive. Of course this is so. Otherwise God would not be God. He is allowing His enemies to thrive only in order that His friends may be chastised for their faithlessness, or infidelity (that is us!).

Notice also the importance of completely Catholic doctrine that makes no compromises with the errors of the world. No one can resist an enemy while half sharing his principles. Catholic doctrine especially is a unity which suffers no diminution. It is so coherent that to deny any part of it is to make it all fall to pieces. We must learn to think with the Church on all questions, especially on social questions, because this is where the enemy has been breaching the Church's defenses over the last 200 years; on liberty, equality, democracy, socialism, freemasonry, communism.

It is noteworthy that whenever retreatants strengthen their faith with the Spiritual Exercises, they frequently wish to deepen their grasp of Catholic doctrine. To answer this desire especially of former retreatants, we are planning to include by way of experiment in this summer's extended series of Ignatian retreats a seminar on the encyclicals, which will be three days' more or less intensive study of the great Popes' teachings on some of the social questions in particular.

Seminarians are also planning to take part this year in the January 22 Pro-Life March in Washington. It is several years since the seminary last went as a group.

The Ridgefield Letters

Before the march itself starting at 12 noon, this letter may reach some of you in time to inform you that the seminary will be offering a Latin Tridentine Mass on the 11th floor of the Washington Hotel on 15th Street and Pennsylvania Northwest, scheduled for 11 a.m. You are welcome to attend.

And for your own Latin Masses, let us know if you would like photocopies which we have had made up of a handsome colored set of the three altar cards used by the priest on the altar itself. First come, first served (as supply is limited), on a donation basis.

And may you all have a truly Happy New Year, that is to say a New Year in which you make giant strides towards Heaven. Our years in this "valley of tears" are for nothing else. God love you and bless you and your families during this month of the Holy Family.

NO. 45 | FEBRUARY 1, 1987

Death of John B. Williamson

MY FATHER, JOHN B. Williamson, died on January 4. What a mystery, the life and death of a single man! One soul, one world, one eternity!

He died at the age of 83, quietly and peacefully, in a Catholic nursing home run by Irish Sisters where my mother could visit him every day, but he did not openly profess the Catholic Faith before dying...

He had been gently sinking for the last few years, and for the last several months had been very fortunate to be able to stay in the nursing home where the sisters looked after him as well as he could have been looked after. Thank you for all your prayers which obtained for him at least a happy departure from this world, and, let us hope, a happy entry into the next... God knows.

Visiting the funeral parlor on the eve of the funeral, my mother said, as her hand gently caressed the last thing she could touch of him, the simple tablet bearing his name on the closed coffin: "He was a good man. He looked after me for 50 years. That is something." Youngsters, hold your marriages together, because there is no substitute for staying together, until death do you part.

The Ridgefield Letters

Also on the eve of the funeral, his sister, my aunt, reminiscing on their ancestors and their childhood in the early years of this century, had called up a whole vanished era: the thriving industry of Victorian England, horse-training and show-jumping in the Edwardian Midlands before the arrival of horse-boxes, travels in the Far East before the sun set upon the majestic British Empire. Now England, her Midlands and her Empire are filled with very different people having very different preoccupations. The stage of this world has emptied of one generation of actors and filled with the next –

> All the world's a stage,
> And all the men and women merely players.
> They have their exits and their entrances,
> And one man in his time plays many parts...

Yet how these fleeting players cling to their brief time on stage! How they come to love their companions in the limelight, their theatrical costumes, their flimsy stage-props, as though the play would go on forever! But one or two curtain-falls and it is over, the next play starts, with the next after that already waiting in the wings, and so they are rapidly disappearing down the long corridors of oblivion. When my aunt in turn leaves us, who will remember generations of our history? Who will recall a whole world of Victorian loves and Edwardian lives, just as vivid then as our own are to us now? And who will be interested?...

God has filled this world with beautiful things, all tiny reflections of His own infinite Goodness. One generation of human souls after another learns to love these things, and attaches itself fiercely to them, but how many learn to love their Creator? Yet that is the only question.

Richard N. Williamson

My dear father – "After life's fitful fever he sleeps well." "My darling, thine the peace, mine the memory," wrote his wife on a card amidst the flowers she left at his grave. Many thanks to every one of you that has said a prayer for him, or for the repose of his soul. More could not be done for him. Of your charity, pray still my mother may receive the gift of the Catholic Faith.

And so the next generation's play has come on stage, and its alarms and excursions resound throughout the theater. Being in Europe recently I was able to pay a brief visit to Archbishop Lefebvre in Switzerland. He will not be coming to the United States this spring for Ordinations or Confirmations, because there is only one candidate for the priesthood from Ridgefield this year, and the Archbishop has much other travelling to do, so Michigander Daniel Cooper will be ordained in Switzerland instead, on June 29.

However, His Grace does plan to be here again for Ordinations in the spring of the following year, 1988, if God gives him strength. Notice then that he is still planning himself to perform the Society's ordinations, so long as he can. He sees the Pope as being determined to continue in the disastrous direction of the interreligious meeting of October in Assisi, which meant for JP2 like the beginning of a new age of the Church. The next such meeting is projected for Tokyo, and if any Cardinals are protesting in private, the Pope is paying no attention to them. The Archbishop considers that the Pope's abandoning the Catholic Faith for the new religion of Liberalism is providential insofar as more and more Catholics – and priests of the Society – are coming to realize that in the normal course of human affairs there is no way in which Rome can be brought to reason. Cardinal Gagnon for instance (who has lost any influence he had in Rome since he became outspoken for Tradition) says: "I think Monsignor Lefebvre's work is blessed by God, so let him

The Ridgefield Letters

decide for himself what he has to do – there is no reason why the Society should not develop as Providence indicates." – this Cardinal was not shocked at the idea of an eventual consecration of bishops.

However, the Archbishop says that he has something like a visceral difficulty over the prospect of cutting with Rome, which would be the result of such a consecration: "Up till now," he says, "God has enabled me to steer between the reefs and shoals of these difficult questions, keeping the Society in unity and balance, so unless I feel pushed to perform a consecration, I shall not do it. I think that when I have to do it, God will give me a sign, so, as long as I have a little health, there is no immediate urgency." In other words the Archbishop is still waiting for a clear sign to consecrate bishops, as he has for some years now been waiting. Fortunately the Archbishop is still on stage! But say a prayer for the repose of the soul of Mother Marie-Gabriel, Archbishop Lefebvre's natural sister and co-founder with him of the SSPX, who died in France on January 26.

Good news of the seminary: your great generosity over Christmas and the New Year has enabled us to pay off the entire principal outstanding on the seminary's local mortgage which was enriching the bankers at the usurious rate of interest of 14 per cent per year. Between 1983 and 1987, you have thus saved the Seminary's benefactors from paying, between 1987 and the year 2000, well over $210,000 in interest! Well done, and thank you! We still have some $80,000 principal to pay off on another mortgage taken out in Michigan on the seminary's behalf, but that is less urgent because the rate of interest is "only" nine per cent! Heaven help us from such usury! It is a real slavery. Thereby hangs a tale which I mean one day to tell: in very brief, God is letting us be enslaved by the money we worship. How I hope not to have to borrow from the banks, if we build here in Ridgefield!

Richard N. Williamson

Enclosed the latest Retreats flyer. Notice we are asking the ladies to wear a skirt or dress (cf. Deut. 22: 5), and we are asking anyone flying out to book a flight leaving no sooner than three hours after the end of the retreat. The Encyclicals Seminar running from July 23 to 26 will be built around the analysis and explanation of five or so major encyclicals on great errors of today: liberalism, freemasonry, socialism, modernism, communism. Participants will have to read and study, but the seminar should certainly deepen their grasp of today's Church and world crisis.

This winter is cold, and my! – was it ever cold and wet for seminarians taking part on January 22 in the Pro-Life March in Washington, D.C., which took place in an uninterrupted snowstorm! However, the seminarians all seem to have found it worthwhile to take part, and with a few hours' sleep caught up, emerged none the worse for wear. A fuller report will be found in the next Verbum.

Keep warm, and let not charity grow cold either, especially amongst those of the household of the Faith (Gal. 6: 10). In gratitude for your prayers for my parents, I will offer a triduum of Masses for all your and your families' intentions, on February 23, 24 and 25.

Thank you, and bless you.

NO. 46 | MARCH 3, 1987

"Rome" – Appearance Without Substance

THE MAIL HAS been overflowing my desk! Firstly, many thanks for numerous cards and letters of sympathy and condolences which you sent me for the death of my father, and for Masses you have had said for him. The cards and letters were not quite as numerous as at Christmas, but they were still too many for me to answer one by one! Please may each of you accept here my sincere thanks for such a testimonial to your faith and charity!

Then secondly, a number of you have also written to ask about reports appearing in many supposedly Catholic newspapers of a "massive defection" of seminarians from the main seminary of the SSPX in Ecône, Switzerland. Fifteen to twenty seminarians are reported to have quit over Archbishop Lefebvre's strong stand against the October meeting in Assisi, and Rome is reported to have established a Spiritual Center, or kind of halfway house between itself and Tradition, to receive them.

Here is the truth. Back in May of last year, a group of seven seminarians was dismissed from Ecône by the Rector, Fr. Alain Lorans, because they had been for several months breaking the Seminary Rule and actually conspiring with Novus Ordo priests and bishops to pull a large number of seminarians out of Ecône and start another seminary which would be both Traditional and acceptable to Rome. "They were mistaken or they were positively deceived," said Fr. Lorans, "because the so-called Traditional centre set up to receive them in Rome is no more nor less than a disinfection chamber, a sort of sieve with which to sift out of the young men coming from Ecône their last remaining traces of Tradition." Ironically, some of the Liberal French bishops were deceived too, for the same reports told of them being stricken with panic lest the halfway traditional house in Rome should attract some of their own few remaining seminarians! Only their guilty conscience could have deceived them, because two grains of common sense would have told them that today's Rome can no more run a Traditional house than a fox can run a hen-coop!

Today's Rome . . . what is today's Rome? Why does it keep giving out such contrary signals? Because we are living in a world in which, as the agents of the Antichrist gain more and more the upper hand, things are less and less what they appear. We are constantly being deceived. Words are being given new meanings, institutions are being given a new content. Let me illustrate with a sorry tale from my own country, England.

In a most interesting article entitled "Treason Has a New Meaning" from the January issue of Ivor Benson's South African monthly *Behind the News*, Benson starts out from the extraordinary fuss that was made recently by the British Government to stop a book from appearing in Australia which was written by a high-up former member of Britain's reputed secret service, MI-5, and which risked uncovering once more a number of Soviet spies and traitors inside MI-5, including its very head for

The Ridgefield Letters

nine years, one Sir Roger Hollis! This scenario of treason in high places, Benson says, can be paralleled in nearly all countries of the West. As Roosevelt and Truman covered up for the spy Alger Hiss, as Canadian premier Lester Pearson covered up for the KGB agent Herbert Norman, as Harold Macmillan covered for the traitor Kim Philby, so, most recently, Prime Minister Margaret Thatcher – supposed right-winger and nationalist – has covered up for the Soviet mole, Sir Roger Hollis.

Going on to ask why and how the British upper classes could produce such a string of traitors at that time as Burgess, Maclean, Philby, Blunt and now Hollis, Benson quotes a celebrated British historian, Professor Arnold Toynbee, addressing an international gathering in Copenhagen in June 1931:

> We are at present working discreetly but with all our might to wrest this mysterious force called sovereignty out of the clutches of the local national states of the world. All the time we are denying with our lips what we are doing with our hands, because to impugn the sovereignty of the local national states of the world is still a heresy for which a statesman or a publicist can be, perhaps not quite burned at the stake, but certainly ostracized and discredited.

Benson goes on to quote the recent reactions of two genuine British patriots. The journalist Peregrine Worsthorne wrote an article entitled "My Country, Right or Wrong?" in which he bitterly deplored British policies which have left him with a feeling of being a stranger in his own country, and he remarked, "It would not be difficult for me to be disloyal to this country." The politician Enoch Powell had this to say: "My country, right or wrong, is all very well. I would subscribe to the principle. My trouble is that I wonder if I any longer have a coun-

Richard N. Williamson

try at all." (Of course Catholics know that my country, right or wrong, is a false principle, and that the Faith alone can harmonize the true interests of my homeland with those of every other man's homeland. Nevertheless Worsthorne and Powell do at least love their country, whereas Toynbee's is a program of lies and deceit to betray it).

As Benson concludes, the word "treason" has changed its meaning. It no longer means betraying one's own nation. It means now betraying the international revolution, the anti-national ideal, of which the Soviet Union has for 70 years been the flaming symbol. Such is unquestionably the secret mentality of numbers of our present leaders, pretending in public to lead us one way for as long as they have to pay lip service to the old set of values, but deep down ready to lie, deceive, betray, break any of God's Ten Commandments, in order to bring us in line with the new set of values.

Thus we live in a world giving itself over to the Antichrist where between the appearances and the reality there is a great gulf fixed. Judged by the old set of values, the supposed "upper" classes of men like Philby, Burgess, etc., could in reality hardly sink lower; a "Sir" Roger Hollis is in fact a skunk; such and such a prominent leader is in truth a pre-eminent liar; a "Professor" is a teacher of treachery; the media are prime means of <u>dis</u>information (see above); "education" has become a veritable sewer of intellectual and moral corruption, and "my country" has been turned into a mere slogan to deceive me.

And my Church? – What have they done to her? In truth, since on the Catholic Church ultimately hangs all the old set of values, then in no domain was it so important for the godless and lawless revolutionaries to penetrate, to empty out the substance, <u>but to maintain the appearances so as the better to deceive the people</u>. And if the people were not watching and praying, not re-

The Ridgefield Letters

membering our Lord's own words to judge by the fruits (Mt. 7: 15–20), to "judge not according only the appearances, but judge just judgment" (Jn. 7: 24), then the people were easily deceived.

So just what is "today's Rome?" Judged by a just judgment of its fruits, it is the appearance of the leadership of the Catholic Church, without the substance or reality. How easy to transpose to our situation as Catholics the remarks of Powell and Worsthorne on their country: "We would subscribe to the principle of Rome. Our trouble is, we wonder if we any longer have a Rome at all . . . It would not be difficult for us to be disloyal to this Rome." The parallel with the Church is striking, and illuminating. In brief, if Archbishop Lefebvre were to consecrate bishops without Rome's authorization, he might be cutting with the appearances of Rome, but never with its Catholic substance or reality. Prudently however, he still waits.

For our own part, how are we to keep our grip on the reality and substance of things, and not slide with the whole world around us into the Antichrist's diabolical dreamland? Firstly, by prayer, which grounds our soul in the Supreme Reality, God, who is Being itself, more intimate to us than we are to ourselves; who is Truth itself without the least trace of a lie, who cannot deceive nor be deceived. The more a soul prays, the less it can be deceived.

Secondly, by attendance at Mass – but celebrated in a rite without falsehood – where our soul is present at the supreme reality of Calvary. Who can consciously be in the Real Presence of the Sacrifice of the Cross and still dream away the things that matter – God's love, the soul, sin and redemption? Profit by the Archbishop's Lenten Letter enclosed, in which he encourages amongst other things more frequent attendance (if possible) at Mass. There Our Lord Himself gives us light and courage: "Let not your heart be troubled. You believe in God. Believe also in me." (Jn. 14: 1)

Continual thanks for your great support of the seminary, news of which you find in the *Verbum* enclosed. Remember us in Lent, and may you profit by the holy season and advance in wisdom and in grace. What else matters?

NO. 47 | APRIL 1, 1987

Communism, The Rotting of Christendom

THE ENCLOSED SPECIAL issue of *Verbum* concerns communism. We are sending it to you at this time because of the recent showing on American television screens of the miniseries *Amerika*, a fictional dramatization of a takeover of the United States by Russia with the help of the United Nations. This miniseries was reportedly defective in various ways, but it did serve to reawaken interest in the problem of communism, on which our media of disinformation habitually put us to sleep.

Typically, before *Amerika* was shown, the liberals or anti-anti-communists made a tremendous fuss to keep it from being shown, or else to reduce the danger of anyone being woken up. The Chrysler Corporation was persuaded to withdraw its sponsorship of the series, one of the leading actors took part in advertisements promoting the United Nations, and so on.

Already in 1937, Pope Pius XI in his great encyclical on communism, *Divini Redemptoris* denounced as two reasons for its rapid spread "a truly diabolical propaganda," and "the conspiracy of silence of a large part of the non-Catholic press of the world," a conspiracy of which he said much could be attributed to reasons of shortsighted politics and just as much to the influence of "various occult forces which have long sought the destruction of the Christian social order."

Indeed communism is no more nor less than the final rot of decomposing Christendom, the just chastisement for our own godlessness. Archbishop Lefebvre has said that the Second Vatican Council, held from 1962 to 1965, will be branded with infamy for having failed to denounce communism, "the most monstrous error ever thought up by Satan." This failure, or refusal, was no doubt due to the treacherous Moscow-Vatican agreement of 1962.

Fr. Oliver Oravec speaks about communism in this *Verbum* from direct and firsthand experience. Originating from Slovakia, his ministry is now in Canada. He is a good friend of the SSPX, and has paid several visits to the seminary here. His message must be heeded, and the requests of Our Lady of Fatima must be fulfilled, otherwise we shall simply have deserved everything coming to us.

For there is not nothing that we can do. The Society's Superior General, Fr. Franz Schmidberger, in his enclosed Letter no. 32, announces a major Society pilgrimage to Fatima for the Feast of the Sorrowful and Immaculate Heart of Mary, on Saturday, August 22, of this year, the 70th anniversary of the apparitions of Our Lady at Fatima.

And if you cannot cross the Atlantic, there are always the Spiritual Exercises of St. Ignatius, the Mother of God's own antidote for all kinds of spiritual poisoning since the Protestant Reformation. See in the Superior General's Letter a moving testimonial to these Exercises.

At Ridgefield, the Easter retreat for men is close to filled and the eight summer retreats are fast filling. If the

The Ridgefield Letters

seminary moved out for lack of space, and if Ridgefield became a year-round retreat house, it would not seem to be a moment too soon. Such a move is possible, because it might well be less expensive than continuing the building program here. In any case we are always grateful for your uninterrupted generosity.

Some of you inquire after the seminary's lawsuits, provoked by the priests who broke away from the Society nearly four years ago. Alas, these lawsuits drag on, because our adversary and his lawyers do everything they can to stop them coming to court where he knows he must lose. Out of five decisions so far, four were humiliating defeats for them and the fifth an effectual defeat which he wrote up as a victory. I spare you the details. Let him afford us a little laugh:

I do think that had he been captain of the Titanic with three funnels out of four under water, he would still have been on the stern screaming to a bemused audience that they were not going to sink. Then had he survived the sinking, with the seaweed still in his mouth he would have come up with a series of utterly convincing arguments to prove that it was not he that had hit the iceberg but the iceberg that had hit him! To prove his point, back on dry land he would have had his Manhattan lawyers take the iceberg to court for damages, and if anyone had ventured to say he was crazy to sue an iceberg, he would have turned round and sued them for libel! As it is, his lawyers must be laughing until they cry – all the way to the bank. After all, he must be finding someone to pay them! Poor someone.

At the Seminary we are now preparing for Holy Week. Holy Week is the best time of year to remember in today's ever-worsening crisis of the Church how wise was the scandal and foolishness of the Cross (I Cor. 1: 23). Our Lord seemed to lose out completely, but it was the devil who once and for all was defeated. Let us never for-

Richard N. Williamson

get that God's ways are not our ways, that it is on the way of the Cross that we must follow Him, and that however much we are tempted to think He does not know what He is doing, still He is right, and we will make a great mistake if we ever abandon Him or His one and only Holy Catholic Church. How sorry the Apostles must have been afterwards, to have run away in the Garden of Gethsemane!

May you have a Blessed Holy Week, if this letter reaches you in time, and in any case a Joyful Eastertide.

NO. 48 | MAY 4, 1987

Assisi Explained: Hell is Empty!

AN INTERESTING LETTER was made public recently in Germany. It was written on December 3rd of last year by the Catholic Vicar General of Berlin to a layman, Herr Gierczyk, who had written a month beforehand to the Holy Father personally, asking if he could or might take part in Masses celebrated by Catholic priests in the St. Peter's Chapel of the SSPX in Berlin. Here is the letter:

> Dear Herr Gierczyk,
> The Secretariat of State of Pope John Paul II has forwarded to me the letter you addressed to the Holy Father on November 9, 1986, and has asked me to give you an answer –
> To the question you put to the Holy Father: the priests of the Society of St. Pius X are validly ordained Catholic priests. The Catholics who follow Archbishop Lefebvre belong to the Catholic Church. Whoever attends Mass in St. Peter's Chapel does indeed fulfill his Sunday obligation, but at the same time he is acting against the unity of the Church, of which the Sacrament of the Holy Eucharist is sign and cause. Hence

Richard N. Williamson

> you cannot be forbidden to attend Mass in St. Peter's Chapel, but you cannot be advised to do so either. Having thus fulfilled my superiors' orders,
> I remain cordially yours,
> Johannes Tobei, Vicar General.

Of course whoever knows the teaching of the Church has always known that Society priests are valid priests, that those who follow Archbishop Lefebvre are in the Catholic Church, and that no one can be forbidden to attend a Society Mass. What is unusual is that a high-ranking official of the Novus Ordo Church should admit as much! Naturally, he also inserts the criticism of Traditionalists for acting against the unity of the Church, but the conclusion he draws from it that they "cannot be advised" to attend a Society Mass is remarkably weak when compared with the fulminating prohibitions to attend which we have up till now heard from so many Novus Ordo bishops and vicars-general. *Deo Gratias.*

For at the beginning and end of his letter, this Vicar General seems to underline that he is acting under orders coming from on high. This is in line with a few other indications we have from Rome that Cardinal Ratzinger and JP2 do not want the SSPX to be broken up or to disappear, because they need the Society as a counterweight to the extreme radicals "within" the Church. If this is their way of thinking, it is all too human and political, it is not the thinking of Catholics, who will take their stand on God's Truth and let Satan's chips fall where they may. However, it is to the credit of these leaders' Catholic instincts if they do not want to see the radicals tearing the Church apart, and these instincts of theirs are surely being used by God to write straight with the crooked lines of their all too human politics – and of their deadly liberal principles.

The Ridgefield Letters

Just how deadly these principles are, Catholics must realize, so as to be forewarned and forearmed. The still surviving Catholic instincts of these liberal churchmen may be enabling God to shield, for instance, the Society, but their implicit-explicit liberal principles (no objective, unchanging truth; no coercion by any divine law) have enabled Satan to ravage the Church, and there is much worse yet to come.

Hence the length of this letter. It encloses the full text of the official theological justification of the October Day of Prayer in Assisi, delivered as a speech in Rome on December 22 of last year before the assembled cardinals, archbishops and bishops of the Roman Curia. This speech and our analysis are difficult reading. Take courage! Your Catholic Faith, and Christendom, are on the line!

The essential error is naturalism, or the emptying out of the supernatural. Another word for it is modernism, or the disfiguring of Catholicism to make it fit the naturalist modern world. Our Faith tells us that the sole purpose of the whole natural order, of human souls and bodies and all the animal, vegetable and mineral creation all around us, is that the natural human souls, when they come to separate at death from their bodies, should contain God's sanctifying or supernatural grace, with the supernatural virtues of faith, hope and charity. Whatever a man's merely natural gifts and achievements, if he dies without supernatural grace, he damns himself to eternal hellfire. Now because Adam fell from God's grace, we are all of us born in original sin without grace, and because Jesus Christ alone restored man to grace, we must all of us without exception accept the supernatural gift of faith in Christ, convert to Him, and receive His sacraments, starting with baptism, to preserve and increase supernatural grace in our souls. Hence our absolute need of His Catholic Church, sole authorized and normal dispenser of the Redeemer's supernatural sacraments and sanctifying grace.

See now in the speech of December 22 what has become of this entire structure of supernature, or grace. It has been entirely made void! Lest we be accused of distorting by omission or quotation, you have in your hands the entire text, as printed in the January 5 issue of the weekly English edition of the *L'Osservatore Romano* (#969), pages 6 and 7. Only the title has been changed, lest you be seduced by the smooth words!

Judge for yourselves if this is a fair summary of the essential first ten sections:

1. Just before commemorating Christmas, my mind goes back to the outstanding religious event of the past year, Assisi, where the divinely established but hidden unity of mankind became visible, despite men's divisions.

2. To expound the full significance of this great event, we must interpret it in the light of Vatican II, which was both fully Traditional and fully in touch with modern needs.

3. Vatican II connects the identity and mission of the Church with the radical unity of all men, consisting in their having been all created by the one God, in His image, on one plan, to go to Him, a radical, fundamental and decisive unity dwarfing men's differences.

4. This one plan centers on Jesus Christ outside whose work no one can remain, as he died for all, wills all men to be saved and – Vatican II – is in some way in contact with all men. Assisi showed this unity.

5. To bring about this divine unity of creation and redemption, the differences arising merely from human weakness must be overcome, because, however unaware men are of their radical unity, still Jesus Christ "has in a certain manner united himself to every man" – Vatican II.

6. Hence the Church's identity and task consist in her working to heal the merely human divisions, and to form the People of God, to whose catholic unity all belong or are oriented.

7. Vatican II invited the Church to discover in all religions the traces of this hidden but radical unity which Assisi manifested in the living, albeit incomplete, communion of all the religions' representatives there. Thus Assisi fulfils Vatican II's commitment to ecumenism.

8. For Vatican II's Decree on Ecumenism tells how Catholics are already united to other Christians through faith and baptism; its Declaration on non-Christian religions tells us "to recognize, conserve and promote the spiritual, moral and social values that are found in them," because all men are oriented by God to Himself.

9. By thus putting into practice Vatican II's teaching on the unity of all men, Assisi has reinforced the very identity and self-awareness of the Catholic Church, which now better understands this divine unity.

10. Through all her multiple forms of ministry, active and contemplative, the Church works to bring about the unity and reconciliation of all men, and now by an Assisi-style ministry too, etc . . .

This landmark speech says that Assisi reinforced the very identity of the Catholic Church (#9). Archbishop Lefebvre says that Assisi is destroying it. Someone must be way wrong. They cannot be both right.

Let us summarize still further the essential argument: the Catholic Church's main business on earth is to form the People of God by bringing together all men in the unity of their God-given creation, redemption and orientation to God. Men may be unaware of this unity often lying hidden within their nature, but beside it, all man-made differences are of little account, so the Church's function is to bring it out – hence Assisi. Still more briefly, men's religious differences matter little, we are all one with God by our mere nature.

But if man-made differences are so unimportant (#3, 5, 6), then the sins of schism, heresy, disbelief and infidelity matter little, indeed sin is rather to be regretted than blamed (#5). Then neither faith in Jesus Christ matters much (#8), nor does conversion to Him, because however bitterly we may refuse Him, still He has somehow united us to Himself (#5). So schism, heresy, sin, faith, conversion, are all of little account!

Moreover, if the misuse of our free will is unimportant because – albeit unawares (#5) – we cannot remain outside the work of Jesus Christ (#4) and we all belong at least by orientation to the Catholic Church (#6, 8), then all men are in effect saved by their nature alone. Then no one having human nature can be damned, so hell is empty, sanctifying grace is not necessary, original sin is not worth mentioning, free will and its choices are inconsequential (what scorn for man!), the Cross and the sacraments must be mere symbols, and the Catholic Church is needed only to proclaim that man is great by his nature alone (#6, 7, 8, 9, 10)! In brief, forget about anything supernatural, or above the order of nature – nature on her own (#4, 7, 8, 9) brings us to God.

Now it may be objected that the speaker does not openly commit the heresy of naturalism, that the consequences spelled out above are not explicit in what he says, that he would repudiate them if they were put before him.

As to the speaker in person, this may be true. If so, then he would lack the obstinacy in denying known truths of Faith which is necessary to make him a formal heretic, especially if there is nobody in authority above him to admonish him. However, if he were to repudiate the clear implications of his own words, then while escaping the charge of formal heretic, he could not es-

The Ridgefield Letters

cape the charge of grave inconsistency, of having a mind adrift between Catholicism and naturalism, which is not a Catholic mind.

But as to his <u>words</u>, they still mean what they say. Are they not consistent with one another throughout this speech? Are they not moreover fully consistent with the actions of Assisi? Are they not in addition wholly consistent with certain teachings of Vatican II? (How could the claim that Vatican II was perfectly Catholic in its documents survive the reading of such an anti-Catholic speech <u>built</u> (#2) on quotes from the documents of Vatican II?).

In truth, just as the liberal Catholic is a walking contradiction, so this speaker is consistently inconsistent. If then he occupies a high enough position in the Church to be addressing the assembled Cardinals, and if not one of them is known to have protested against such a speech, then the whole official leadership of the Church would seem to have cut adrift from its supernatural moorings. No wonder if the poor Catholic in the pew is almost hopelessly confused! And thank God for at least two bishops who raise their voice in clear and Catholic protest! They are a sheet-anchor for the whole Church, and the two very best friends of the Holy Father, who may seem to be shielding them by his <u>instincts</u> but is surely fated to cause them much more hardship yet by his <u>principles</u>. He is in very grave trouble, but as Heaven told the little children of Fatima, we must pray for him all the more. And we must fasten our spiritual seatbelts.

A flyer from St. Mary's, Kansas, presents the grand annual opportunity to visit and get to know St. Mary's, a great refuge for Catholics in the middle of the USA. And next month you will receive a flyer for the second series of three tapes made by Bernard Janzen and myself, on Obedience, the Priesthood, and the Seven Ages of the

Church, but send for them now if you like – $4 a piece or $10 for the set.

All is well at the seminary. Seminarians are just returning for the last part of the school year, beginning with the lovely month of May, when each evening in honor of Our Lady they will be praying the Rosary in front of the Blessed Sacrament exposed, for your intentions. No one but Jesus will have inspired His Church to dedicate to her the loveliest month of the year. Mother of the Church, pray for us!

NO. 49 | JUNE 1, 1987

The Fifth Age of the Church

TWO INSPIRING VIDEOCASSETTES are coincidentally being put into circulation at the same time within the United States by the SSPX. The first is entitled *Priests for Tomorrow*. It comes from the Society's motherhouse in Ecône, Switzerland, and it is a beautiful presentation of the life of Archbishop Lefebvre, the origins of Ecône, and ceremonies by which the Catholic seminarian ascends to the priesthood. "Too beautiful," was one journalist's begrudging comment at the cassette's first showing to the Press in Switzerland. This cassette absolutely needs to be smuggled into Novus Ordo seminaries, in fact it is a powerful advocate for Catholic Tradition wherever it is shown. It was professionally made, it has been professionally translated into English, and it is available for $20 from the Society's headquarters in the USA.

The second videocassette is entitled *Sign of Hope*, and it comes from Ridgefield. It is a presentation of seminary life and of seminarians, where they come from, why they come, and what they think lies ahead of them. The interviewer is Fr. Bourmaud who has become almost a professional producer in the producing of this tape, and the result is truly a sign of hope. For anyone wishing to know what Ridgefield

Richard N. Williamson

is about, this is an excellent presentation. It shows that the good Lord has not, after all, handed in His resignation! The Catholic priesthood does have a future. Beware, we have as yet no version for Beta or non-American VCR systems, but the VHS version is available from the seminary here for a suggested donation of $20.

Also available from us is the second series of three audio tapes on the *Faith in Crisis*, which like the first series takes the form of question and answer between Bernard Janzen and myself. The enclosed flyer presents the three topics discussed. His favorite might be the tape on obedience, mine might be the Seven Ages of the Church, but we would have to recommend – modestly, of course – all three!

The Seven Ages of the Catholic Church is an idea drawn from a quasi-inspired commentary on the first fifteen chapters of the book of the Apocalypse, written in about 1640 by an outstanding German priest, the Venerable Bartholomew Holzhauser (I have seen his commentary in German and French, but never in English – TAN books, are you there?).

According to Holzhauser's pattern, we would now be approaching the end of the Fifth Age, that of the progressive destruction of Christendom by the working out of the ferment of Protestantism. There would follow only the relatively brief Sixth Age, or final triumph of the Catholic Church and then the also brief last age, or the arrival of the Antichrist. If we said the end of the world could be for around the years 2030 to 2040, we could easily have got the dates wrong, but Holzhauser's overall reading of the Church's history from its beginning to its end most logical and persuasive.

It is also pacifying. As the ruin of Christendom continues to be engineered all around me, I shall not be worried that God has made a mistake or lost control; I can see that through the unprecedented decadence of our Fifth Age, He is harvesting for Heaven a generation

The Ridgefield Letters

of saints also without precedent in any of the previous four Ages of the Church. Let the Sixth Age, the triumph of the Immaculate Heart of Mary arrive in God's good time; all I need do is not miss the opportunities provided by my own circumstances to become one of those saints. So the continuing bad news will not unduly worry me. In March, Rome replied to Archbishop Lefebvre's October 1985 "dubia," or thirty-nine doubts, questioning the Vatican II Decree on Religious Liberty, with a fifty-page document which says that, yes, the Council's doctrine on religious liberty is a novelty, but it is in continuity with Tradition. In other words what breaks with all Catholic Tradition, continues it! Or, between man's doing as he likes and having to do as God likes, there is no contradiction. Or, water is dry, and circles may be square.

Now such nonsense is easy to speak and easy to write, because neither the airwaves on, which we speak, nor the paper on which we write make any resistance to our words. It is only the facts which will unfailingly demonstrate such contradictions to be unlivable. Poor Cardinal Ratzinger! Poor JP2! If they love the Church, they are due for much more distress and disappointment before they realize she cannot be defended by diminishing one jot or tittle of her all-time teachings. That is a lesson which the liberals never want to learn. They dream and dream and dream of coming to terms with the world. Our Lord on the contrary says, "Heaven and earth will pass away, but my words will not pass away." (Mt. 24: 35)

Our Lord's unchanging words for the modern world will be the subject of the experimental Encyclicals Seminar for men running from July 23 to 26 at Ridgefield. Participants will receive in advance a packet of five papal Encyclicals, analyzing major modern errors in depth. The doctrinal long weekend will be designed a little like a retreat to help participants find what Cardinal Ratzinger has surely lost – the integral objective truth on the nature of man, God and society, which man disregards, or dissolves at his peril, and which is the only hope for the world of tomorrow.

Nor will Our Lord's promises pass away. The card here enclosed for June, month of the Sacred Heart, carries the incredible twelve promises made by him in 1675 through St. Margaret Mary, to all souls that will practice the devotion to His Heart. Let threatened families remember the second and ninth promises; let suffering and anxious souls heed the third and fourth; let priests take to heart the tenth; but most incredible of all is surely the twelfth, often known as the Great Promise: in return for a worthy Holy Communion received on the first Friday of nine successive months, Our Lord promises "the grace of final repentance," in other words, Heaven!

How could Our Lord make such a promise? Because He knew that as the Fifth Age advanced, the devil would invent more and more distractions to divert men from the one thing essential, the saving of their souls. Then let a Catholic have but the faith and humility to believe in the promise of his God, together with the perseverance to carry through with Communion on nine first Fridays, and he is sure of saving his soul. The Sacred Heart has said so. End of argument! And our thanks to the distributors of this card who remind us of Jesus' divine love and generosity towards us!

No decision has yet been made to relocate the seminary, but we may decide to buy a building at any moment. To ensure that we can make a down payment over and above our current expenditure, you might like to pledge your regular support of the seminary with the enclosed Pledge card. It entails no obligation. It does bring this letter to you each month by first class mail instead of by bulk mail.

In any case, thank you for your great support up till now. St. Joseph has – with your help – looked after us!

NO. 50 | JULY 1, 1987

Episcopal Consecrations Pondered

THE END OF June and the beginning of July is the seminary's season of thanksgiving – another school year completed, in this case another year of tranquility, taking over thirty seminarians one year closer to the Catholic priesthood. How many and special graces for which to thank God from whom they came, and His Mother through whom they came!

At this school year's end, instead of holding a picnic in the seminary yard, the seminarians made a three-day field trip to Boston. Three nights of marvelous hospitality were provided by the Traditional parishioners of Fr. John J. Keane in West Roxbury enabled us to visit during the day firstly, the Freedom Trail in Boston, secondly the battlefield and various warriors' homes of Lexington and Concord, thirdly Plymouth Rock and other Pilgrim sites in "America's hometown," Plymouth. We had the good fortune of having interesting guides who taught us all a good deal of American history and literature.

Now it is extremely difficult to make Catholic heroes out of the 17th century's Protestant pilgrims, the 18th century's radical revolutionaries or the 19th century's literary liberals. Yet seminarians were fascinated. Here was the modern world taking shape before their eyes, disintegrating as the virus of Protestantism bit deeper and deeper. As the guide pointed out the monuments, it seemed as though one wave after another of crusading radicalism radiated out from Boston. From the first half of the 19th century there was the statue of Horace Mann, key founder of the secular public school system, and we know what fruits that has borne. Even in the second half of the same century when the Catholic Irish and Italians were taking over Boston, it was still out of Boston that Mary Baker Eddy founded her sect of Christian Science. And today, if we think for instance of a certain family whose name begins with K, should we say that the Irish converted Boston or that Boston has radicalized its Irish . . . ? So many secular liberal hopes. So many inexorable disappointments.

Yet we had been put on notice: we cannot serve two masters; Our Lord founded His Church on Peter; if we will not gather with Him, then we will scatter. Still we thought we knew better. That is why we built, ignoring His design. That is why what we built is crumbling in ruins. In the US Congress we see going on a suicidal war-dance to destroy patriots, and in the US Government a suicidal paralysis by liberalism seemingly of any will to resist the on-set of the killer disease, AIDS. Why is liberalism so suicidal? Because to deny objective truth and divine law is to turn away from God, Light of the World, the Way, the Truth, and the Life. It is correspondingly to embrace lies, darkness, and death.

Oddly enough, the seminarians were not at all depressed. In Plymouth Plantation they greatly enjoyed grilling – or attempting to grill – the actors who played the part of Pilgrims in 1627, and who gave as good as they got! (Plimoth or Plymouth? The guide explained that it was in those days the mark of an educated man

The Ridgefield Letters

to spell any word in several different ways, whereupon one seminarian was heard to observe that he had some very educated fellow seminarians!) Truth to tell, Catholics will still love these United States when the logical heirs of Protestantism have sunk in their suicidal hatred of them.

And so the seminarians have departed on vacation. One day it was Fr. Bourmaud, Dan Cooper and Ed MacDonald to Ecône, for Dan Cooper's ordination on June 29 with fifteen other new priests for the Society. From Ecône Ed MacDonald was due to depart for India, to spend an apostolic summer with Fr. Welsh and Brother Bernard. The world may be crumbling in ruins, but where there is the Faith, there is still the missionary spirit. Brother Bernard has written us a daunting description of the poverty and living condition in India, worse he says than the worst he ever knew in Africa, but he is very happy to be there. He notes, for instance, the <u>innocence</u> in the Indian children's eyes...

Nor is Archbishop Lefebvre daunted. Ordaining sixteen new priests for the SSPX at Ecône on June 27, and seven more in Zaitzkofen on July 5, he will allow no suicidal liberalism within the Church, or spiritual AIDS as he has called it, to paralyze his defense mechanisms! Admire in the enclosed *Verbum* his logic – only this time a logic of life and not a logic of death – as he thinks through an eventual consecration of priests to the episcopacy to ensure the continuation of confirmations and ordinations: Rome is so losing the Faith, that only the Society's seminaries are not infected with a modernism which kills the Catholic priesthood. Now the Archbishop says he is drawing towards his end and he knows of no other bishop thus far who will come forward to ordain the Society's priests after he is gone. He could leave seminarians to their own devices, but then after all that God has done for the Society, it would not seem

Richard N. Williamson

God now wants to drop it. The Archbishop has, morally speaking, no access to the Pope so long as he is enclosed in modernism, and so the only remaining solution is an eventual consecration of a few of the Society's own priests with bishop's powers.

For there is here no question of bishops with any territorial jurisdiction, no question of setting up any kind of parallel Church, no question of any "sedevacantism" affirming that the Pope is not Pope. On this point read and reread the top right hand corner of page 4 of this *Verbum*, how Liberal Catholics are the worst enemies of the Church, yet not necessarily thereby excommunicated or out of the Church. The Archbishop has always taken this position. It is the only position that corresponds to the full reality of this incredible crisis of the Church. It is an accurate position, rooted in the wisdom of Pius IX and St. Pius X and it is of immense importance, for if we underestimate the modernists' liberalism, we shall follow them in their errors, but if we deny altogether their membership of the Church, we risk dissolving the visible Catholic Church as instituted by Our Lord. The Archbishop clearly has no such intention. Rather, as soon as the Pope were to come to his Catholic senses, the priests of the Society with bishops' powers would happily lay these powers back in the Holy Father's hands, and, with the grace of God, resume their duties as normal priests, if that was the Pope's wish.

Now sufficient for the day is the evil thereof, but who in the meantime can fault the Archbishop's judgment or logic, unless one denies that there is a crisis at all? But such deniers are not living in the world I for one am living in! On a more practical level, the Society's high school in St. Mary's, Kansas, is very anxious to find some house parents for the next school year starting in August. Remember that Don Bosco promised special graces from

The Ridgefield Letters

God for those who take spiritual care of youngsters in our child-pampering, child-neglecting age.

The Dean of the College Facility at St. Mary's is also seeking personnel, students for its Institute of Catholic Higher Education two-year Arts Course. It would be a wise young Catholic who devoted two years to really learning about his Faith, whatever he was then to do. We must offer to many of you an apology for the now four-month delay in getting to you copies of the first series of *Faith in Crisis* tapes. The problem was entirely with our suppliers. We hope it has now been resolved. Be a little patient yet, and you will have the tapes. The second series is also proving popular.

For the summer, the seminary now changes into its retreats mode. Of the eleven retreats, only two are booked out so far, but the others are over all eighty per cent booked. Register soon. Who knows if next summer it will still be possible to do a retreat? For the autumn, still no decision on a move of the seminary. Please pray for this intention, because the incoming vocations will make this building again very crowded in September. And do not forget to support the truest of patriots, your future Catholic priests.

For these beautiful summer days, thank God, but do not spoil them with immodest fashions. Christians must have nothing to do with the undress almost universal today. July is the month of the Precious Blood. Think why Our Lord shed it before choosing what you wear. And may He bless you and guard you and yours from all wiles and onslaughts of the devil, who even, or especially in the summer heat, never sleeps.

NO. 51 | JULY 30, 1987

Answered Prayers

OUR PRAYERS HAVE been answered...
We have found the new seminary for which we have been searching these past several months, and after some negotiating, we have it at a very reasonable price.

Built as a Dominican novitiate in the early 1950's at a cost of one and a half million dollars in southeast Minnesota, the handsome stone building would cost today many more millions to replace. Together with over one-hundred acres of land (mostly farmland), it is ours for $400,000!

Of course, it will need some repair work (for instance, $31,000 to repair the roof), but there will no expensive alterations because it could almost have been designed for our purposes!

With single-room accommodation for about eighty-five people, it is neither too big nor too small. It has a lovely chapel in marble and stone, and a grand hilltop view over the surrounding countryside. Above all, its distinctively religious atmosphere and character strikes visitors immediately and will make of it a jewel in the crown of the worldwide SSPX.

The Ridgefield Letters

However, WE NOW NEED YOUR HELP! We need an immediate war-chest with which to undertake the necessary repairs and cost of installing ourselves in the new quarters. The US District of the Society would like to take over Ridgefield as soon as possible – hence this swift appeal.

And, we would wish to close on September 30 without having to take out a usurious mortgage. Can we?

With the next regular monthly newsletter, you will have some pictures of the new seminary. If only 700 of you could donate $750, we could have easily most of what we need.

It is a lot to ask, we know, but if it is too much for you, then please help as you can. The seminarians are offering their lives to serve the Faith and your children's salvation – won't you add your sacrifices to theirs? God love you and reward you!

NO. 52 | AUGUST 10, 1987

A Handsome Dominican Building

TO MANY OF you, many thanks for giving our Building Fund a really flying start! If a picture is worth a thousand words, the enclosed flyer should be worth several thousand words to tell you what you are buying. One of you from western Wisconsin just wrote:

> Yesterday after Mass we went to see the Seminary's new location in Winona. We were taken on a grand tour and got a good taste of its history. Oh, Father, what a find for all of us! Truly, all of our prayers have been answered – mightily! After seeing the place we were left speechless.

Today, the Seminary Priests' Letter to Friends and Benefactors found the right words for our own impression of the new seminary: "It will be a jewel in the crown of the worldwide SSPX! Amen." It is interesting that, as in Ridgefield the Society took over a building formerly belonging to the Jesuits, so in Winona we are stepping into the heritage of the Dominicans. When the seminary

The Ridgefield Letters

leaves Ridgefield (surely not before Christmas – it all depends on the repairs needed in Winona), we shall leave behind us a retreat house where retreats are given such as the true Jesuits of St. Ignatius used to give.

For in Ridgefield, two Society priests will continue to provide Mass in Connecticut and upstate New York at the missions presently served from the seminary, and these priests will also be opening, not a moment too soon, the Society's first full-time retreat house in the United States. Now since the collapse of the Jesuits (memorably related in Malachi Martin's recent book *The Jesuits*, which is thoroughly to be recommended), in how many places can souls find the old-fashioned closed retreats they know they need, and of which the Jesuits used to be the masters? Well, when the Ignatian Fr. Jean-Luc Lafitte arrives in Ridgefield, watch out for ignition!

And when St. Thomas Aquinas Seminary arrives in Winona, it will – always with the grace of God, and never without it – establish a truly thomistic house of formation for priests. Now of thomism, (philosophical and theological studies according to the mind of the Church's greatest Doctor, St. Thomas Aquinas), the Dominicans – St. Thomas' own order – used to be the masters. Indeed Pope Benedict XV said that the Dominicans' greatest glory was less to have engendered St. Thomas than to have remained faithful to his teaching ever since him. But where are those Dominicans today? With noble exceptions, today's Order of Preachers is anything but faithful to St. Thomas.

And now comes into St. Peter Martyr Priory, former novitiate of the Dominicans' central American Province, the Society's lowly St. Thomas Aquinas Seminary, where the studies may not be highly intellectual, but where they are solidly thomistic. Who can not see here the action of God sustaining His Catholic Church? As the Jesuits and

Richard N. Williamson

Dominicans throw away their pearls of great price, so the outcast SSPX picks them up to preserve them for another generation. Pray for us that we do not drop them in turn. Let us at least be able to hand them back to true Jesuits and true Dominicans when these rise again from their present ashes! Pray, because prayer is what matters.

A great American priest, Fr. Charles E. Coughlin, as the famous "Radio Priest" of the late '30's and early '40's of this century, swung into action and took the Catholic battle right out into the public arena until the Church's enemies had him silenced – through the Church's own hierarchy! A few years later he was visited by a young priest seeking advice. "Father," he replied (in so many words), "go home, and each day prepare to say your Mass, say Mass, and for the rest of the day give thanks for having said Mass." Fr. Coughlin was speaking from experience of the relative uselessness, already forty years ago, of what most men call "action." For we are, by the Lord God Himself, being driven back on the supernatural. Merely natural weapons He is letting fall to pieces in our hands.

One naval spy recently made a whole U.S. ocean defense system obsolete. Nor will any amount of brilliant technology, nor even brave and patriotic lieutenant-colonels, succeed in defending us from enemies designated by the Lord God of Hosts to chastise us. On the other hand, one anguished prayer from good King Ezechias, and the exterminating angel cut to pieces Sennacherib's otherwise irresistible invading army – Isaiah 37. We are in a spiritual battle, and we must resort to spiritual and supernatural weapons: prayer, penance, denial of self, the state of grace. These alone are today efficacious. They are absolutely efficacious.

"The king is not saved by a great army: nor shall the giant be saved by his own great strength. Vain is the horse for safety: neither shall he be saved by the abun-

The Ridgefield Letters

dance of his strength. Behold the e yes of the Lord are upon them that fear Him: and on them that hope in His mercy." (Ps. 32: 16–18) And the weapon of weapons, then? A 50-bullet machine gun given by Our Lady to St. Dominic: The Holy Rosary. May the Dominican stones of Winona help give you priests who will never themselves drop, nor ever let you drop, the Most Holy Rosary of St. Dominic and of the Blessed Virgin Mary, and may she keep you and your families safe under her unfailing protection!

NO. 53 | SEPTEMBER 10, 1987

Three Items of Good News

AT LEAST THREE items of good news: Firstly, a major candle was lit in the darkness when at Fatima in Portugal on August 22 last, Feast of the Sorrowful and Immaculate Heart of Mary, Archbishop Lefebvre, heading an official pilgrimage representing the entire SSPX, solemnly consecrated Russia to the Immaculate Heart of Mary. Over fifty priests, forty-six from the Society, and some 2,000 laity from all over the world were present for the consecration which took place after an all-night vigil and a Solemn Pontifical High Mass at an altar improvised in a field, just like the field nearby where Our Lady originally appeared in 1917 to the three children of Fatima, and which is now a huge and impressive paved sanctuary.

Of course it is idle to give to this act any more significance than one bishop's action has in the Universal Church. Turn over this page to see the wise and modest words to this effect in the fourth paragraph of the beautiful text of Russia's consecration, pronounced by the Archbishop. Nevertheless, with this trailblazing act the Archbishop and his Society have together done the least, and the most, they could do: the least, because with the graces we have received to understand Fatima and the

The Ridgefield Letters

importance of Russia's consecration, we could not do less; the most, because passing for a handful of outcasts, we could not do more. In any case, such a consecration is certainly the way the Universal Church must, sooner or later, go. The Archbishop's and the Society's act can only draw down upon all of us great graces from the Blessed Virgin Mother of God.

Next piece of good news, the seminary's Building Fund for the new seminary in Winona is forging ahead! In Fatima three weeks ago Archbishop Lefebvre promised me a check, and our Superior General, Fr. Schmidberger, gave me an envelope filled with banknotes – both wanted to be amongst the 700 generous donors we called for. In fact at the time of writing, just over 1,000 of you have already given us $329,000, bringing us close to the immediate purchase price! That is wonderful. If your generosity does not slow down, you will start funding the repairs, an unknown at present, but the final repair bill could be of the order of another two or three hundred thousand dollars. Thank you all very much. May God repay you with good priests out of Winona in the future. Your generosity surely deserves them. And do not fear the Society abandoning our chapels or Mass centers in the East. These will continue uninterrupted even when the seminary moves West.

Third item of good news – the long drawn-out battle in the law courts in the Northeastern United States between the Society and the group of priests that split away in 1983 is terminating next month in a settlement. Archbishop Lefebvre and Fr. Schmidberger (who actually negotiated the settlement) are both very happy with it, because the Society can at last leave behind a most unhappy episode and do the work it is meant to do, of rebuilding the Church. Like all settlements this one is a compromise, but to have fought to the bitter end for our complete rights would have enriched the lawyers much more than the Church. However, let no one be deluded that the Society and the breakaway priests are reconciled. A key point in the settlement is that they may in no way use the name of St. Pius X in their "association," and if, as they requested, they use the name of St. Pius I or St. Pius V, then for the next 18 months they must at the same time make it clear that they have nothing to do with Archbishop Lefebvre's SSPX. We would be grateful for notice of any infractions of this ruling, because the differences between the Society and these priests are not insignificant, as some would pretend.

What the Society stands for, you see in brief in the enclosed flyer, just reissued in color. Ask us for as many as you like, because we have a good supply on hand. Remember this month Archbishop Lefebvre in your prayers. It is the month of the 40th Jubilee of his consecration as a bishop. And may God bless you!

NO. 54 | OCTOBER 1, 1987

Episcopal Consecrations Decided

MORE GOOD NEWS: the seminary in Minnesota has been bought, and it now belongs to the SSPX. In just under two months you have contributed to our Building Fund a sum of $402,008, enabling us to purchase Winona without a mortgage. That is a remarkable achievement.

Even more precious in God's eyes will be the sacrifice many of you must have made. After all, the Lord of Lords might have inspired one or two souls well endowed with this world's goods to put up the entire sum. Instead He sent St. Joseph to knock on many doors. After all, He wants many souls to store their treasure in Heaven. To all of you, many thanks.

I cannot help quoting from another visitor's reaction to the Winona building:

> Words fail me in trying to tell you my impression of the magnificence of the place, the holy atmosphere, and how perfect this will be for the Society... We came away from there so thrilled to see how the Church is going to be able to continue through the Society and

Richard N. Williamson

the good priests who will come from this seminary. Surely anyone going there can see the Hand of God in this whole affair, from the day the first shovel of dirt was turned, and how He has enabled the Society of St. Pius X to inherit the legacy that was left by the Dominicans who built this place high on the bluff overlooking the river valley.

What a place! What a view! What an opportunity for the Society! There are just not enough words in my poor vocabulary to describe my enthusiasm – for the future of the Church, for the future of the Society, and for the future of the Catholic people who cling to Tradition and their Catholic faith. I hope that the Archbishop will be able to see what is there on the high ground overlooking the valley and far off to the east and the lands of Wisconsin. Just imagine how thrilled he would be!

What a find! You should have no problems at all raising the necessary funds to get this place running again, and you should keep telling everyone who can help what a good find it is. It would seem to me that to duplicate at today's costs what you have bought, would take at least twenty times the amount. It is almost unbelievable that this most perfect place can become the Society's seminary, and your words, 'a jewel in the crown of the world-wide SSPX', tell it all.

Mark you, to get the repairs going without delay, we have had to borrow temporarily, so if you made a pledge, or if that envelope you meant to send is still there, please send it in. For a start, roof repairs are costing some $30,000 and replacement of the boilers another $60,000.

But repairs are forging ahead! If any of you would like to help on a voluntary basis, even just one month at a time, we will pay for your travel. For the moment there is nowhere convenient to lodge the ladies, but if you are male, single and skilled (or willing to learn a skill), there will be no lack of work for several months – ring Mr.

The Ridgefield Letters

Peter Sardegna (who is in charge of works). What a joy to take part in rebuilding on Stockton Hill, please God, a Fortress of the Faith!

For in Rome the crisis of the Faith only deepens. Enclosed you find the text of Archbishop Lefebvre's sermon of June 29, at this year's priestly ordinations in Ecône. In it you read how he announced in public, albeit in guarded terms, his decision to consecrate some auxiliary bishops, because he considers that the sign he was waiting for from Providence to do this, has come.

What sign? Firstly, the abominable ecumenical meeting in Assisi of last October; secondly – and still graver – Rome's reply to the Archbishop early this year defending against his objections submitted two years ago on the novel doctrine of Vatican II on religious liberty.

Why is the latter sign still graver? Because, as the Archbishop explained to Cardinal Ratzinger in their meeting at the Vatican on July 14 of this year, it is graver to lay down false principles than it is simply to put them into practice. When the Cardinal then continued to defend the falsehoods of Vatican II, the Archbishop said he and the Cardinal could never come to an agreement, because while Our Lord Jesus Christ means everything to the Society, Rome on the other hand is stripping Our Lord of His rights over men's consciences.

The Cardinal was still anxious to arrive at some agreement, so a mere two weeks later he wrote to Archbishop Lefebvre to propose for the Society official recognition, its own seminaries with the Tridentine Liturgy of John XXIII, and a Cardinal-Visitor to perform ordinations (thus solving the problem of episcopal consecrations), only . . . only this Cardinal-Visitor would "guarantee the orthodoxy" of teaching in the Society's seminaries, and he would have the final word on who gets ordained or not.

Richard N. Williamson

Now who cannot see that to accept these conditions giving to a Cardinal from modernist Rome control over doctrine and ordinations, would be to hand over the Society's seminaries, bound hand and foot, to modernism? In which case, is Cardinal Ratzinger a fool to have made such a mistake, or a villain to have laid such a trap? Dom Putti's answer was, "They are all delinquents." Yet surely the gifted mind that showed such a concern for the Church as in *The Ratzinger Report* is the mind of neither a complete fool nor a complete villain.

Then <u>how</u> can the Cardinal make a proposal to the Society calculated to destroy in its seminaries exactly what his anxiety to keep the Society as a counterweight to the radicals is seeking to preserve? Answer, because as his writings <u>also</u> show, the poor Cardinal believes in evolving truth, and has no grasp on a fixed, unchanging truth. Hence he cannot begin to understand the Archbishop or the Society, for whom the Way, the Truth, and the Life is unchanging, yesterday, today, and forever, Our Lord Jesus Christ. The Cardinal and the Archbishop are like on different mental planets. In brief, <u>if</u> the poor Cardinal still has the Catholic Faith in his heart and intentions, he has certainly lost all grip on it in his mind and actions. Such is the depth of perversity of modernism. As has been well said, the end-times will be characterized by men doing evil, thinking they are doing good. In any case, whosoever today would defend the Catholic Faith must hope for no cooperation, and fear no sanction, from this Rome.

Where will it all end? The Archbishop may continue the dialogue, always in the charitable hope of enlightening Rome, but finally he will act. And if he proceeds to consecrate bishops, will he and they be excommunicated? Maybe, but the excommunication, like that of St. Athanasius by Pope Liberius in 359 AD, would merely rebound against its perpetrators. But won't the people be

The Ridgefield Letters

hopelessly confused? Patience. Men may be crushed, but not the Truth. When the Pharisees complained to Our Lord of His disciples hailing Him as Messiah, Our Lord replied that if His disciples were to be silenced, the very stones of the street would rise up to proclaim the Truth (Lk. 19: 40). Whichever way this conflict turns, the Truth will always be there and recognizable, for those that seek Him. "Heaven and earth shall pass, but my words shall not pass" (Mt. 24: 35). "Behold I am with you all days, even to the consummation of the world" (Mt. 28: 20).

We will not lose hold of the Truth if we pray, especially through the Mother of God with the Most Holy Rosary. Catholics may have their priests taken away, but not their rosaries, if they know how to use them. During October, month of the Holy Rosary, include a prayer for those priests who are being taken away – like broken on the wheel – by the revolutionary Novus Ordo.

And may God bless you and keep you. Fear not, the Truth is mighty and will prevail.

NO. 55 | NOVEMBER 1, 1987

Chronology of Contacts with Rome

WE ALWAYS KNEW that sooner or later Archbishop Lefebvre would be back in the news. The media being as treacherous as they are, the seminary's telephone has been ringing for the past two weeks with query after query as to the recent negotiations between the Archbishop and the Vatican. Here then for clarification are the facts, with the sequence of events going back to their origin in the Second Vatican Council:

December, 1965: the Second Vatican Council issues a *Declaration on Religious Liberty* which gravely departs from Catholic doctrine.

October, 1985: Archbishop Lefebvre submits to Rome a 138-page document listing 39 "dubia," or grave doubts against this departure from Catholic doctrine.

February, 1987: Rome makes a 50-page reply to the Archbishop's "dubia," justifying the Council's false teaching on religious liberty.

July 14, 1987: Archbishop Lefebvre takes to Cardinal Ratzinger personally in Rome a collection of documents proving how unsatisfactory has been this reply of Rome.

The Ridgefield Letters

The Archbishop highlights the diametrical opposition between the Society's aim of restoring all things in Christ, and Rome's present policy of liberating society from the rights of Christ.

July 28, 1987: The Cardinal writes to Archbishop Lefebvre proposing to "legitimize" the SSPX and the Tridentine liturgy, on condition that a Cardinal-Visitor from Rome will effectively control the Society and its seminaries.

End of August 1987: The Archbishop lets Rome know that the Society cannot relinquish its seminaries to such a Visitor, because, again, Rome's present liberalism and the Society's Catholic Faith are incompatible.

September 4, 1987: The Archbishop in a conference to Society priests at Ecône talks of Rome in very severe terms: Rome has apostasized, the Roman churchmen quitting the Church, their program of dechristianizing society is an abomination. He has not yet decided to consecrate bishops to save the Faith, but he holds all objections to such consecrations to be soluble.

Mid-September 1987: The Archbishop is on the brink of announcing at the 40th Jubilee of his episcopacy, on October 3, that he will consecrate bishops before the end of the year.

September, 1987: Rome, thoroughly alarmed at the prospect of such a consecration, sends a note to the Archbishop that the proposed Visitor's sole function will be to work out a canonical status for the Society (in other words, he will not have control over the seminaries).

October 1, 1987: On these terms, the Archbishop agrees to a visitor. His Jubilee Sermon at Ecône on October 3 is of a guarded optimism Rome concerning relations with Rome.

October 17, 1987: The Archbishop and the Cardinal meet once more in Rome to finalize an agreement on the Apostolic Visitor, not yet named. The press release

Richard N. Williamson

issued at the end of the meeting says that the Visitor's task will be "the gathering together of information needed to help define the terms of a canonical regularization of the Society of St. Pius X. In the fulfilling of this function, the Apostolic Visitor will depend directly on the Holy Father."

<u>October 29, 1987</u>: At the Synod on the Laity in Rome, Cardinal Ratzinger announces the nomination of the Visitor: Cardinal Edouard Gagnon.

<u>November 1987</u>: Cardinal Gagnon is due to visit the Society's motherhouse, the seminary in Ecône, Switzerland. Upon this sequence of events there are several comments to be made. Note firstly that in accepting a Visitor to gather information, the Archbishop has not "given away the store," nor compromised, nor backed off in any way, and whoever thinks he ever will is not a good judge of men. The Archbishop has merely agreed to delay fixing a date for the consecration of bishops, a delay well worth it if Rome's authorization for the consecration can possibly be obtained, but a delay which will not be prolonged beyond next year.

Note on the other hand that by agreeing to send a Visitor to Ecône, Rome has not given away its modernism either. The Visitor can make a report, a report can be spiked, the months can slip past... In fact, the Archbishop has said, it will take a miracle for Rome to authorize this consecration of bishops.

Now miracles are rare, but this one may be hoped for on two grounds: firstly, the Society's official pilgrimage in August to Fatima, honoring the widely dishonored request of the Mother of God for the Consecration of Russia to her Immaculate Heart, will surely have obtained a measure of her powerful intercession for the Society. Secondly, the Catholic Church's indefectibility must place some limit upon how far the Lord God will allow <u>His</u> hierarchy to break with <u>His</u> truth. Now only

The Ridgefield Letters

one who knew the mind of God could say for certain whether that limit has yet been reached, but it is surely not far off now. The Lord God will intervene at some point.

Indeed, is it not by divine inspiration that Rome is showing itself so alarmed at the prospect of a consecration of bishops? After all, traditional Catholics are so relatively few that Rome could easily refuse to give Archbishop Lefebvre the time of day. Indeed, if Rome was as wholly villainous as some people claim, it would merely rejoice in the consecration formalizing the Archbishop's "schism," and giving them the long dreamt of excuse to "excommunicate" him. Yet here is Rome sending as Visitor, on the Archbishop's terms, the Cardinal most sympathetic of all towards the Society, Cardinal Gagnon . . . What to make of it? . . .

Does Rome have a bad conscience, realizing that if it had done its duty, the Archbishop would not now find himself being driven to this extreme? Did the Pope's latest American journey make him realize that the Society's Catholic vitality is not something the Church can afford to throw away? Do the Romans realize that, despite all their maneuvering, an eventual "schism" will be blamed on them? Do they fear that if they push the Society out into the cold, the Church's center of gravity will lurch leftwards, leaving them virtually defenseless against the radicals amongst them whose only strong-principled opponent they will have eliminated? And which way will Rome jump?

Amidst so many questions and so many uncertainties, two things remain certain: the Truth cannot change, and the Truth – in the Catholic Church – cannot lose. Rome may twist and dodge and turn, and the Archbishop will adapt to the situation they create, but he has not deviated from his course of defending the Faith, and nothing indicates he ever will. And even if he did, the Lord God would merely raise another standard-bearer of Tradition, which is Truth, to take his place. This banner cannot fall. Therefore "fear not, little flock, for it hath pleased the Father to give you a kingdom." (Lk. 12: 32) Instead "pray without ceasing" for the Pope, for the Romans, and for the Archbishop, and in the months and years to come, admire how the Lord God, while fully respecting the free will of each one of us, will be nonetheless surely and firmly saving His Church. We are watching a literally divine Master at work!

At the seminary we are now well into the new school year, more crowded than ever, for we have had to find room for thirteen brand new seminarians, a fourteenth returned from five years ago, and a fifteenth come over from the Novus Ordo. And we risk having to still find room for a sixteenth, another seminarian returning from years ago, and a seventeenth, a late vocation from South Africa. We have bought Winona in the nick of time, where repairs are forging ahead, also the repair bills! Especial thanks to all those of you who have made real sacrifices to help us. Your letters are most edifying. However, beware of thinking of moving near Winona if you are hoping for a parish situation like in St. Mary's, Kansas. You will have the Mass of course, but, for the rest, a seminary must guard its relative seclusion.

Also needing more room are the Carmelite nuns of Phoenixville, Pennsylvania. Closely connected to the Society and using exclusively the Tridentine Mass, they are also receiving more vocations than they can accommodate. Hence the raffle-tickets that a number of you on Society mailing lists have received. The Carmelites deserve our support, for we all benefit by their prayers.

May Our Lord increase your Faith, inspire you with Hope, and enkindle your Charity.

NO. 56 | DECEMBER 9, 1987

The Archbishop Will Consecrate Regardless

THIS CHRISTMAS WE are sending you a card which we hope is a little present in itself. Certainly the Novena of Masses of which it speaks is a present to you all. It is the least we could do at the seminary in return for your gift to us of the magnificent seminary building in Minnesota. The Novena will run from the Midnight Mass of Christmas to January 2, inclusive. It comes to you with our very best wishes for above all your spiritual health and happiness for Christmas and the New Year.

What will the New Year bring? What will it not bring? At any rate the closing of the old year brings relatively good news for the Society from Europe. Cardinal Gagnon has just terminated his one month visit to various houses of the Society and of kindred Traditional movements in Switzerland, France and Germany, and he will no doubt be depositing by Christmas on the Holy Father's desk a report highly favorable to the Society.

Just before beginning his visit, the Cardinal excused himself from visiting any Society houses in the New World or in the United States because his time was too short. In fact, after just the first eight days of his visit, he told members of the Society that he already had enough positive elements in hand to be able to conclude his visit then and there, but he wished conscientiously to complete it as planned.

So he next set off for France, where on Sunday, November 24, he almost took an official part in the celebration of the Solemn High Mass at the famous Traditional church of St. Nicolas du Chardonet in Paris, run by Society priests. He was only prevented from doing so by a last minute intervention from the very highest quarters in Rome: the Holy Father and Cardinals Ratzinger and Casaroli met together and decided that it would be better to avoid such a provocation to the French bishops. So Cardinal Gagnon's place in the ceremony was taken by his colleague on this visit, Msgr. Perl, an official of the Congregation of Divine Worship. <u>Both of them said only the Tridentine Mass in Society houses for the duration of their visit.</u>

Proof that a different wind is blowing in Rome is offered by the fact that on that same Sunday, at the very same time, <u>Cardinal Lustiger of Paris</u>, normally no traditionalist, <u>was celebrating a Tridentine Mass in another church in Paris</u>. The battle of the Mass is virtually won? If so, that is Archbishop Lefebvre's doing.

But will the Pope be able to settle the question of the Mass and the Society as several things indicate he would like to do? The mere mention of the name of Cardinal Casaroli, archenemy of Sacred Tradition, and of the French bishops, archpromoters of modernism, reminds us how fierce the opposition will be in the Roman Curia and amongst the world's bishops, to any papal approval of the Tridentine Mass or of the Society associated with it. Here is what Archbishop Lefebvre wrote to me in a letter dated November 20:

> I think that as his visit continues, Cardinal Gagnon is more and more convinced that we are right to be

doing what we are doing. However, if his visit is useful, it is not the answer.

We shall have to find a form of institution to protect us from the Roman Curia and the diocesan chanceries. In Rome we shall need a secretariat or commission, composed of members agreeing with what we think and do, to help the Society set itself up with three bishops chosen from within the Society, to form like an "Armed Services' Vicariat," with all the powers necessary to continue our work, independently of all other bishops. A way must be found for all Traditional movements and initiatives to normalize their juridical situation so that they can continue to ask for the help of our own bishops.

The whole thing is to know whether Rome, that is to say the Pope, will have the courage, despite the howling set up by the bishops and the Roman Curia, to grant us such a degree of independence. There are several Cardinals who will support Cardinal Gagnon. But it will not be easy. Already the episcopates are getting together to prevent a solution.

In any case, if they do not give me the authorization to consecrate bishops, I shall do it without authorization. This is the most practical and pressing point. Let us continue to pray, especially to Our Lady of Fatima.

The solution here envisaged by Archbishop Lefebvre, a personal prelature, like an Army Vicariat for instance, is from the point of view of Canon Law a very flexible formula and may be the best suited to the needs of the situation. Whereas a local bishop has jurisdiction over Catholics in a given locality, or geographical diocese, a personal prelate has jurisdiction by his person over Catholics in some way connected to him. Thus an Army Vicar has in person direct jurisdiction over army chaplains or priests and through them over Catholic servicemen and their families attached to that army. Thus Archbishop Lefebvre or his successor would have full powers of a diocesan bishop firstly over the Society priests and their faithful, but also over priests and faithful outside the Society who would resort to him because of their attachment to the Traditional rite of Mass. He would be in effect an alternative Ordinary or bishop for all such Traditional priests and faithful, without their necessarily having to quit the diocese to which canonically they normally belong. Such a solution has the great advantage of largely corresponding to an already existing and honest state of affairs. Will it come about? That depends upon God's grace and men's free will. It is, as always, and more than ever, a question of prayer.

A great way to pray is to do the Exercises of St. Ignatius for five days. On last month's flyer for the Exercises of December 26 to 31, we forgot to mention they are for men, age 18 and upwards. There are still vacancies. Come to the help of Mother Church by taking this major step in your own sanctification, and come to the help of the seminary by filling out the enclosed pledge card.

And may the Child Jesus amidst all the trouble and turmoil, grant you the peace, light and joy of the Christmas crib. Do not miss the little poem on the back of the card!

NO. 57 | JANUARY 10, 1988

Liberalism Against the Family

JANUARY IS THE month of the Holy Family, because of today's Feast of the Holy Family. This feast was instituted by Popes Leo XIII and Benedict XV a little under 100 years ago to help defend the family against the onslaught of Liberalism.

For indeed the family is the instrument designed by God for the making of men, from conception to adulthood. Hence to unmake men, the devil will attack the family, and to redeem or remake mankind, the Divine Savior began by giving a sublime example, extended over thirty years, of family life. Here is what Pope Leo XIII taught in 1892:

> No one is unaware that private and public prosperity depend principally on the constitution of the family. The community's welfare will be measured by the virtues which have taken root in the family and by the extent of the parents' zeal for inculcating in their children – by doctrine and example – the precepts of religion. For it is of the greatest importance that domestic society not only be firmly constituted, but also that it be ruled by holy laws and that the religious spirit and the principles

—243—

of Christian life be carefully and constantly developed. It is evidently for this purpose that the merciful God – wishing to accomplish the work of the restoration of humanity which had long been awaited – so prepared the details and the manner of Redemption that from the beginning this work would present to the world the august form of a divinely constituted family, in which all men could contemplate the most perfect model of family life and an example of every virtue and sanctity.

Such was the family of Nazareth . . . constituted in such a manner that all Christians, of every condition and race, can with a little attention, easily find therein a motive for practicing every virtue and an invitation to do so. In fact, fathers of families have an excellent example of vigilance and fatherly protection in Joseph; the Most Holy Mother of God is an admirable example and pattern of love, modesty, of the spirit of submission and perfect faith for mothers; in the person of Jesus, who "was subject to them," children have a divine model of obedience to be admired, venerated and imitated.

These family roles, distinct but complementary, are so deeply inscribed in the way we humans are, that all common sense, nature and tradition rise up against our society's unmanning of the father, unwomaning of the mother, and dismantling of parental responsibility. Here is God Himself teaching through the Apostle's words what the Holy Family had taught by example:

Wives, be subject to your husbands, as it behooveth in the Lord. Husbands, love your wives, and be not bitter towards them. Children, obey your parents in all things: for this is pleasing to the Lord. Fathers, provoke not your children to anger; lest they be discouraged.

(Colossians 3: 18–21)

The Ridgefield Letters

Here is God's own charter for the family, to rewrite which is an insanity. And if it be objected that there are a thousand good reasons why today's wives cannot be cherished or husbands obeyed, why for instance today's mothers cannot stay at home and make and mind the babies that God sends them, then the only reply is that there are a thousand good reasons why our present civilization cannot survive. In all creativity there is nothing to compare with creating people, as God has obviously designed women to do, which takes not only nine months but nineteen years, and then some. Yet women are allowed, or made, to feel that to be "creative" they must put the kids in daycare centers and "fulfill their personalities" in the marketplace jobs alongside the men? Behold the suicidal deathwish, yet again, of Liberalism.

The punishment for disregarding God's plan for the family is all around us. Most interesting testimony came recently from a Chicago university professor, Allan Bloom, analyzing in his surprising bestseller, *The Closing of the American Mind*, why today's students are more or less incapable of whatever a university is really about. Being absolutely free, democratic, and equal, they are so open-minded to all ideas, he notes, that their minds are closed to there being any truth – hence the title of his book. Most interestingly, Bloom is a liberal, yet he traces the dissolution of his individual students, back through their lack of family life, to the dissolution of authority in society at large by democratic Liberalism. As the principle of authority in politics was replaced by the principle of consent, so paternal and parental authority in the family was inevitably weakened; as freedom and revolution were glorified, so family ties and bonds were progressively discredited; as equality leveled down social rank, so hierarchy and obedience in the family were further discounted. From democracy, the family of consent – "Johnny, put on your shoes, please"; from liberty, the "sexual revolution"; from equality, women's lib and feminism.

Thus what started with the politics of consent Bloom observes to have led through the disintegration of the family to a generation of social solitaries, unbelievably "nice," free and equal, but rootless, shiftless, aimless, unable to commit themselves though yearning for commitment. The students Bloom finds most typical of this social solitude, and most to be pitied, are those whose parents divorced. A few sample quotes: "Divorce has a deep influence on our universities because more and more of the students are products of it, and they not only have problems themselves but also affect other students and the general atmosphere. Although . . . people want and need to create a general will out of the particular wills, those particular wills constantly reassert themselves. There is a quest, but ever more hopeless, for arrangements and ways of putting the broken pieces back together. The task is equivalent to squaring the circle, because everyone loves himself most, but wants others to love him more than they love themselves. Such is particularly the demand of children, against which parents are now rebelling . . .

> Children may be told over and over again that their parents have a right to their own lives, that they will enjoy quality time instead of quantity time, that they are really loved by their parents even after divorce, but they do not believe any of this. They think they have a right to total attention and believe their parents must live for them. There is no explaining otherwise to them, and anything less inevitably produces indignation and an inextirpable sense of injustice.

Bloom goes on:

> I am not arguing here that the old family arrangements were good or that we should or could go back to them. I am only insisting that we not cloud our vision to such an extent that we believe that there are viable substitutes for them just because we want or need them . . . All our (Liberal) reforms have helped strip the teeth of our gears, which can therefore no longer mesh. They spin idly, side by side, unable to set the social machine in motion. It is at this exercise in futility that young people must look when thinking about their future.

Eloquent testimony from a liberal to the havoc wrought by Liberalism! He dare not openly defend the old-fashioned family, but at least he is honest enough to recognize and relate the tragedy of its dissolution.

Youngsters, before you marry, grow up enough to realize that the Hollywood spooning-swooning-crooning bit lasts three weeks, three months if you're lucky, so that when it's over you need to have a lot in common with your partner if your marriage is to last, and last, it must, firstly to obey God, secondly to avoid spiritually wrecking your children. So choose a partner not only by fancy, but also by reason, one above all with whom you share the Faith, so that you will never disagree over accepting whatever children God sends you, nor over one of you being the fond breadwinner and the other the obedient homemaker. Then marry sacramentally to obtain God's blessing and indispensable grace for your union, and when you marry, pray the Rosary every night and prepare for a life of sacrifice, whereby you will put into the family more than you take out of it, giving life and education to your children, and a home eventually even to your own parents. You want nothing to do with immaturity, Hollywood, the Justice of the Peace, contraception, state schools, or nursing homes! And when you are not exhausted, you will realize you are as happy as you can be in this vale of tears, for our destiny is not here below but in heaven! And oldsters, never tire of dinning such old truths into young ears! Allan Bloom said it all when he said in so many words that the true family is a school of selflessness, whereas modern ideas are systematized selfishness. Pray one day he be given the gift of the Catholic Faith.

No news yet from Rome. We shall be immensely grateful if the SSPX obtains a green light, but we are not holding our breath: we are praying, and trusting God to do as He knows best with His Church.

Enclosed the latest *Verbum* devoted entirely to the new seminary in Winona. It will be a magnificent facility when the renovations are finished. We expect to move out there at the end of the school year, end June, early July. A retreats schedule for retreats at Ridgefield this summer, from July onwards, you should receive with the February letter. And if for a scrapbook or a catechism class or whatever, you would like any more of the cards that came with the December letter, let us know, we have plenty to spare.

Thank you for your generosity at Christmas, helping a good deal with the renovations in Minnesota. May God bless, guard and guide you, and your family life!

NO. 58 | FEBRUARY 2, 1988

The Consecrations are Justified

ELEVEN SEMINARIANS WHO entered this seminary last autumn received today the cassock, and so appear to the world from now on like priests. Henceforth, however young they look, they are liable to be addressed in public as "Father" by good souls who make no fine distinction between priests and brothers and seminarians – these all wear the uniform of the servants of God, and they stand out in the world as signs of contradiction.

Their cassock by its mortified black contradicts the world's bright pursuit of vain pleasures, by its length and looseness the brevity and tightness of the world's immodest fashions. The cassock is a non-stop sermon without words, so effective that anti-Catholic legislators have more than once singled it out for attack. How often, alas, Our Lord's enemies seem to know Him better than do His friends! May He grant perseverance to His eleven new soldiers! Archbishop Lefebvre has said that in today's world each vocation is a miracle. When we consider the forces aligned today to corrupt youth, that is surely no exaggeration. Parents, you have been warned to check your children's music? Now, check also their computers! An article told in the *Washington Times* a few days ago how youngsters can buy pornographic computer programs, or key into filth if they just know certain numbers! – what a world!

Yet the vocations continue. I am under the impression that we have had this year several more enquiries than at the same time in previous years from young men interested in entering the seminary next autumn. Now this may be because of the magnificent facility that your ongoing generosity and a happy team of thirteen workers are putting together for us in Winona, but I doubt if that is the reason. Certainly the campaign of prayer for vocations launched by the Society's U.S. District Superior, Fr. François Laisney, will have had something to do with the increase in interest – keep up those prayers, for remember always, you will have the priests of your prayers. Most likely, the recent hopes of some agreement between Rome and the Society must be drawing towards the Society some young men to whom it previously seemed off limits.

But how are those hopes? The news is that on January 5 Cardinal Gagnon gave to the Pope his full length Report on his one month official visitation of the Society carried out in November and December of last year, but by the end of January he was still waiting to be received in audience by the Holy Father to discuss the Report. As Archbishop Lefebvre said in a sermon given in Paris on December 13: "Rome we hope will come to our aid in a positive way and will let us extend and spread the benefits of Catholic Tradition, clearly recognized by Cardinal Gagnon. But I am not sure that that will be the case. Throughout the modernized and modernist Church, the mind-poisoning theories of modernism have such weight at the present time, that I would not be surprised if they seek by all means in their power to make us draw closer to them and to their spirit of the Council. That is what I am afraid of." And he said that any such proposals of a compromise with modernism "we would refuse. We wish to remain Catholic. We have not fought for twenty years in order to give up the fight and join the ranks of those losing the Faith."

And so it is possible Cardinal Gagnon and his report will continue to wait. For how can ecumenical Rome (Assisi, Kyoto, etc.) approve of the Society which so vigorously and consistently attacks all of its ecumenical pomps and works, all of its enthusiastic commitment to heading up a one-world Church? On the other hand, how could Rome disapprove of the Society's faithful continuation of the Catholic Church's two-thousand year Tradition without radically discrediting its own last claim to be Catholic? Hence, ever since the Society emerged into public view in the mid-1970's, ecumenical Rome has been on the horns of a dilemma: it cannot approve, and it cannot get away with disapproving.

Of course the dilemma is of Rome's own making. Jesus Christ says, "I am the Way, the Truth, and the Life." Today's ecumenism says (in actions if not in words), "All religions are good, there is no absolute Truth." Hence the ecumenical servant of Christ is a walking contradiction, resolvable only by his abandoning either of this false ecumenism or of Christ.

However, Rome, especially with the support of the vile media, could live with the dilemma, so long as the Archbishop and his Society quietly puttered on towards their extinction with the passage of time. So long as the Archbishop was mortal, delaying tactics kept Rome in the driving seat. Hence Rome's policy for eleven years, from 1976 to 1987, was one of masterly inaction.

But when the Archbishop threatened last June to consecrate bishops and so perpetuate the living testimony to the falsehood of this ecumenism, then Rome's dilemma rapidly became acutely uncomfortable. For an unauthorized consecration of bishops calls, by Canon Law, for excommunication. Now this forces the issue. For if Rome excommunicates, Rome discredits not only its Catholicism, but even its ecumenism, for it will be disowning its very own! On the other hand if it fails to excommunicate, it discredits not only its own discipline and law, by tolerating their flagrant violation, but, again, even its own ecumenism, by leaving unpunished such a flagrant anti-ecumenist!

Hence the rapidly reopened dialogue in July of last year, and a flurry of activity, and some until then unheard of concessions on the part; of Rome, to cut the Archbishop off at the pass, and prevent him from forcing the issue to the point of excommunication. Hence Cardinal Gagnon's visitation, resulting in a report which may be spiked but is bound to leak out, documenting objectively the fruitfulness of Catholic Tradition, and the injustice of its prolonged oppression.

Thus the threat to consecrate produced this report and put the Archbishop in the driver's seat, which is where he belongs, as long as he serves the Truth and Rome does not. Hence he was right to threaten to consecrate, he will be right to go on threatening (the latest projected date is for the end of June), and he will be right eventually to consecrate. In the Catholic Church, the Truth cannot permanently lose, and lies can only temporarily win. Thus Cardinal Oddi said in private last November that in a few years' time the post-conciliar "Church" will have rotted completely away. Our Lord built His Church well. Only, we have to be courageous and to take an unflinching stand on His Truth. Pray for an end to the Holy Father's misguided ecumenism, and for no end to Archbishop Lefebvre's courage!

If everything goes according to plan, the seminary will move out to Minnesota towards the end of June, be-

The Ridgefield Letters

ginning of July. At that time Fr. Jean-Luc Lafitte with one other Society priest will move into Ridgefield and begin operating it as the Society's long-needed full-time retreat house. Notice however that Fr. Lafitte is making no plans yet for the shorter three-day retreats. This is mainly because he is convinced that the five-day retreats yield much better fruits. We only hope this schedule reaches you in time for you to be able to plan your vacation time around taking off the full five or six days.

Since the settlement of the Society's litigation last August, the Society is now in complete and tranquil possession of the properties in Ridgefield, Connecticut and Armada, Michigan. In a year's time it recovers clear possession of another two valuable properties, the churches in Detroit and Minneapolis. Of the remaining nine properties in litigation, the breakaway priests recover the one most important to them, at Oyster Bay Cove on Long Island, only by having to pay the Society $350,000 plus interest on a mortgage over five years; for the church building in Norfolk, Virginia, they have had to pay $25,000. The remaining seven properties out of the thirteen, generally rather less valuable, are theirs.

They have also been forced by the settlement (they would say, they have "consented") to stop using the name of the "Society of St. Pius X," which is why a sign has come down in front of the Society's former building in Rochester, New York. The settlement further stipulates: "In the event that any of those (the break-away priests') corporations choose to adopt the name "St. Pius V" or "St. Pius I," then those corporations shall, for 18 months from the date of this settlement, include a statement in any printed matter which incorporates that name, that the organization is not affiliated with Archbishop Lefebvre's Society of St. Pius X." Now these priests have announced their intention to use the title of "Society of St. Pius V," so in the attempt to prevent confusion in

—253—

people's minds, we would be grateful to know of any instances where they use this title without making clear – as they consented to do – that their "loose association" of St. Pius V has nothing to do with the Society of St. Pius X.

Poor Catholics! What confusion! But truth will win out. In St. Augustine's memorable words, quoted by the Council of Trent, "God never abandons those who have not first abandoned Him." Not all the confusion in the world, nor all the dissension or distraction or division ever stirred up by the devil, can keep away from the true God a soul intent upon making its way to Him. May cleaving to Him be our firm prayer and intent through the coming holy season of Lent.

Weak Arguments Against the Consecrations

WE MAY NOT and must not apologize for coming back on the question of the imminent consecration of bishops by Archbishop Lefebvre, because it is – with good reason – a question now causing concern to many Catholics who truly love their Church.

For instance just recently a nationwide newsletter launched to defend the Tridentine Mass, and a reputable semi-monthly conservative Catholic paper, both published an open letter addressed by a distinguished French Dominican priest, Fr. Bruckberger, to Archbishop Lefebvre, begging him not to go ahead with these consecrations. Similarly several readers of this letter sent us a copy of an article by Fr. Robert Graham from the February issue of the Knights of Columbus magazine, *Columbia*, declaring that the Archbishop is on the brink of schism with this intention to consecrate.

The latest news to hand of the state of negotiations between Rome and the Archbishop or the Society, is that Cardinal Gagnon has seen the Pope, and the Pope has handed over the question to Cardinal Ratzinger, who has in turn handed it over to canon lawyers for study of the canonical problems involved.

Like the rest of us, the Archbishop himself seems to waver between hope that Rome will do what is right by Tradition ("charity hopeth all things"), and the expectation that it will not ("charity endureth all things," or prepareth to endure them!). Thus at the end of his February 3 interview with the French newspaper *Figaro*, reprinted on the sheet enclosed, the Archbishop was hopeful, but when he wrote to recommend for publication the "brief but excellent" study of Fr. Pozzera, here enclosed on the same sheet, he said, "We must not be under any illusions. The Vatican remains more than ever an instrument of destruction of the Faith. How can we cohabit with the disciples of the Father of Lies? We need a miracle." And the Society priest in Italy closest to what is going on in the Vatican has written to me, "we need not one miracle but several miracles." So of course we continue to pray, sincerely hoping for the best but prepared for the worst.

Meanwhile let us look at the arguments of Fathers Bruckberger and Graham, firstly Fr. Graham.

Interestingly, the whole first half of his one-page article is in defense of Rome's having sent Cardinal Gagnon at all to make a visitation of the Society! As though the grave accusation against Rome was not that it is deserting Tradition, but that it is even still talking to Tradition! What a perspective!

Fr. Graham goes on correctly to say that the issue at stake is not just the Tridentine Mass, nor even the canonical status of the "wild-cat" Society – has Fr. Graham ever read the documentation in Michael Davies' *Apologia pro Marcel Lefebvre* of the perfectly canonical erection and un-canonical, Soviet-style, "dissolution" of the Society? But let that question pass. He correctly situates the heart of the problem as doctrinal: the Archbishop's repeated and specific accusations that Vatican II, and subsequent events in the line of Vatican II, represent a "great betrayal of Catholic teaching."

And what does Fr. Graham answer to these accusations? Not one single word! He recognizes that Archbishop Lefebvre is more than willing to specify his accusations, but for himself he merely lists the heads of accusation, declines absolutely to go into them, and concludes that the Archbishop is threatening "grim and tragic" prospects of schism.

Fr. Graham has not one single argument! Now since when was Catholic truth short of arguments against real heretics and schismatics? When ever did the true Church fail to refute the fallacies and sophistries of her enemies'? Now for Fr. Graham, discretion here may be the better part of valor, but his declining to argue what he recognizes as the issue is not a sign that he is on the side of the truth. He is a Jesuit in good standing with the Society of Jesus. To understand what has happened to the once great Society of Jesus read Malachi Martin's invaluable *The Jesuits and the Betrayal of the Roman Catholic Church*, now available in paperback,

Fr. Bruckberger for his part is a venerable French Dominican in his eighties. He begins his plea to the Archbishop not to consecrate by laying out his credentials as – he says – one of the Archbishop's most valiant defenders in his resistance to the faithless destruction of Catholicism in the wake of Vatican II. He even calls the Archbishop "a truly great bishop."

But then he goes on, "Today, I am assured that on all those points where he conducts a legitimate battle, Msgr. Lefebvre has received from the Vatican the most definite and formal assurances. But in the meantime his original claims have been extended, even displaced. It seems that he has even reached the point of contesting the legitimacy of John Paul II as Pope."

Richard N. Williamson

In plain American, the Archbishop is "upping the ante." But who cannot see that whereas ten years ago, to defend the Faith, the Archbishop at 72 might have contented himself with asking for the Tridentine liturgical books and canonical standing for the Society, its seminaries and himself, today on the contrary, at age 82 the same defense of the same Faith requires that he insist upon obtaining in addition bishops for Tradition, properly shielded from all modernist enemies? Would Fr. Bruckberger say it was the Archbishop's fault that in these ten years not one other "truly great bishop" (except maybe the equally aged Msgr. Castro de Mayer) has stepped forward to offer to ordain the priests who will guarantee Tradition? In which case who is responsible for the "upping of the ante?" If today the Archbishop settled for a Traditional liturgy and priests but with no bishops of their own shielded from modernism, would he not, with his own departure from this life drawing normally so close, be abandoning into the hands of its enemies the Tradition Fr. Bruckberger so praises him for having defended?

Fr. Bruckberger then compares at length the Archbishop's resistance to Rome and to the Pope with that of the heretical Jansenists and their leader, Arnauld, in 17th century France. However, while Fr. Bruckberger expresses much pious and entirely Catholic feeling in love of the Church, against schism and for the Pope, the only argument he has for comparing the Archbishop to the heretical Jansenist is both men's unyieldingness and conviction of being right! Dear Fr. Bruckberger, was St. Athanasius right or wrong to be unyielding in his resistance to Pope Liberius? The question is not simply whether a churchman's stand is unyielding, but what he is taking his stand on. Fr. Bruckberger may be a friend while Fr. Graham would pass for a foe of the Archbishop, but both alike fail to tackle the central issue of doctrine.

There is in fact no comparison between the heretic stubbornly resisting orthodox Popes, and the Archbishop faithfully resisting liberal Popes (however well intentioned these may be).

A Catholic is a Catholic not by nationality, color of skin, sex or class, but by his faith, by what he believes in, and what he believes in is certain definite doctrines. Did or did not the man Jesus Christ rise from the dead? Is He or is He not God as well as man? Do I or do I not have a moral right to practice any other religion than the one He instituted? Do or do not the recent Popes believe in a gravely erroneous doctrine of religious liberty, apt wholly to undermine, if they could be undermined, the very foundations of the Catholic Church?

The Archbishop's stand in defense of the Catholic Faith is first and foremost doctrinal, as Fr. Graham has the intelligence to realize. As for the argument of schism, read Fr. Pozzera's text enclosed. When your neighbor's house is burning down, you need not ask his permission to walk across his lawn with a fire hose! When the captain of the liner has in a fit of madness plunged the ship into darkness, you do not need his permission to switch on the emergency lighting system, nor to keep it switched on until he comes to his senses. Such permission is implicit in the nature of the liner, in the absolute needs of thousands of passengers and in the very functions of the captaincy itself. And with the Archbishop now aged 82, bishops that Tradition can rely on are becoming absolutely necessary to keep the emergency lighting system of the SSPX switched on in the liner of the Church.

Since 1976, the Church's situation has grown so much worse that many good priests who at that time contested the Archbishop's continuing to ordain Society priests in "defiance" of Rome, now recognize he was right. Give the situation just a little longer to evolve on its present course, and many good priests like Fr. Bruckberger who now contest his consecrating bishops will soon be recognizing that he was right. It is not the Archbishop who is "upping the ante!"

God love you readers of this letter, because many of you, as I know from your letters, see clearly the need for these consecrations. Not that you rejoice in defying Rome, nor that you have any intention of quitting the Church, but that needs of His Church which God has hidden from the wise Dominicans and prudent Jesuits, he has revealed to His little ones, "Yea, Father, for so it hath seemed good in thy sight." (Lk. 10: 21) Then in the months to come fear not, and let not your hearts be troubled within you, but remember to sift argument from emotion, truth from slogans, Catholic doctrine from mere abuse.

Your faithful support of the Truth is taking concrete form in the renovation of the seminary's new home in Winona, Minnesota. Everything indicates it is going to be a magnificent facility, ready soon at very reasonable cost. However the bills for the renovation are coming in, and we would like some help. We presently owe $100,000 to friends, and we will soon owe more for the renovations to be finished in the next few months. Do not put yourselves into debt, but can you help us out of it? Thanks always every one of you that contributes regularly.

All is well at the seminary. Fr. Bourmaud has just finished recording with seminarians another musical tape. It will be called *Reign Jesus and Mary*. Pray that between now and the summer Bernard Janzen and I succeed in getting out a long-projected flyer on obedience, and a tape on the new consecrations.

And pray through March, month of St. Joseph, to this great Patriarch, and Patron of the Church. It was only because he was so virtuous that he underwent such agony of mind and heart on seeing that Mary was pregnant with a child not his (Mt. 1: 18–25). Had he cared less either about God's Law or about Mary, he would have had no such problem. Because he cared about both, he underwent anguish until God in His good time revealed to him the solution. Likewise we and the Archbishop would have no problem if we cared little either for the survival of Tradition or for belonging to the Church. If then to form St. Joseph for the role of father to Jesus, God let him go through agony, why should not we also have to undergo some perplexity and distress? God knows what He is forming us for, such a storm as . . . let us be patient and pray to St. Joseph.

God bless you and love you.

NO. 60 | APRIL 2, 1988

The Story of Dorothy

GOD IN HIS boundless goodness is giving us another spring. Heedless of that goodness, most men continue on their wicked way. Let me for Eastertide tell you a tale of a soul, much as it was told to me.

Dorothy died in June 1987, on the Feast of Corpus Christi. She was an unusual lady that one does not see too many of.

Born of German parents 89 years ago in the United States, she never married, taking care of her parents on the farm in their later years. She then worked in a furniture factory, finishing by hand the fine points of furniture that the machines do not do. A daily communicant, she would go to Mass before going to work, and if she could not make the early Mass, she would in those days fast all day at work so as to be able to receive Communion in the evening.

She spent little on herself, wearing for the most part used clothes so that she could save, and help educate priests, and build mission chapels and convents. Nobody knows how much she helped all over, except that here and there she let things slip out. When after Vatican II things started to go downhill, she became worried, and would only support priests and causes that

The Ridgefield Letters

never changed from the old ways. She would drive far to attend the Latin Masses.

Before she came here a niece of hers named Lisa was injured as a child and developed seizures. The motor-part of her brain was also hurt so that she walked only with a walker, very poorly, and she had to be dressed and cared for in every way. Lisa was then put in an institution by her parents, where she got worse.

When Dorothy was 62, she decided to retire, to take Lisa out of the institution and care for her. She always took Lisa along to Mass and to Holy Hours in the afternoon, and as a decent Mass became harder and harder to find, she finally moved here. This was because she learned of an 85 year old woman needing someone to take care of her as she was poorly. So in return for room and board and a little salary, at the age of 74, Dorothy began looking after this old woman and Lisa in an over 100 year old house with no modern conveniences, bad plumbing, just the old dish-pan methods, like the old-timers used to live on the farms. The L.P. gas was not enough to heat the house, so Dora cut and stacked cords of wood to prepare for winter, mowed and fixed leaks in the roof.

Then she was told she did not belong at Mass in the local church because she refused to leave her pew to shake hands for the sign of peace, especially during the week, when so few were at Mass that she would have had to walk across the church to do so. Also the priest changed the locks so that she could not make her Holy Hours, usually from two to four or five o'clock in the afternoon. He would not give her a key, telling her that only important people could have keys. So she left.

Now the nearest center with a regular Sunday Latin Mass was two hours away. For a year she drove the four hours each Sunday, but then it became too much for her, so she began attending the Latin Mass of a retired priest in a private chapel close to home. She had been told she could not attend the Mass of this priest who had been excommunicated for letting himself be made a bishop by the Palmar de Troya group, although he had seen the light and left them when Clemente made himself "Pope" upon Paul VI's death. But Dorothy was by now in her 80's so she finally had to give in. Also she could make her daily Holy Hours with Lisa. She had a great devotion to the Blessed Sacrament, and would read in a loud whisper all the prayers and the Rosary, so that her niece could mentally follow as she could not read. There were so many prayers she said, and when she got home she would say some more.

She lived poorly, mending by hand her clothes, bought only from second-hand stores or given to her and her niece. She looked thin and poor and out of style so all thought she was very poor. They also ate poorly after the old lady she took care of died. The renter went on renting the house to Dorothy because as everyone said at the time, in that condition it could not be rented to anyone else. She chose to stay because it was out of the way, quiet, and the Latin Mass, getting by 1979 pretty impossible to find, was close by. She only had one good eye to drive with.

When she herself got cancer and was almost sure her one good eye would go blind, which it did for three good months, she arranged for her funeral, gave the rest of her money to good Traditional causes, rather than let the State or her relatives have it, and in November of 1986 went with her niece into a nursing home. For years she had prayed that her niece would be cured so that she could care for herself, or that God would take both of them at once. Since there was a 40-year age difference, most of us felt that would hardly happen unless they got killed in an accident together.

In the nursing home they continued to pray together and a Traditional priest was able to bring them Holy Communion each week. Then due to government cutbacks the niece could not stay with Dorothy and had to be moved to a private home which most likely was less expensive. Lisa liked it, but the woman running it was Protestant, so Lisa missed someone praying with her. Her mother, still alive, did not want Lisa home, but gave instructions to the Protestant that the Traditional priest must not be allowed to come and give her the sacraments, only a Novus Ordo priest could come, which he did once a month. This troubled Dorothy. She must have prayed even harder. Lisa could not speak well, so could not defend herself against these arrangements.

Dorothy still had two younger sisters living, who old as they were, were so against Dorothy giving her money away to Traditional groups and attending the Latin Mass that they tried to convince her that she was out of the Church, and that she sinned by giving money to Traditionalists and following them. Dorothy said her sisters were both well off, but they were angry because they felt she should have left to them whatever she had left over. It was by spending so little on herself that she saved up to send money each month to help others, when she could have rented a better place to live in. Things got very bitter between her and her relatives. They blamed her friends for convincing her to give her money away like that. The truth is that the rest of us were hardly aware what she was doing until she asked our help to send out her money according to her wishes, as she was too tired herself. She said her relatives were too worldly and nagged her as though she did not know a thing.

The end did not seem far off when for a week she was unable to eat or swallow. Her weight was down to 80 pounds. On the contrary Lisa was doing well, had gained a little weight and looked better than ever. Then on June 18 Lisa had a seizure, which was not uncommon, but it was followed by two massive heart attacks, and within 20 minutes she was dead. We were all shocked that she went so suddenly, but not Dorothy as she had prayed for that. When we told her, she just said quietly, "Now I can go," and she seemed relieved that her prayers had been answered.

Ever since she had been unable to read the calendar herself, she had been asking us when the next feast day was coming, because she said she was going to die on a big Church feast day. Two days after Lisa's death she died in her sleep, on the Feast of Corpus Christi. Her niece can never have committed a serious sin in her life, being brain-damaged from the age of five, so we could just see her waiting for Dorothy to come.

The Novus Ordo priest where Dorothy came from objected to burying her from church on the grounds that she had left the Church, but apparently the bishop gave a dispensation for her burial when he was told that a Novus Ordo priest had visited her and she had renounced the other Mass, which was not true. In any case we had a Latin Funeral Mass for her on the day of her burial. She had her wish.

She had inherited nothing and worked for all she had. She was a hard worker. People marveled how she could do what she did at her age. She went without meat three times a week most of her life. Her prayers must have been pleasing to God for nobody ever thought her niece would go before her. When she entered the nursing home, the doctors had given her two to three months to live, but she lasted until the Feast of the Blessed Sacrament before whom she had spent so many hours all her life, making hours of reparation.

Dear friends and benefactors, the world is plunging to its ruin and the Church into chaos all around us (no news, incidentally, from Rome, concerning the Society), but in all this suicidal frenzy there is nothing that can stop us, if we wish, from loving God and saving our souls. Dorothy simply prayed, and did her duty, and more, day by day, as God gave her to do it.

May the beauties of spring be for you all a small image of the beauty of the risen Christ, triumphant over the world, the flesh, and the devil!

NO. 61 | MAY 1, 1988

The Consecration of Russia

AT THE TIME of writing, still no news from Rome on the state of negotiations between the Vatican and the SSPX over the re-establishing of official recognition of the Society's standing within the Church. From Society headquarters in Switzerland we learned in mid-April of the appearance of a glimmer of a possible solution, but above all we were asked to pray.

For indeed, independently of the Society, great events are in gestation. I hope many of you receive the excellent quarterly magazine, *The Fatima Crusader*. In its latest issue, an excerpt is quoted from a prophetic dream of St. John Bosco in 1873, including the sentence, "before two full moons shall have shone in the month of flowers, the rainbow of peace shall appear on the earth." Interestingly, a friend of ours planning to be in Fatima for this May 13 learned from his travel agent that the Holy Father might be there on the same day. And to another friend recently meeting Cardinal O'Connor of New York and asking him if he would ask the Holy Father to consecrate Russia to the Immaculate Heart of Mary, the Cardinal replied, "I am sure he will do it soon." Now "the month of flowers" is normally May, and May of this year has two full moons, on the 2nd and

31st, an occurrence which will not happen again until well into the 21st century, in other words well beyond the 19__ deadline set for the renewal of the Papacy and the Church by St. John Bosco in another famous vision. Could then this month, May 1988, be the month of the long-awaited and absolutely necessary Consecration of Russia by the Pope to the Immaculate Heart of Mary? Could this consecration be Don Bosco's "rainbow of peace?" Speculation.

God knows. We do not need to know: "It is not for you to know the times or moments which the Father hath put in his own power," said Our Lord (Acts 1: 7). However, He did deign to tell Sister Lucy in 1931 that the Consecration, though very late, would at last be done, and so to it apply the words of Hamlet concerning the special providence in the fall of a sparrow: "If it be now, 'tis not to come; if it be not to come, it will be now; if it be not now, yet it will come: the readiness is all." And so these tantalizing bits of prophecy bring us back exactly where Our Lord wishes us to be brought back – "Watch and pray" – the readiness is all.

It is interesting to note that the Mother of God did not ask the Pope to perform this Consecration of Russia in union with the <u>Mass-centers</u>, but in union with the <u>bishops</u> of the world. Now thanks be to God for the Catholic Faith of those of us who cling to the true Mass, and for the existence of these centers from which the true Mass will be poured back into the main body of the Church. Nevertheless the bishops remain the fulcrum of Jesus Christ's Church, however undermined or contaminated with modernism He gave His Mother to foresee they would do, by the time it would be too "late." This is why Archbishop Lefebvre is unquestionably right to have been striving all these years to bring back to Tradition the Cardinals, Archbishops and Bishops in Rome, however hopeless the task may have seemed.

The Ridgefield Letters

This is also a major reason why the seminary may well have been right to participate in a Marian Year Procession and Benediction on December 6 last year in the nearby archdiocese of Hartford. The decision to participate was mine. It has just been violently attacked in a bulletin known to a few of you. I would not stake my eternal salvation on the rightness of decision, but interesting questions are raised which concern all of us striving to keep the Faith, so let me describe the event and lay out some of the arguments:

The unofficial invitation to the seminary to participate came to me from a member of the Waterbury clergy who was one of the organizers of this one-off Marian Year ceremony. The official program given us beforehand enabled us to foresee a minimal risk of exposure to Novus Ordo modernism. After all, what clergy that disregards the Holy Eucharist and the Madonna will organize a grand-scale Rosary, Sermon and Benediction, preceded by Marian Procession? And so it turned out. The only non-traditional feature I can now remember was introduction of women into the sanctuary (where there was no Novus Ordo table in view, only the beautiful and unvandalized high altar), to lead in various languages the decades of the Rosary. Regrettable, but hardly infectious!

On the positive side, it was an inspiring and beautiful occasion; a tribute to the Faith of the clergy of Waterbury; a demonstration of the Catholic Church's unrivalled power for good over the people; an evocation of what the Church in America once was in a multi-national Catholic city like Waterbury, and proof of what the Church in America could again so easily be, if only the clergy would always give such a lead! For seminarians, many lessons in few hours!

Imagine the scene: the long village green of downtown Waterbury, on a crisp and clear December evening, where the stars in the cold night-sky are imitated closer at hand by the township's Christmas decorations flecking the canopy of trees over the green. From the basement of the grand Church of the Immaculate Conception giving directly onto the green there slowly emerges, led by a dozen national flags, a procession of thousands of Catholics carrying candles, singing, and praying, before and behind a float of the Madonna held shoulder-high, on which she is picked out by torch-light amidst a bank of flowers. Slowly the procession makes its way round the green, to be engulfed again in the body of the church.

Now Catholics from Catholic parts of the world may be used to such a spectacle, but, for me, such a procession in the heart of an average sin-sodden modern city was a marvel. Amidst all the pornography and abortions, thousands of humble folk for a few hours exchanging the misery of their television set for the tranquil but animated happiness of honoring the Blessed Virgin Mother of God! What a prospect of joy for the angels in heaven! What balm and relief for the ravaged Mother's Heart! What a flow of graces of spiritual warmth, faith and hope from her divine Son for so many of her children, especially her priests! We had come to honor and love her. I can hardly believe she was unhappy that we were there.

But here come the arguments. We should not have taken part because the procession was organized by the Conciliar Church? Good for the Conciliar Church to have organized such a procession! Because we were co-operating with clergy who daily defile holy places? Some defilement, such a procession! Because we were adoring a doubtfully consecrated host? Find me a modernist rite of Benediction, or even a modernist who puts on Benediction! Because we were practicing a false ecumenism? The seminarians were edified by these Catholic people, and the people and the clergy were much edified by seeing our old-fashioned seminarians. Because it was a precedent for accepting the Novus Ordo Mass? Benediction is not Mass, and one swallow does not make a summer! Because this fraternizing with the Novus Ordo betrayed the back-and forth complicated inconsistency typical of the zig-zagging Archbishop Lefebvre and his unprincipled SSPX? Ask Rome whether the Archbishop is inconsistent! Ask Cardinal Ratzinger whether the Archbishop zig-zags!

These poor enemies of the Archbishop (I do not mean the modernists, but priests like the writer of the bulletin who betray their father in the priesthood and then do not even have the grace to leave him alone) – what they cannot grasp is that it is Rome which zig-zags and not the Archbishop, because whereas the Archbishop is balancing attachment to Peter's Rome and attachment to the true Faith which complement one another, today's Rome is oscillating between love of Liberalism and fidelity to Catholicism which contradict one another.

As for the bulletin writer's qualifications to tell what is Catholic, judge for yourselves: He is founding his own Religious Congregation of nuns, all by himself, answering to no one, and without anyone else's control! For he himself has such control over his some twenty "nuns" that I am told only one girl got into his "convent" and succeeded in getting out again. It would be funny if it was not becoming tragic. When, only recently, thoroughly alarmed parents succeeded in getting a daughter of theirs out for a while who had for the last seven months been on the tranquillizer Librax (Clindex), such was his concern that he sent flying seven-hundred miles after her the "Sister Superior" who clamped onto their daughter and made it clear to the parents that if they wished to separate her from their daughter, they would have to physically assault her. And she took their daughter back to the "convent." Such tactics sure minimize the loss of "vocations," but they are about as Catholic as Dr. Jim Jones of Jonestown, Guyana. Parents, if ever a girl of yours expresses an interest in joining the *Daughters of Mary*, I advise you to learn rapidly how kids have to be de-programmed that get caught up in the Moonies. I have for some time been convinced that this poor man has lost his mental grip on reality, but he sure has some people hornswoggled! Pray for him.

Patience. Not everyone is losing their grip. Dr. Malachi Martin, ex-Jesuit, and world-renowned Catholic writer, authorizes me to announce that, depending on which way events turn he will write a comprehensive article on the forthcoming consecration of Society bishops, to show that in no case will the Archbishop be going into schism, rather he might be committing a mortal sin if he did not consecrate, given the absolute need for certainly valid priests and Masses.

Remember Our Lady during her "wonder-beautiful" month of May. The perversity of men makes her infinitely sad but it does not confuse her. She prays, and she remains deeply in peace.

With thanks for your ongoing generosity, much needed for the renovations in Winona, and with all good wishes in Our Lord.

NO. 62 | JUNE 1, 1988

Will Rome Approve of the Consecrations?

THIS JUNE PROMISES to be some month! June 30 is the fateful day for the consecration of Society bishops at Ecône in Switzerland, and at the time of writing it is still unresolved between Rome and the Society whether these consecrations will have Rome's official approval or not.

The reports appearing in the press on the state of the negotiations are distinctly confused. Early in May the *Philadelphia Enquirer* for instance reported that Archbishop Lefebvre and Cardinal Ratzinger had signed an agreement on May 5. In the middle of May, the Archbishop confirmed on a radio program in Europe that he had indeed signed an agreement, but he said there were certain points still to be cleared up, while on May 23 a Vatican spokesman said that no "definitive agreement" had been reached, but as soon as one was reached, it would be announced (*National Catholic Register*, June 5).

On June 1, a Californian friend told me "from a highly reliable priestly source" that a final accord was reached on May 24, whereby the SSPX was to be recognized, the Archbishop's suspension was to be lifted and Rome was

—273—

to grant permission for one bishop to be consecrated for the Society on August 15. However, no such accord has, between May 24 and the time of writing, been officially announced, either by the Society or by Rome, so I think we must assume there are still "points to be cleared up," whatever they may be.

At this point it is much more important to pray than to be listening for the latest rumor, because a crucial moment in Church history has arrived: will the Church authorities, by approving the Society's bishops, take the decisive step back to Catholic Tradition without which – as we well know, but they do not – the Catholic Church cannot survive?

We may hope that Rome will finally approve the consecrations. The Pope's letter of April 3 to Cardinal Ratzinger in which he pressed for an understanding to be reached, was made public, maybe to anticipate opposition from the Liberals to any such understanding. Negotiations must have begun soon after for an agreement to have been signed on May 5, which is significantly the Feast Day of one of the greatest heroes of Catholic Tradition, Pope St. Pius V.

Now, that common agreement seems not to have been final, but an impetus and momentum towards agreement seem to have been generated, which can only help. For instance, if the accord of May 5 (and of May 24?) contained terms granting approval to the Society and the Archbishop, how could Rome now convincingly disapprove of them? Any such terms once signed by Rome represent a concession to the truth which Rome can with difficulty take back.

Nor may Rome wish to take them back. Opening his arms wide to all creeds on the horizon, the Holy Father may sincerely wish that Archbishop Lefebvre be not excluded from his pluralist embrace. Such is the logic of his ecumenism. Similarly, that Luther's exclusion from the Church was the Catholics' fault is a lie, but if this Pope by for instance his official visit to the Lutherans in Rome indicates he has any sympathy for such untruths, may he not regard himself as bound to avoid excluding Archbishop Lefebvre from the Catholic Church? The logical Liberal knows that he must crush the truth as being his only real adversary, but the well-meaning Liberal will embrace even truth. Such an attitude certainly fits the Pope's letter of April 8, and is grounds for hope that he will insist on overriding what looks to him like minor obstacles in order to avoid what looks to him like a major threat of schism.

For your own part, I am sure that a large number of you would welcome an agreement with immense relief. Whatever ill we may have to say of Rome, nevertheless which of us as Roman Catholics wishes to go through even the mere appearance of being cut off from it? However, none of us can be wishing for an agreement at absolutely any price. There would be a price too high to pay – the placing in peril of Catholic Tradition.

Say what you will about the twilight of semi-approval, semi-disapproval in which the SSPX and the Tridentine Mass have officially existed for the last several years (rather more disapproval than approval, to put it mildly!), you have to admit that the corresponding independence from control by the Liberals has enabled the Catholic Mass and priesthood to be preserved true to their nature. Nay, the faith of many Catholics, including probably our own, has been so strengthened and purified by this trial, that were God to decide the trial must be extended and even intensified by a failure of these present negotiations, I am sure most of us would not change course but would simply ask God for the grace of continued endurance, without bitterness or sectarianism.

So our independence from the modernists, even if it has meant our apparent detachment from the official

Church, has not been the worst of evils. On the contrary an agreement failing to safeguard Tradition would certainly be the worst of evils. For why have we been enduring and battling all these years, except to preserve the essentials of Jesus Christ's one true Church? What do we have to offer the official Church except those essentials? What use would we be to the official Church without those essentials? What use would it be to them to reabsorb us if they do not at the same time reabsorb Tradition? Such a dissolution of our opposition may precisely be the Modernists' dream, some would even say it is Rome's purpose in these negotiations, but be that as it may, we at least know that our abandoning Tradition would be their disaster.

Hence, dearly as we ourselves might long for an end to our status as outcasts from Rome, we cannot long for an agreement at any price. To take one example: if it is true that around May 24, Rome agreed to approve the consecration of one bishop for the Society, that is a great concession, but would one be really enough, to safeguard Tradition? Could not one alone slip from the Truth, as many good men have done? Or could not one alone easily be made to meet with an "accident?" Whereas to arrange three "accidents" would be rather less convincing...

Without any doubt, much the best judge of what agreement will or will not sufficiently safeguard Tradition and the Faith is, by his past record, Archbishop Lefebvre. How many times over the last thirteen years, since the going began to get tough in 1975, have we not been tempted to wish that he would not take the tough decision to climb still craggier heights? Yet each time we followed him, were we not delighted to find ourselves emerging into another sunny Catholic upland, where our children for instance could breathe clean Catholic air? Were he a modern leader, one of the many who follow their followers, he would have taken a rest from climbing long ago, to regain his peace and good standing within the official Church. Instead he has taken the heroic decisions, and the heroic decisions have been right. In conclusion, it is for the sake of the entire Catholic Church that we must now close ranks behind Archbishop Lefebvre in the hour of what may be his greatest trial. He has never failed us yet. Why should he now?

This June is also the month of the seminary's move to the Midwest. On the morning of June 21 there will be a High Mass here for the Feast of St. Aloysius Gonzaga, Patron Saint of seminarians, at 10 a.m., after which there will be a farewell lunch party, outside or beneath the new chapel. Bring your own dish. You are all invited and welcome. Besides bidding farewell to the seminarians, you will be able to admire the resplendent new white polyvinyl cladding of the new chapel. Faced with alternatives of either pulling down the entire structure and certainly losing well over half a million dollars, or laying out another $40,000 to shield the exterior, the Society has chosen the latter course. We have had to borrow from the bank to do it, but at least now what has been already spent is protected, and we retain the option of an eventual use of the building. If there was an agreement with Rome, who knows how soon the church might be filled?

Then on June 22 one truck should be enough to move to Winona what worldly goods the seminary will be taking with it. In fact we are leaving behind us everything that St. Ignatius Retreat House will need to start into immediate operation in July, because it makes little sense to pay to move things to the Midwest and have to replace them in the East instead of simply buying them (or often being given them) in the Midwest. However, there are still serious expenses involved in our westward migration, so I do beg of you to be as generous as ever with your monthly gifts. For several months now the

Richard N. Williamson

seminary has been running two establishments – we are presently running on empty! Thank you in advance!

In Winona, the renovations are mostly done, but voluntary workers alongside the seminarians will be very welcome throughout the summer. The renovations have been costly, and to complete them without interruption we have had to borrow. Patience. There are no ordinations at Ridgefield this summer, but two former seminarians of Ridgefield, Rev. Mr. Peter Lemay of Rhode Island and Rev. Mr. James Doran of Michigan, are due to be ordained priests by Archbishop Lefebvre in Ecône on June 29, and they will both be serving you soon, in Idaho and Kansas unless plans change. In addition the Society is planning in August to import into the United States one or two newly ordained priests from abroad. America is being looked after, as best the Society can. The harvest will come.

A note for priests: at Ridgefield there is a Priest's Retreat from the evening of Monday, July 18, to midday Friday, July 22. All priests are welcome (except to celebrate here the Novus Ordo Liturgy). Come under a pseudonym if you like. No questions asked. Similarly any and all priests are welcome to visit the seminary in Winona, from July onwards, and to stay overnight, or several days. No questions! Just answers! Lastly we are enclosing the text of the music on the seminary's latest tape, *Reign Jesus and Mary*. Order from Ridgefield or from Winona. And during June, beg the Sacred Heart to give light and strength to one great Archbishop . . .

INDEX

A

abortion, 48–50
absolute Truth, 251
Adler, Manfred, 159
adultery, 164
Africa, 217
Agenzia Adista, 157
Ahern, Daniel, 26
AIDS, 216
American Carmel, 121
Amerika, 199
The Angelus, 3–4, 18, 34–35, 70, 105, 185
Anglicanism, 134
Anglicans, 157
Antichrist, 129, 176, 194, 196, 197, 212
The Antichrist (Fr. Miceli), 25
anti-modernism, 16, 56, 57
Apologia pro Marcel Lefebvre (Davies), 256
Argentina, Argentine
    SSPX's ordinations in, 123–127
Arian crisis, 129
Armada, 5, 34, 101, 253
Arnauld, 258
Arnold, Matthew, 148–149
Assisi Prayer Meeting 1986, 153, 173–177, 184, 231
    explanation of, 205–210
    false ecumenism, 161–164
    flyer on, 166–172
    Lefebvre on, 207
        letter to Pope, 173–174
attendance at Mass, 64–65, 197–198
Austin, Rev. Gerard, 56
authority, 2, 9, 25, 31, 78, 99, 100, 126
    of John Paul II, 100
    of Lefebvre, 78

B

Babinet, Fr., 124
Baggio, Cardinal, 44
baptism, 205, 207
Bea, Cardinal, 95

Becker, Judge, 153
Behind the News, 194
Benediction, 269, 270-271
Benedict XV, Pope, 223, 243
Benson, Ivor, 194-196
Bernard, Brother, 217
Berry, Fr. Eugene, 1-2
Bethlehem, 179-180
betrayals, 36-39
Bishop of Bishops, 136
Bishops' Conferences, 61-62
Bitzer, Fr. Gavin, 126
blasphemy, 163
    films, *see* films
Bloom, Allan, 245-247, 248
B'nai B'rith International, 95
Bolduc, Fr., 28
Boston, seminarians visit to, 215-216
Bourmaud, Fr. Dominique, 178, 211, 217
Brandler, Fr. Christopher, 89
Bravo, Cardinal, 154
Bruckberger, Fr., 255, 256, 257-258, 260
Bugnini, Msgr. Annibale, 96
Building Fund, 221-222, 227, 229

C

Calvi, Roberto, 44
Canada, 87
Candlemass of the Feast of the Presentation, 74
Canon Law, 241, 252, *see also* Church Law
    New Code, 22, 24-26, 96-97
        Archbishop Lefebvre on, 24-25, 98-100
        Canon 204 #1, 99
        Canon 336, 99
        Canon 493, 71
        Canon 653, 1
        Canon 681, 1
        Canon 844 #4, 99
        Canon 1055, 99
        Canon 2242, 71
        Canon 2341, 36
    Old Code, 36
Cardinal Mindszenty Foundation, 154
Carmelites
    nuns/sisters, 25, 35, 91
        of Phoenixville, Pennsylvania, 116, 238
Casaroli, Cardinal, 157, 240
cassock, 249

Catholic Church, 12-13, 15, 90, 196-197, *see also* Rome
    division and disorder within, 21-22
    Fifth Age of, 212-214
    gift of indefectibility, 129
    identity of, 206-207
    infallibility, 128-132
    Sixth Age of, 212, 213
    spiritual war, 118-119
    unity of, 163-164, 204
Catholic girls, *see also* girls; women
Catholic hierarchy, 12-13
Catholic Liberals, *see also* liberalism, liberals
Catholic Liturgy, *see* Liturgy
Catholic schools, 29
Catholic Tradition, *see* Tradition, Traditionalism
Cekada, Fr. Anthony, 1, 36
Central America, 223
Chalard, Fr. Du
    SSPX Consecration to Immaculate Heart, 65
chaos, 149
charismatics, 105, 157, 158
charity, 93, 163
Charlestown, 91
children-rope-bank parable, 161-162
Christendom, 200, 204, 212
Christian marriage, *see also* families; Holy Family; marriages
Christian Science, 216
Chrysler Corporation, 199
Churchill, Winston, 101
civil corporations, 13
clergy
    Waterbury clergy, 269-270
The Closing of the American Mind (Bloom), 245
collegiality doctrine, 95
Collins, Fr. Joseph, 2
Columbia
    mudslide in, 121
Communism, 67, 95, 154, 164, 192, 199-202
Conciliar Church, 13, 16, 96
    mentally stricken, 103-107
Conciliarism, Conciliarists, 15, 90
consent, 245-246
contraception, *see also* abortion
Cooper, Michigander Daniel, 190, 217
Coughlin, Fr. Charles E., 224
Council of Trent, 109
Counter-Reformation, 167
Cuomo, Mario, 49, 50, 51

D

Dalai Lama, 185
Dante Alighieri, 167
Daughters of Mary, 272
Davies, Michael, 106, 256
death, 139–141
de Castro Mayer, Bishop Antonio, 19, 22, 125, 126, 145, 169
      joint statement with Archbishop Lefebvre, 184–185
Decree on Ecumenism, 207
defectors, 36–39
Delaplace, Fr. Pierre, 7
de la Tour, Fr., 28, 34
de Mallerais, Bishop Bernard Tissier, 54
democracy, 245–246
De Smet, Fr., 46
Devil, 57
      century of, 30–32
de Vriendt, Fr. Dominique, 120
dialogue, 158
Die Freimaurer und der Vatikan, 159
disciplinary regulations, 25
dissident priests, 1–2, 13, 36–37, 36–39, 73, 77–78, 85, 112
divine law, 205, 216
Divini Redemptoris, 199–200
divorce, 246, *see also* families
doctrinal split, April 1983, 83–87, 227–228
doctrines, belief in, 259
Dolan, Fr. Daniel, 1, 36
Doran, Fr. James, 278
Dorothy, story of, 262–266

E

Ecumenical Council of Churches, 95
ecumenical prayer meeting at Assisi, *see* Assisi Prayer Meeting 1986
ecumenism, 21, 31, 43, 95, 96, 105–106, 110, 136, 144, 146, 158, 161–165, 166–167, 207, 251, 252, 274, *see also* religious liberty
Eddy, Mary Baker, 216
Emily, Fr. Jacques, 86–87
Encyclicals Seminar, 192, 213
English Catholic bishops
      and Rome, 134
Epinay, Fr. Pierre, 125
Episcopal Consecrations
      decision, 229–233
      ponderation, 215–219
Episcopal Manifesto, 19–20
European Episcopal Conferences, 134

"ex cathedra" infallibility, 128
Express, 73
extremism, extremists, 111

F

Fahey, Fr. Denis, 25
Faith in Crisis (audiotapes), 107, 212, 219
Faith's ebb and flow, 148–150
false ecumenism, 161–165, *see also* Assisi Prayer Meeting 1986; ecumenism
false religions, 105, 175–176, 185
families
        and liberalism, 243–248
The Fatima Crusader, 147, 267
Fatima, Portugal, 226, 267
Feast of the Immaculate Conception, 53, 60
females, *see* women
Ferraro, Geraldine (Mrs. Zaccaro), 48–49
Fifth Age of Catholic Church, 212–214
films, 116
Foley, Fr. Gregory, 89
foreign priests, 45–46
Forrest, Keith, 154
        and his wife, 93–94, 97
fortitude, 113
France, 240
freedom, *see also* liberalism, liberals
        of worship, 50
Freemasonry, Freemasons, 21–22, 90, 105, 192
free will, 208
fundamental novelty, 24

G

Gagnon, Cardinal Edouard, 76, 91, 119, 161, 174, 190–191
        visit to SSPX, 239–240
              Archbishop Lefebvre on, 240–241
              report to Rome on, 250–251
German Evangelical Church Council, 134
Germany
        Catholic bishops
              and Rome, 134
Gerspacher, Fr. Loren, 89
Gibbons, Judge, 153
God
        law of, 49–50
        obeying, *see* obedience
        Word of, 176

Goettler, Fr. Wolfgang, 7, 41
Gonzales, Fr. Alberto, 126
Gonzalez, Cardinal, 174
Graham, Fr. Robert, 255, 256–257, 259
Graham, Mrs., 154
Gratias, Deo, 204
gratitude, 40–42
Great Promise, 214
Groche, Fr., 124
Gurriri, Rev. John, 56

H

Hail Mary (film), protest against, 116
Herrick, Robert, 139
Hesson, Fr., 170
Hiss, Alger, 195
Hogan, Fr. Gerard, 103
Hogan, Fr. John, 26, 33
Hollis, Sir Roger, 195
Holy Family, 244, *see also* families
Holy Matrimony, 84, *see also* marriages
Holy Orders, 84
Holy See, 15, 66, 68, 71, 109–110, 157
Holy Week, 201–202
Holzhauser, Bartholomew, 212
Horton, Mrs., 154
Housman, A. E., 138, 140–141
human rights, 95, 164

I

I Accuse the Council, 114
Ignatian Spiritual Retreats, *see* Spiritual Exercises of St. Ignatius
Il Poema dell' Uomo-Dio (The Poem of the Man-God), 183–184
Immaculate Heart of Mary, 14, 213, 226
    International SSPX Consecration to, 52–54, 59, 60–63, 64, 66
immortality, 139–141
India, 217
Indianisation, 80
Indult of October 1984, 156
    sign of hope, 55–59
    weighing, 64–69
infallibility
    of the Church, 128–132
Interreligious World Prayer Meeting, Assisi, *see* Assisi Prayer Meeting 1986

J

Jansenists, 258
Janzen, Bernard, 209, 212, 260
Jenkins, Fr. William, 2, 36
The Jesuits and the Betrayal of the Roman Catholic Church (Martin), 223, 257
John Paul II, Pope, 9, 12, 30, 36, 45, 53, 62, 84, 96–97, 145, 161, 167, 185, 190, 204, 209, 213, 218
    appearing and speaking in a Protestant church, views about, 21
    befriending false religions, 146
    extraordinary authority, 100
    praise to Luther, 96
    visit to the Synagogue in Rome, 184
John Paul I, Pope, 44
Johnston, Emily, 170
John XXIII, Pope, 22, 99
Jones, Jim, 272
Joseph, Brother, 32

K

Keane, Fr. John J., 215
Kelly, Fr. Clarence, 1, 13, 14, 27, 28, 36
KGB, 157, 195
Koenig, Cardinal, 22

L

Lafitte, Fr. Jean-Luc, 223, 253
Laisney, Fr. Frantois, 34, 35, 88, 250
La Reja, 123–127
Lefebvre, Archbishop Marcel, 1–2, 9, 14, 34, 36, 41, 66–68, 71, 76, 79, 83–84, 250–251
    40th Jubilee of his episcopacy, 235
    80th birthday, 113–117
    accusation
        of schism, 255, 259, 272, 275
    accusations, 15–16
    appeal addressed to Cardinals in August, 174–175
    on Assisi International Prayer Meeting, 207
        letter to Pope concerning, 173–174
    authority of, 78
    balance of, 15–17
    on Cardinal Gagnon's visit, 240–241
    conference in Nantes, France, 134
    consecration by
        anxiety over, 133–139
        arguments against, 255–261

Richard N. Williamson

        of bishops, 191, 197, 239–242
        possibility of approval of Rome, 273–278
        of Russia to the Immaculate Heart of Mary, 226–227, 236
        threatening, 251–252
    conversation with Fr. Kelly, 27–28
    dubia regarding Declaration of Religious Liberty, 234
        Rome reply to, 213, 234
    in Eastern United States, 15
    endurance, 276–277
    Farmingville, visit to, 18
    fear of, 143–147
    flyer on ecumenism, 166–172
    fortitude and courage, 114
    handing over to Fr. Schmidberger, 5–6
    on hopeless of Rome, 94–97
    insistence on Tradition, 97
    inspiration of, 115
    interview in *Figaro*, 256
    interview in France (1983, Spring), 16
    joint statement with Bishop de Castro Mayer, 184–185
    letter to Mr. Madiran, 145
    L'Osservatore Romano, 95, 135, 206
    meeting with Cardinal Ratzinger, 75–76, 109, 234–235, 235–236
    opening of the Society-attached American Carmel, 120–121
    position on New Code of Canon Law, 24–25, 98–100
    Press Conference (1983), 28
    and Rome, 18–19
        exchange of letters between, 98
    St. Thomas Aquinas Seminary, visit to, 18
    on Second Vatican Council, 200
    sermon at Ecône on Easter Day, 145
    in SSPX' first ordinations in the Argentine, 124–126
    on Synod of Bishops (November-December 1985), 105
    testimony in property dispute lawsuit, 91–92
    unswerving, 27–29
    US visit, comforted by, 88–92
    video on life of, 211
    vision of, 113, 114
Lemay, Rev. Peter, 278
Leo XIII, Pope, 30–31, 53
    on family, 243–244
liberalism, liberals, 15, 45, 56–58, 77, 90, 96, 107, 108, 128, 186, 190, 192, 199, 216–217
    against family, 243–248
Liberius, Pope, 232
liberty, *see* liberalism, liberals
liturgical reform movement, 24, 100

Liturgy, 84, 95
Liturgy Secretariat of the U.S. Conference of Catholic Bishops, 56
Long Island, 2, 5, 14, 18, 24, 39, 41-42, 73, 121, 253
Lorans, Fr. Alain, 193-194
L'Osservatore Romano (Lefebvre), 95, 135, 206
Louisville Faith Baptist School Crisis, 29
Luciani, Pope, 43-44
Lustiger, Cardinal, 240
Luther, Martin, 85, 100, 274-275

M

Mac Donald, Ed, 217
Macmillan, Harold, 195
mafia, 76, 157
Magisterium, 99
    Extraordinary, 99
    Ordinary, 99
Major Ordinations ceremony, 144
Mamie, Bishop, 71
man-made differences, 207-208
Mann, Horace, 216
Marcinkus, Archbishop, 44
Marian Year Procession and Benediction, Hartford, 269-270
Marie-Christiane, Mother, 35, 121
Marie-Gabriel, Mother, 191
marriages, 134-135, 188, 247, *see also* families
    destruction of, 30, 31, 32, 135
    mixed marriages, 134
    Swiss marriage law, revision of, 135
Martin, Malachi, 223, 257, 272
Martyrs of the Coliseum, 150
Marxism, 164
Mary, 200, 261, 268
    experience of birth of Jesus, 178-182
Mayer, Archbishop Augustin, 62, 65, 119
May Ordinations (videotapes), 107
McGlynn, Judge, 152-153
McMahon, Denis, 26
media
    power of, 165
Men's Three-Day Retreat, 101
Mexico
    earthquake in, 121
Miceli, Fr. Vincent, 25
mistrust, 37-39
mixed marriages, 134
modernism, modernists, 15, 16, 45, 62, 111, 119, 158, 192, 205, 217-218, 232, 240, 251, 269, 275-276

Mohammedans, 135
Moreno, Garcia, 52–53
Mormons, 157
mortality, 139–141
Mortalium Animos, 162
Moscow-Vatican agreement of 1962, 200
mosque construction, in Rome, 96
Mother Church, 21, 57, 71–72, 128
motherhood, *see* women
Mroczka, Rev. Tom, 23, 26
Mystical Body of Christ, 31, 163, 169

N

The National Catholic Reporter, 49
nationality, and Faith, 45–46
naturalism, 205, 208–209
nature, 140
Nelson, James, 46
New Mass, *see* Novus Ordo Mass (NOM)
Newsday, 73
New York Times, 49, 174–175
Nicaragua, Communist Revolution, 154, 164
Noè, Archbishop Virgilio, 56, 65, 157
non-Catholics, 156–157
Norman, Herbert, 195
Northeast District Incorporation
    restart of missions, 5–6
    and Society of Saint Pius X
        consolidation, 5–6
        division amongst the priests, 1, 13
Novus Ordo Mass (NOM), 14, 15–16, 41, 55, 58, 68, 85, 98, 105, 114, 128–132, 204

O

obedience, 107, 110
O'Connor, Archbishop John J., 48, 49, 50, 51, 267
Oddi, Cardinal, 47, 65, 91, 174, 252
Old Testament, 15
oneness of the Church, 163–164, 164, 204
Open Letter to the Pope, 19–20
Opus Dei, 71, 105
Oravec, Fr. Oliver, 200
Ottaviani Intervention, 100, 114
Our Lady of Fatima, 200
Our Lady of La Salette, 100
Our Lady of Lujan, 125

P

pacifism, 158
Palazzini, Cardinal, 91, 174
papacy, 16, 110, 268
papal infallibility, 128–129
parents, *see also* families
    responsibilities of, 249–250
Paul VI, Pope, 43, 55, 56, 57–58, 65, 68, 99, 114
Pax priests, *see* Liturgy
Pearson, Lester, 195
Peek, Frank, 103
Peek, Fr. James, 103
penance, 121–122
Pentecost, 136
Perl, Msgr., 240
Petit, Fr., 23, 54
Philadelphia Enquirer, 273
Philby, Kim, 195
pilgrims, 215–216
Pius IX, Pope, 53, 110, 128, 162–163
Pius X, Pope, 81, 110
Pius XI, Pope, 161, 164, 199
Pius XII, Pope, 22, 67, 135
Plymouth Plantation, 215, 216–217
poems, poetry, 138–141, 148–149
politics, 48–51
Pontifical Biblical Institute, 157
Pope, *see also specific popes*
Pope John's Council (Davies), 106
pornography, 250, 270
Portugal
    flyer on ecumenism, 168–170
Powell, Enoch, 195–196
Pozzera, Fr., 256, 259
prayers
    power of, 197
Priests for Tomorrow (videocassette), 211
progressives, 108
Pro-Life March in Washington, D.C., 186, 192
property disputes, 8, 73
    Connecticut and New York property cases, 165
    lawsuits, 36, 51, 91–92
        Oyster Bay Cove, 16
        against Oyster Bay Cove, 26
    litigation, 73
    Northeastern United States
        settlements, 227–228
    Pennsylvania Federal Court's ruling, 78, 81, 112, 120, 152–153

Philadelphia ruling, 91, 176–177
rulings and verdicts, 152–153, 201
settlements, 253
Protestantism, 13, 49, 212, 215–216, 217
Putti, Dom, 156, 232

R

radicalism, 204, 215–216
rational soul, 140
Ratzinger, Cardinal Joseph, 10, 22, 61–62, 65, 75, 76–77, 96, 204, 213–214, 231–232, 240
    on Archbishop's movement, 109–111
    and the Council, 108–112
    Fr. Schmidberger's meeting with, 65–66
    interview to an Italian journal, 108
    Lefebvre's meeting with, 234–235, 235–236
    meeting with Archbishop Lefebvre, 75–76
    refusing Archbishop Lefebvre's views on new Code, 98–100
    reply to Solemn Warning, 144
The Ratzinger Report, 232
rebellions, 1–2, 13, *see also* dissident priests
reconciliation with Rome, 110
Reign Jesus and Mary (audiotape), 260, 278
religious liberty, 95, 96, 105–106, 144, 213, 231
retreats, *see also* Spiritual Exercises of St. Ignatius
Revolution, *see* Vatican II
Rifan, Fr. Fernando, 169
Rizzo, Fr. John, 89
Roe v. Wade (1973), 49
Roman Curia, 76
Rome, 16, 44, 75–79, 217, 231, 237–238, *see also* Catholic Church
    appearance without substance, 193–198
    and Archbishop Lefebvre
        dilemma over consecrations, 251–252
        dubia on Declaration of Religious Liberty, 234
        dubia on Declaration of Religious Liberty, Rome's reply to, 213
        exchange of letters between, 98
    chronology of contacts with, 234–238
    horrendous of, an insider's description, 155–160
    New Code of Canon Law, *see* Canon Law, New Code
    Spiritual Center, 193
    spiritual war, 118–119
    SSPX
        sanctions against, 76–77, 231–232
        undoing of ban on Freemasonry, 22
Romero, Msgr. Antonino, 157
Roosevelt, Franklin D., 195

Russia, 53
    consecration of, 267–272
    Lefebvre consecration of, 226–227, 236
    Orthodox bishops of, 95

S

Sacred Tradition, 240
St. Aloysius Gonzaga Fund, 6
St. Athanasius, 129, 232
St. Augustine, 46
St. Boniface, 46
St. Cyprian, 164
St. Dominic Barberi, 46
St. Don Bosco, 218–219, 268
St. Gregory's Church, 185
St. Ignatius' Spiritual Exercises, *see* Spiritual Exercises of St. Ignatius
St. John Bosco, 267, 268
St. Joseph's Shrine, Armada, 34, 39
St. Margaret Mary
    Our Lord's twelve promises, 214
St. Mary's College, 29
St. Mary's, Kansas, 28–29, 34, 35, 209, 218–219, 238
St. Maximilian Kolbe, 60
St. Nicolas du Chardonet, Paris, 240
St. Peter Martyr Priory, 223
St. Peter's Church, 184–185
St. Philip Neri, 159
St. Thomas Aquinas, 140
St. Vitus, 150
Sanborn, Fr. Donald, 1, 2, 6, 36, 38
sanctifying grace, 69, 206, 208
Santa Maria degli Angeli's Church, 185
Santa Maria Maggiore's Church, 185
Sardegna, Peter, 231
Sarto, Bishop, 81
Satanism, 30, 33, 205
Schmidberger, Fr. Franz, 5–6, 8, 9, 22–23, 25, 34, 35, 57, 88, 116, 142, 200, 227
    comments on Vatican's Decree of October 3, 1984, 55–59, 61, 64, 65
    meeting with Cardinal Ratzinger, 65–66
    petition on Decree, 80
    and petition to Rome against Vatican October 1984 Decree, 72
    SSPX Consecration to Immaculate Heart, 53, 64, 66
    in SSPX' first ordinations in the Argentine, 125
SCSF, *see* Seminary Continuous Support Fund (SCSF)
Second Vatican Council, *see* Vatican II
Secretariat for the Unity of Christians, 95

sedevacantism, sedevacantists, 13, 218
seminarians
    life of, 151-152
        video on, 211-212
Seminary Continuous Support Fund (SCSF), 8, 10, 63
Serra, Fr. Junipero, 46
Seven Ages of the Catholic Church, 212
Shawinigan, Quebec, 54
Sign of Hope (videocassette), 211-212
Silvestrini, Msgr., 157-158
Siri, Cardinal, 174
Si Si, No No, 156, 157, 184-185
Sister Lucy of Fatima, 53, 268
Sixth Age of Catholic Church, 212, 213
Skierka, Fr. Martin, 2
socialism, 192
    international socialism, 105
Society of Saint Pius X (SSPX), 23
    accommodation issues, 7-8, 219
    agreement on Visitor, 235-236
    American Carmel attached with, 121
    appointment of priests and vocations, 7-8, 10
    Argentina, first ordinations in, 123-127
    buildings and property problems, 8
    Cardinal Ratzinger's proposal for legitimization of, 235
    Connecticut seminary, 6
        lawsuit against, 120
    consecration of auxiliary bishops, 231
    Consecration to the Blessed Mother of God, 59, 60
    Consecration to the Immaculate Heart of Mary, 52-54, 59, 60-63, 64, 66, 267-272
    dependency within the Church, 71
    doctrinal split, 83-87
    Dominican building (Winona), *see* Winona seminary
    Farmingville chapel, 14, 18, 121
    Holland, first church in, 25
    intercontinental flavor, 103-104
    La Reja seminary, *see* La Reja
    Maryknoll Novus Ordo seminary, 127
    massive defection of seminarians, 193
    and Northeast District Incorporation
        consolidation, 5-6
        division amongst the priests, 1, 13
    official recognition, 231, 267
    Oyster Bay Cove, 13, 27, 253
    property disputes, *see* property disputes
    question on taking part in Masses in the St. Peter's Chapel, Berlin, 203-204

    retreats, 101, 107, 165, 186, 200–201, 219, 223, 248, 278, *see also* Spiritual Exercises of St. Ignatius
        Ladies' Three-Day Retreats, 101
    Ridgefield, 81, 83, 97, 101, 223
        Easter retreats, 200–201
        property, disputes and lawsuits, 170
    and Rome
        chronology of contacts, 234–238
    South Americans' support to, 64
    Spiritual Exercises, 4, 23, 26, 39, 51, 54, 63, 81, 177, 186, 200
    triple petition
        number of signatures, 86
    in the USA
        split in, *see also* dissident priests
    Winona, *see* Winona seminary
    Zaitzkofen, 217
Society of St. Pius V, 253–254
South America, 67
    support to SSPX, 64
Spiritual Center, 193
Spiritual Exercises of St. Ignatius, 101
    Easter Week Ignatian Exercises, 146–147
Spring and joy, 138–142
Stapleton, Judge, 153
State and Church, tussle between, 48–51
Stickler, Bishop, 91
Stickler, Cardinal, 174
submission, 77
supernatural grace, 205–206
supernatural weapons, 224–225
superstitions, 185
Swiss Bishops' Conference, 135
Switzerland
    marriage law, 135
Synod of Bishops (November–December, 1985), 104–105, 111–112, 118–119, 126–127, 133–134, 136

T

Teilhardian Omega Point, 158
Thatcher, Margaret, 195
Thiandoum, Cardinal, 174
Thomism, 223
Tobei, Johannes, 203–204
Toynbee, Arnold, 195
Traditional priests, unity of, 31
Tradition, Traditionalism, 33–34, 37–38, 43–44, 45, 57, 58–59, 70–71, 75–76, 97, 98–99, 110, 204, 239, 256, 274
treason, 194–196

Tridentine Mass, 41–42, 55, 57, 61, 107, 238, 240
    in Latin, 186
    Vatican's Decree of October 3, 1984, 55–59, 61, 64, 65
        oppositions against, 67–68
        petition of the SSPX to Rome, 70–74
    video recording of, 78–79
Truman, Harry S., 195
Tucker, Lou, 149

U

Una Voce International, 105
United States, 216–217
    Congress, 216
unity of Christians, 163–164
Universal Church, 226–227
usury, 191
utopia, utopians, 114, 158

V

Valtorta, Maria, 183–184
Vatican II, 15, 24, 61, 65, 66, 75, 77, 95, 98, 106, 111, 144–145, 206–207, 231, 257, *see also* Conciliarism, Conciliarists
    Decree on Religious Liberty, 213, 234
    documents, 99
    fidelity to, 109, 110, 111
    Freemasonry, *see* Freemasonry, Freemasons
    orderly continuation of, 106
    revolution, 106
Vatican's Decree of October 3, 1984, 55–59, 61, 64, 65, 75, 76
    American bishops' oppositions against, 68
    oppositions against, 67–68
    petition, 80
    petition of the SSPX to Rome, 67–68, 70–74
Verbum, 16, 32, 59, 88, 93, 116, 144, 148, 183, 192, 199, 200, 217, 218
Villot, Cardinal, 44
Violette, Fr. Jean-Louis, 54
Virgil, 139–140
vocations, 103

W

The Washington Post, 56
Waterbury clergy, 269–270
Welsh, Fr., 217
Wickens, Fr., 142
Willebrands, Cardinal, 95
Williamson, John B., death of, 188–190
Winona seminary, 201–225, 221–225, 227, 229, 260

migration and its expenses, 277-278
purchase of, 220-221
renovation of, 248, 260, 278
repair of, 230, 238
visitors' reactions, 222, 229-230
Witnesses of Jehovah, 157
women, 245
Word of God, 176
Wordsworth, William, 139, 140
Worsthorne, Peregrine, 195, 196

Y

Yallop, David, 43-44
youth, youngsters, 249-250

Z

Zapp, Fr. Thomas, 2
Zionism, 105
Zoungrana, Cardinal, 174